The Democratic Dilemma
of American Education

Dilemmas in American Politics

Series Editor: **Craig A. Rimmerman**, Hobart and William Smith Colleges

If the answers to the problems facing U.S. democracy were easy, politicians would solve them, accept credit, and move on. But certain dilemmas have confronted the American political system continuously. They defy solution; they are endemic to the system. Some can best be described as institutional dilemmas: How can Congress be both a representative body and a national decision maker? How can the president communicate with more than 250 million citizens effectively? Why do we have a two-party system when many voters are disappointed with the choices presented to them? Others are policy dilemmas: How do we find compromises on issues that defy compromise, such as abortion policy? How do we incorporate racial and ethnic minorities or immigrant groups into American society, allowing them to reap the benefits of this land without losing their identity? How do we fund health care for our poorest or oldest citizens?

Dilemmas such as these are what propel students toward an interest in the study of U.S. government. Each book in the Dilemmas in American Politics series addresses a "real world" problem, raising the issues that are of most concern to students. Each is structured to cover the historical and theoretical aspects of the dilemma but also to explore the dilemma from a practical point of view and to speculate about the future. The books are designed as supplements to introductory courses in American politics or as case studies to be used in upper-level courses. The link among them is the desire to make the real issues confronting the political world come alive in students' eyes.

BOOKS IN THIS SERIES

The Democratic Dilemma of American Education: Out of Many, One?
Arnold Shober

The New Citizenship: Unconventional Politics, Activism, and Service, Fourth Edition
Craig A. Rimmerman

"Can We All Get Along?": Racial and Ethnic Minorities in American Politics, Fifth Edition
Paula D. McClain and Joseph Stewart Jr.

The Lesbian and Gay Movements: Assimilation or Liberation?
Craig A. Rimmerman

Onward Christian Soldiers? The Religious Right in American Politics, Third Edition
Clyde Wilcox and Carin Larson

Claiming the Mantle: How Presidential Nominations Are Won and Lost Before the Votes Are Cast
R. Lawrence Butler

Voting for Women: How the Public Evaluates Women Candidates
Kathleen A. Dolan

Two Parties—or More? The American Party System, Second Edition
John F. Bibby and L. Sandy Maisel

The Role of the Supreme Court in American Politics: The Least Dangerous Branch?
Richard L. Pacelle Jr.

Money Rules: Financing Elections in America
Anthony Gierzynski

The Accidental System: Health Care Policy in America
Michael D. Reagan

The Image-Is-Everything Presidency: Dilemma in American Leadership
Richard W. Waterman, Robert Wright, and Gilbert St. Clair

The Angry American: How Voter Rage Is Changing the Nation, Second Edition
Susan J. Tolchin

Remote and Controlled: Media Politics in a Cynical Age, Second Edition
Matthew Robert Kerbel

Making Americans, Remaking America: Immigration and Immigrant Policy
Louis DeSipio and Rodolfo de la Garza

From Rhetoric to Reform? Welfare Policy in American Politics
Anne Marie Cammisa

No Neutral Ground? Abortion Politics in an Age of Absolutes
Karen O'Connor

Payment Due: A Nation in Debt, a Generation in Trouble
Timothy J. Penny and Steven E. Schier

Bucking the Deficit: Economic Policymaking in the United States
G. Calvin Mackenzie and Saranna Thornton

The Democratic Dilemma of American Education

Out of Many, One?

Arnold Shober

Lawrence University

WESTVIEW PRESS

A Member of the Perseus Books Group

Westview Press was founded in 1975 in Boulder, Colorado, by notable publisher and intellectual Fred Praeger. Westview Press continues to publish scholarly titles and high-quality undergraduate- and graduate-level textbooks in core social science disciplines. With books developed, written, and edited with the needs of serious nonfiction readers, professors, and students in mind, Westview Press honors its long history of publishing books that matter.

Find us on the World Wide Web at www.westviewpress.com.

Every effort has been made to secure required permissions for all text, images, maps, and other art reprinted in this volume.

Westview Press books are available at special discounts for bulk purchases in the United States by corporations, institutions, and other organizations. For more information, please contact the Special Markets Department at the Perseus Books Group, 2300 Chestnut Street, Suite 200, Philadelphia, PA 19103, or call (800) 810–4145, ext. 5000, or e-mail special.markets@perseusbooks.com.

Library of Congress Cataloging-in-Publication Data
Shober, Arnold F., 1976-
   The democratic dilemma of American education : out of many, one? / Arnold Shober.
      pages cm
   Includes bibliographical references and index.
   ISBN 978-0-8133-4536-9 (hardcover : alk. paper)— ISBN 978-0-8133-4537-6 (e-book) 1. Education and state—United States. 2. Democracy and education—United States. I. Title.

LC89.S495 2012
379.73—dc23
                                                                                        2011047235

10 9 8 7 6 5 4 3 2 1

for Gretchen

Contents

8. Devolving the Dilemma? **203**

Illustrations

Boxes

Figures

Tables

Abbreviations

AFDC	Aid to Families with Dependent Children
AFT	American Federation of Teachers
AYP	Adequate Yearly Progress
CEA	Colorado Education Association
DPI	Department of Public Instruction
ESEA	Elementary and Secondary Education Act
GADOE	Georgia Department of Education
IASA	Improving America's Schools Act
KIPP	Knowledge Is Power Program
MEA	Michigan Education Association
NAACP	National Association for the Advancement of Colored People
NAEP	National Assessment of Educational Progress
NAEYC	National Association for the Education of Young Children
NAMI	National Alliance on Mental Illness
NCHS	National Center for History in the Schools
NCLB	No Child Left Behind
NEA	National Education Association
NEH	National Endowment for the Humanities
NESIC	National Education Standards and Improvement Council
NJEA	New Jersey Education Association
NTA	National Teachers Association
SCLC	Southern Christian Leadership Conference
TANF	Temporary Assistance to Needy Families
UFT	United Federation of Teachers
OBE	Outcomes-Based Education
WEAC	Wisconsin Education Association Council
WLI	Western Literary Institute and College of Professional Teachers

Acknowledgments

I would like to acknowledge the many people who helped to bring this book together. First, my students at Lawrence University in my education policy seminar and introduction to public policy course deserve thanks for their insight on various permutations of the arguments in this book; two, Jake Woodford and Shin Wei Ting, deserve special mention because they took the opportunity to "rate my professor!" with relish—and made thoughtful, written comments on book chapters. Two of my colleagues in the Government Department, Bill Hixon and Steve Wulf, provided encouragement and read drafts. As they have in the past, John F. Witte and Paul Manna provided invaluable feedback as accomplished scholars in the field of education policy and political science; their suggestions saved me from errors and improved the readability and thoroughness of portions of the book. I also wish to thank my editors, Anthony Wahl and Craig Rimmerman, for encouragement, support, and suggestions for a better product. Despite excellent guidance from all of these, any errors are my own.

1

....

Out of Many, One?

The Democratic Dilemma of American Education

THIS BOOK ASKS THE QUESTION, *How does American educational policy attempt to transmit democratic values democratically?* Democratic governments like those in the United States cannot monopolize what "the people" want, and they face the dilemma of transmitting the norms of democratic government *using* democratic norms. In this context, a norm is a widely shared belief about how governments *should* behave, whether they actually do so or not. The norms discussed in this overview are *inclusion*, *equality*, *participation*, *understanding*, and *self-rule*.[1] Children are taught that democratic governments *include* the interests of as many groups as possible, try to treat everyone *equally*, encourage their citizens to *participate* in the political process, try to use good judgment and *understanding* to make policy, and promise that citizens can *rule themselves*—all at the same time. Frequently these norms are at odds with one another, and throughout American history policymakers have not valued all of them equally. For example, in the late seventeenth century colonial policymakers in Massachusetts valued understanding and self-rule in educational policy far more than they did participation or equality. In the twentieth century inclusion and equality are prominent in federal educational policy, sometimes at the expense of self-rule.

Even among policymakers in the same era, however, shared norms rarely lead them to suggest the same public policy. For example, treating everyone equally makes it very difficult to give citizens a meaningful opportunity to rule themselves. This situation is evident in debates over school spending. Giving every school district the same amount of money to spend per student (equality) can shortchange both inclusion and self-rule. Special-needs students and students in high-poverty areas, for example, may require additional resources to achieve the same level of education as that given to average students, so a law requiring each district to spend an equal amount of money per student would do nothing to help the "needy" students catch up. Likewise, citizens who value public education very highly might want to raise significantly more money for their schools through local taxes, but a statewide limit on school spending or taxation thwarts their self-rule.

Of course most educational policy is not about promoting inclusion or self-rule directly, but rather about using governmental power to encourage citizens to behave in a certain way. For example, contemporary American educational policy tries to serve children of various ethnic or racial backgrounds in the same classroom, give chronically poor school districts extra funding to hire better teachers, and provide parents and students with choices about what they learn and where they go to school. "Encouragement" may be as mild as simply *allowing* parents to choose a school based on its reading pedagogy or arts focus, or it may be as forceful as *requiring* children to attend a particular school to ensure racial integration, even if they live across town. It is in the design of public policy that government policymakers struggle with the conflicts among the norms of democracy. This book shows how American policymakers have wrestled with these dilemmas through the public policy process.

Changes in public policy create new politics, so this chapter begins with a brief overview of four major questions that policymakers must consider when designing policy. Educational governance specifies who decides that a policy problem exists and when, for whom, and how policy decisions are made. American education has a strong federal structure that complicates any educational change; most American educational policy is made at the state and local levels. Federalism means that regional and local governments have autonomy to make some of their own policy decisions. (Chapter 2 presents an overview of American educational governance.)

Next the chapter introduces five norms of democracy discussed in this book and provides sketches of the main educational policies covered in the following chapters. It is important to remember that no educational policy is a pure manifestation of any particular norm of democracy, and other factors, such as school finance, may have as much influence on equality, for example, as on racial inclusion or self-rule.

BOX 1.1   Guiding Questions for Public Policy

Is there a problem? A public policy *problem* exists when the public demands a government solution. Something that is considered a problem now may not have been a problem fifty years ago. Reasons that the public demands government action include effective publicity by interest groups, economic crises, and changing social norms.

When should government intervene? Government policymakers may recognize a problem but not have a good solution. Or "solving" a problem may create political conflicts with other public policy or important voters. Policymakers may choose to intervene when the problem is highly visible, when it affects many people, or when it is politically safe to do so.

For whom should government intervene? A problem may affect many people, but governments have limited time and money. Policymakers may have to limit a government policy to benefit only some of those people. They may make their decisions based on the importance of the policy to targeted individuals, the probability that the policy will be successful, or other political considerations.

How should government intervene? Policymakers have to connect the problem to government action. They have to be sure that whatever legislation government enacts has a real effect on the problem. They have to determine a cause of the problem and create a way to measure inputs to the policy, outputs, and outcomes.

Public Policy

Public policy is the result of four deliberate decisions made by an authority to address an identified problem (see box 1.1): Is there a problem government can remedy? When should government intervene? On whose behalf should government act? What should it do? An "authority" may be voters, a school principal, the school board, the state legislature, a governor, Congress, the courts, or the president.

The first question policymakers must ask is, *Is there a problem?* A *policy* problem means that many people are affected by a particular condition over time. For example, parents may think that a particular math teacher at the local elementary school is a "problem" teacher because he does not enforce classroom discipline or seem to care about student progress, and his continued employment may become a topic for discussion with the local teachers' union and the school board. But unless there are *many* teachers like this, low teacher quality would not be a policy problem (see Chapter 5). Similarly, students who fail to finish high school are likely to have fewer job opportunities, which may be a problem for them individually, but high school dropouts are not a policy problem unless policymakers can identify widespread *patterns* among those students. To do so, they must identify variables that help predict who is at risk for dropping out, such as family poverty, low academic achievement, becoming a teen parent, or being a member of certain ethnic or racial groups.[2] Because these variables are linked to teenagers dropping out of high school, most policymakers would consider the dropout rate a policy problem.

Yet even if many people are affected by some condition, government policy may still be to ignore an issue. For example, some children might benefit from government help, but lawmakers may believe that too few children would benefit, or that there is strong opposition to government involvement, or that individuals acting in a market-like setting could better address the issue.

American education was once subject to official neglect. Many policymakers before the early twentieth century thought that Americans' widespread lack of basic, formal education was not a policy problem, or even if it was, government could not address it uniformly, adequately, or fairly, so parents would arrange for education as best they could. For example, Massachusetts required schooling beginning in the late 1600s, but the law was weakly enforced and did not specify what should be taught. In 1840, in response to a proposal to make Massachusetts' system of education more uniform, that state's House Committee on Education explicitly denied that widely varying educational standards were a policy problem. They reported that, "District schools in a [r]epublican government need no police regulations, no systems of state censorship, no checks of moral, religious, or political conservatism, to preserve either the morals, the religion, or the politics of the state."[3] Although few elected officials hold this view anymore—most politicians now are quick to grab the "education" mantle as their own—Massachusetts' example shows that this was not always the case.[4]

In American history, policymakers have framed the policy problem of formal education in debates over the *provision* of education versus the *production* of education.[5] A government that only *provides* for education would require that children have access to education, whether by attending a school or certifying that they were taught at home. In this situation, government does not specify *how* children are educated. A government that *produces* education does.

Until the end of the nineteenth century, this debate clearly favored pro-vision over production, but policymakers slowly adopted the view that for-mal education was a tool to promote democracy, citizenship, and job skills (see Chapter 6). In that century, children might have attended school if there was one and if their parents thought it was useful. (A choice only some par-ents made during some part of the year; children were often more useful working at home or in a factory.) Later, states required local communities to fund schools for anyone in a certain age range, but they did not require children to attend.[6] But by 1890 half of the states required children to com-plete some formal schooling, and every state did by 1929. By 1944 the U.S. Supreme Court firmly rejected the nineteenth-century view, holding that "the state . . . may restrict the parent's control by requiring school atten-dance, regulating or prohibiting the child's labor, and in many other ways."[7] Thus the provision of education became a *public* policy problem.

Although state and local governments did produce education before the 1940s by collecting school taxes, operating schools, hiring teachers, and constructing school buildings, the Court's ruling fully shifted the policy de-bate to the appropriate means of producing education. Government pro-duction of education does not mean that the government has a monopoly on education—the state of Oregon tried to close all the private schools in the state in the 1920s but was rebuffed by the Supreme Court in *Pierce v. Society of Sisters* (1925); it only means that public schools receive favorable legal treatment. Since the debate over provision has been settled, policy-makers now debate when and how government actors should produce ed-ucation. Policymakers have thus turned to the second question of public policy.

When should government intervene? Policymakers may identify that some problem is widespread, but they may not have the political will to engage in government action. Scholars like John Kingdon have argued that "policy windows" frequently open after crises.[8] One such event was when many Americans panicked after the Soviet Union successfully launched the first artificial satellite, *Sputnik*, in 1957. Somehow the Soviet communists were leapfrogging the free West in math and science. This led directly to the pas-sage of the National Defense Education Act of 1958, which provided some federal money to support improvement in these subjects.

Less dramatically, state governments became increasingly worried in the mid-1970s that their schools were not preparing students for modern em-ployment. The federal government made the point succinctly in 1983 by calling the nation's "mediocre educational performance" nearly equivalent to an "act of war."[9] States increased the number of "academic" courses (math, science, and English) students had to take in the 1980s and supplemented these with more rigorous standards for what would be taught in the 1990s. In 2001 the U.S. Congress passed the No Child Left Behind Act (NCLB), which authorized major changes to federal educational policy by requiring students to take state exams to demonstrate their proficiency in academic subjects. Under the law, students are not graded based on the results, but schools are. If schools cannot show "adequate yearly progress," they may be subject to a variety of sanctions, from having to find and fund tutors for students to school personnel being fired.

The third policy question is, *For whom should government intervene?* Policymakers wander into a political minefield when they decide who should receive help from the government, because one legislator's downtrodden constituents are another's undeserving special interest. (Such *target populations* and the organizations and lobbyists working on their behalf are described in Chapter 5.) Nevertheless, the answer to this policy question shapes what actions the government may take, because policy solutions may not work equally well with all people.

For example, since the 1960s a primary target population of federal educational policy has been students in low-income families, who also tend to have low academic achievement. Yet a large body of research has shown that a student's family situation has more effect on the student's learning than schools or teachers.[10] Children may come from households in which parents have no time for their children because they are working or absent. They may come from a very low-income home that does not or cannot spend money on required school materials or extracurricular activities. They may come from abusive households. They may move between schools multiple times during the year (some schools experience turnover rates in excess of 50 percent during a year!). How much can schools compensate for these students' home situations? Is there another government agency that could address these issues better? Federal policymakers turn to the fourth policy question for answers.

How should government intervene? Observers of American education have little trouble identifying problems that educational policy could address, from low science literacy to teen pregnancy. It is much harder to formulate a response that actually addresses the identified problem, and policymakers have to identify the causes of the problem and balance cost, uncertainty, and political opposition. If the proposed policy is politically feasible, the analysts need to suggest how the policy should be implemented. Who should do what? Who should pay? Finally, a good policy analyst should expect to evaluate the policy after its implementation. Should the government continue what it is doing, or should it change course?

The federal Head Start program is instructive. As one of President Lyndon Johnson's key War on Poverty programs in the 1960s, Head Start sought to prepare students for school by providing health and social services. Federal policymakers argued that low educational outcomes related to poverty were a problem that government could remedy, and they identified who could potentially be helped. They were not sure, however, how to attack poverty directly. Instead, they chose to mitigate some effects of poverty in the hope that children's educational abilities would increase as a result. They argued that Head Start could address low-income children's educational problems through nutrition programs, pre-kindergarten school-readiness classes, and parent-child activities to help parents become interested in their children's educational progress.[11]

Has the policy worked? Researchers have found that Head Start is an unqualified success in the short term. In early school grades, Head Start students do better in academics and classroom behavior than similar children who did not participate in Head Start. Analysts are not as sanguine about the long-term effects of the program, as some studies have found that its effects disappear by third or fourth grade; other studies show just small improvements for some ethnic or racial groups.[12] The federal government's own evaluation of Head Start is decidedly neutral.[13] The mixed evaluations have prompted other policymakers to suggest alternatives. Some evaluators argue that although Head Start does benefit children before they go to school, many students in the program attend poorly performing schools after leaving Head Start. These evaluators suggest that giving parents an option to send their student to a school of their choice might work better than Head Start.[14] Others argue that poor academic achievement is not so much a matter of the schools, but of poor teachers *in* the schools.[15] Others suggest boosting funding for the program, intervening earlier, or increasing Head Start teacher qualifications.[16]

In any case, what the government should do is much less clear than what the problem is, when government should intervene, or even who should be helped. Facing this uncertainty, policymakers must balance conflicting demands on government services, the limits of knowledge, and contradictory policy suggestions. One way they address these dilemmas is by favoring one norm of democracy over another. These norms are introduced in the next section.

Democratic Norms

Compounding the difficulties of designing and implementing policy is doing so within a democratic system. Even if the designers of Head Start could decide on the best way to overcome the effects of poverty on academic achievement and life chances, lawmakers would still have to shepherd the changes through a democratic system. They would have to answer questions such as, "Should parents in the Head Start program be able to change the rules?"; "How much money should go to Head Start participants instead of helping all children in kindergarten?"; and "Shouldn't the state government administer Head Start like it does low-income medical insurance programs?"

Modern democracies thrive on the participation of citizens. Since the 1800s defenders of government-produced, tax-supported education have said that public education uniquely invites all citizens to participate.[17] Elementary schools are usually the smallest in a district to facilitate parent involvement, and school boards tend to be large to reflect diverse community interests in school policy. Many school districts set tax rates through elections. But the participants in each of these opportunities may be different. Parents, community activists, and general taxpayers each have different values for education, and they may not agree on the direction of educational policy. Nineteenth-century boosters of public education were correct in asserting that American education modeled democratic norms, but educational policy was also a showcase for the conflicts between these norms. This section introduces the five norms of democracy discussed in this book—inclusion, equality, participation, understanding, and self-rule—and suggests elements of conflict between them. It also introduces highlights of the major educational policies discussed in the following chapters.

Inclusion

When democracies exclude many people from the decision-making process, governments cannot credibly claim that they are fulfilling both self-rule and participation, and American exclusion of various immigrant groups, women (until 1920), and African Americans (effectively until the 1965 Voting Rights Act) has weakened American claims to democracy. Yet democracy is not static, and each of these groups has been incorporated into the public sphere.

Most of the targets of educational policy, students, do not vote, but schools do emphasize this democratic norm by whom they include in schools and classrooms. Some educational policy scholars contend that schools and school districts still systematically exclude some children from meaningful educational opportunities, and school segregation continues to be a live debate, as shown in Chapter 3.[18] American educational policymakers have struggled with how best to incorporate children from various backgrounds in the same classrooms. African American students have had the most visible struggle. In the 1930s and 1940s courts found that schools provided for African American children were always less well provisioned than similarly situated schools for white students. Scholars also explored the apparent negative psychological effects on students of being sent to a "different" school on account of race. Seeing trouble brewing, some Southern state legislatures, like Georgia's, sought to stave off desegregation by dramatically increasing spending on African American schools through the 1940s.[19] Those efforts were not sufficient for the courts. The Supreme Court held in *Brown v. Topeka Board of Education* (1954) that the difference in quality and negative psychological effects made the separation inherently unconstitutional. This ended legally mandated (de jure) segregation.

The decision did not end actual segregation, however. Instead, policymakers and the courts disputed whether the government's role was to desegregate or integrate schools. Desegregation required school districts to disband schools that had deliberately separated races or ethnicities by having a "black school" and a "white school" in the same neighborhood or drawing district attendance zones to create such schools. Integration, on the other hand, meant deliberately *increasing* the racial or ethnic diversity of a school even when the neighborhoods surrounding the school were not racially or ethnically diverse. Most policymakers agreed that segregation was a problem, but they disagreed about when, for whom, or how government should intervene.

American courts moved slowly to answer these policy questions between 1954 and the early 1970s. Their challenge was to find a way to build educational inclusion through desegregated schooling while preserving aspects of self-rule. The *Brown* decision gave states and districts the slow-burning charge to desegregate with "all deliberate speed." The Supreme Court apparently thought that pushing for faster desegregation would invite a strong Southern reaction that would make it even harder to remedy inequality in the future. The Court tried to diffuse the potentially explosive situation by allowing school districts time to desegregate within the bounds of local politics. This was not to be: Some states toyed with the idea of creating publicly funded private school systems, while others created token desegregated districts by enrolling a handful of African Americans in the white system. As it was, the courts moved slowly to correct obvious attempts in the South to prevent nonsegregated schooling. Although courts ruled the publicly funded private systems out of bounds (*Griffin v. County School Board of Prince Edward County* [1964]), token enrollments of white or black students were generally allowed.[20]

The Supreme Court's patience ran out by 1968, when it decided that self-rule could not trump inclusion. Justice William Brennan wrote that districts had to desegregate "*now*" (emphasis in the original; *Green v. New Kent County* [1968], 439). Very soon thereafter, the courts moved to promote integration beyond desegregation and ordered crosstown busing to remedy racial separation. If African Americans and whites were attending the same schools, the courts argued, their education would be equal.

Despite the court's initial hope of integrating schooling through busing, demographic change and a change of heart in the federal courts have frustrated that desire. After World War II white families left American cities for the suburbs in record numbers ("white flight"). The trend accelerated in the 1970s as busing was implemented, leaving urban school districts that could only be predominantly nonwhite. Detroit, Michigan, for example, was 91 percent white in 1940, 56 percent in 1970, and 12 percent in 2000. Nationally, some 65 percent of African American students and 72 percent of children of Hispanic descent now attend predominantly minority schools.[21] Integrating many of these schools would be impossible without busing from predominantly white suburbs, but the Supreme Court closed off that option in *Milliken v. Bradley* (1974)—only three years after it had approved busing as a remedy. In this case, the Court knew of evidence that discriminatory housing policies kept African Americans out of the suburbs, but its ruling implied that self-rule was more important to democracy than inclusion was. The federal courts proceeded to retreat from desegregation policy, especially in the 1990s, and they have signaled that using race as a factor in assigning children to school at all might be constitutionally suspect (*Parents Involved in Community Schools v. Seattle School District No. 1* [2007]).

But America's changing demographics might turn the tide toward greater inclusion more than all of the courts' efforts. Although some advocates of integration suggest that the end of court-ordered desegregation would lead to a return to racially split schools, the data do not suggest resegregation.[22] Despite continuing high levels of racial and ethnic imbalance in many schools, the rapidly increasing numbers of children of Hispanic or Asian descent have actually increased diversity in school districts in the United States. In 1990, 37 percent of students attended schools that were more than 90 percent white, but in 2000, only 28 percent did. In 2000, white students attended schools that had 5 percent more minority students than they had in 1990.[23] As white students become minorities in Southern and Western states, racial integration is likely to increase.

Chapter 3 shows how American *federal* educational policy has turned on the norm of inclusion perhaps more than any other, as the national government moved aggressively into educational policy only after segregation in schools became a policy problem in the 1940s and 1950s. Policymakers saw inclusion as a first step to improving educational equality, and the federal government quickly tied goals of maximum inclusion to educational equality.

Equality

The second norm that frames educational policy debates is equality, one of the most difficult democratic norms to apply. The difficulty starts with the word. Who should be equal? And what part of their democratic experience should be equal? In American education, policymakers generally talk about two forms of equality: opportunity and outcome.

Equality of opportunity means that children are given access to equivalent educational resources such as qualified teachers, safe classrooms, and similar textbooks. That is, the government ensures that educational resources are the same *before* students start school, and differences in a student's goals, aspirations, and academic achievement are the result of student characteristics, not of the school environment. In the 1960s many policymakers argued that desegregation would improve African Americans' educational achievement and social opportunities, because they and white children would share the same educational resources. (As shown in Chapter 3, however, some scholars argued that the link between resources and educational outcomes was partly explained by nonschool factors that are difficult to influence.)

Equality of outcome, on the other hand, means that students meet the same standards *after* they complete formal schooling. Though government might require a similar basic level of education for all students, policymakers might encourage different curricula, different kinds of teachers, and even different forms of school so long as students reach set goals. Chapter 6 shows how equality of outcome has come to dominate education headlines as federal and state policies have required students to meet academic standards.

Equality is difficult to square with other norms, especially participation and self-rule. Those norms institutionalize inequality, because all citizens do not participate with equal interest or ability, nor do all citizens share the same preferences for public policy.[24] One school may have "better" education than another, either because it has more educational or extracurricular programs (like advanced-placement programs and a well-funded football team) or because it has a more supportive school environment (there are no metal detectors at the doors, and most students stay in school until graduation). These differences are pronounced in American education, because many states allow school districts to adjust their own tax rates and make decisions about curriculum, athletics, and teacher hires. Nevertheless, the theory of pluralism, described elsewhere in this chapter, suggests that democracy can still uphold this norm despite varying levels of individual participation, because interest groups work on behalf of individuals who might be affected by some policies. Although issues of democratic equity occur in many educational policy areas, the norm is central to contemporary policy debates about school funding and school choice.

Policymakers have pressed both equality of opportunity and equality of outcome into service in the debates about American school finance (see Chapter 4). Proponents of higher school funding argued in the 1950s and 1960s that nonwhite students' schools would be improved if they received funding equal to that of white-dominated schools. In the 1970s and 1980s, however, this argument was turned back in federal and some state courts because it seemed to impinge on local decision making—the norm of self-rule. Further, some students seemed to need additional resources to meet the same basic standards, so finance advocates pivoted to the equality of outcome and argued that some students and some schools needed *more* funding to even out American education.

On one level, it is obvious that school funding is inequitable. Although the share of school funding from state and federal governments has increased substantially over the last century, local taxes still account for nearly half of school finances in many states and more than half in some.[25] Colonists and early travelers to the Midwest tended to believe strongly in self-rule and self-taxation. Education was seen widely as an extension of home and religious life, and many parents viewed *any* government involvement suspiciously. Keeping funding close to home meant that parents could keep a close watch on local schools.[26]

Consider the Beachwood City, Ohio, school district. It has above-average residential property values, and 27 percent of its residents hold masters, doctoral, and professional degrees. Local property taxes fund 85 percent of the district's budget, at about $19,900 per child. In contrast, the Perry school district in Allen County, Ohio, has below-average residential property values. Just 2 percent of the residents hold advanced degrees. Even though the state and federal governments cover 33 percent of its school budget (double the percentage of Beachwood City), the district still only spends about $6,600 per child.[27] Should students in the latter district have less than half the amount of funding than those in the former?

Advocates of equalized school funding would say no, but there is no clearly superior policy to distribute funds equally. Policy research discussed in Chapter 4 suggests that school spending itself is only weakly correlated with educational outcomes, so increasing spending, by itself, might not improve the equality of outcomes. Further, the socioeconomic situations of children in the Beachwood and Perry districts are different, meaning that the equality of opportunity will also be different. Requiring equal per-pupil expenditures might overcome the financial disparity, but it could not overcome the potential disparity in opportunity, and requiring that the wealthier district spend less by capping local spending might be seen as an antidemocratic policy because it limits self-rule.

A second policy, school choice, suggests that equality of outcome might be best served by giving students explicitly different opportunities. Proponents of school choice (discussed in Chapter 7) contend that each child is unique, and that promoting a one-size-fits-all school system might actually undermine a child's educational chances, especially the least-privileged students.[28] They further argue that parents should have the ability to make decisions about the educational program to which their children are exposed, a manifestation of self-rule. The controversial school voucher program created in 1990 in Milwaukee, Wisconsin, is an example of this choice. Parents and legislators knew the traditional public school system was in difficult straits. Just over 17 percent of the district's high schoolers dropped out of school in 1992–1993, versus 2 percent for the state as a whole.[29] Its students performed at the 38th percentile on national reading tests, and 7.5 percent of parents wanted to leave the district simply on educational grounds.[30] In response, a handful of determined parents and State Representative Polly Williams pushed through a state-funded program that gave low-income parents a state-funded voucher to spend at a school of their choice, public or private.[31] Williams argued that the program empowered parents when the system failed them. She said, "I did not feel that our children should have to leave their community and go into another community just to be educated. . . . We need to help [low-income] families opt out if the system is refusing to help them with their child."[32]

Critics do not dispute that all children have special needs, but they suggest that school choice can undermine the education of students who are "left behind" because they have parents who cannot or will not choose something different.[33] Some parents do not have the motivation to look for a school that fits their children better, or they may not have the resources to transport their children to those schools—especially if they are poor. Students who live in rural areas may not have any schooling options other than the publicly provided school unless they can be driven dozens of miles. Thus choice might rebalance the scales for some, but the opportunity is not equally available to all. Others criticize choice on the grounds that it compounds a bad school environment by "creaming" the best academic students out of the school, and others allege that school choice will segregate urban schools more than they already are, threatening the Supreme Court's ruling that separate schools are inherently unequal.[34]

The dilemma of equality in a democracy is difficult to resolve theoretically, and it is just as contentious from a policy point of view. Using the four policy questions, most policymakers would agree that inequality of opportunity is a problem for public policy, but there is less consensus on the equality of outcomes. When government should intervene is also difficult to determine: When is inequality too great? When financial disparities are as obvious as those between Beachwood and Perry? When students in one district score more than 25 percent lower on a standardized exam than students in a neighboring school district? Should government intervene in school districts that need help most, those that seem to spend "too much," or both? Finally, should states abolish property taxes and control all funding from the state level? Should government target just low-performing students and schools? None of these policy questions has a clear answer, but Chapter 4 describes how policymakers have tried to balance the desires of local voters, state priorities, and court mandates for educational equality in school finance. Although research on school finance does not answer the questions definitively, the norm of democratic participation helps explain how policymakers have arrived at the answers applied in American educational policy.

Participation

If one were to ask a bystander what "democracy" means, odds are that the answer would be "elections." Indeed, when polling firms try to find how likely "democracy" is to succeed in Afghanistan, Iraq, Chile, or other transitioning countries, they invariably ask about free and fair elections.[35] Elections, though, are an imperfect way to translate democratic preferences into public policy and can distort other democratic norms easily, especially if some voters are systematically more likely to turn out to vote than others. Political theorists of pluralism have suggested that interest groups can mitigate some of these drawbacks to participation. Interest groups also perform key roles in the policymaking process, as some groups research, draft, and advocate for particular responses to the four policy questions.

Elections are one of the simplest ways to incorporate many citizens' preferences into the policy process. Asking "the people" about appropriate ways to address the complexities of equality and inclusion can aid policymakers as they attempt to resolve that democratic dilemma, and the United States holds more elections to decide questions of representation, taxation, animal welfare, marriage, mining, immigration policy, and other issues than any other country in the world except Switzerland. Americans are regularly asked to go to the polls to select more than 510,000 public officials; in 2009, they were also asked to pass judgment on 263 citizen initiatives and legislative referenda.[36] School politics are no exception: 96 percent of school boards are elected.[37]

Elections, though, do not necessarily account for what "the people" want, and voters may not value each democratic norm equally. Critics of contemporary democracy say that it is distinctly nonparticipatory, and they argue that the system is just a cloak for elites.[38] It is not uncommon for local school board races to attract only 20 percent of eligible voters to the polls, and many of these "races" are uncontested—so there is no decision to make.[39] Those who do participate tend to be strongly motivated, either as supporters or detractors.[40] Given the 80 percent nonvoting rate, it is difficult to argue that school elections, in particular, are representative of the public's views on local educational policy.

Political theorists suggest that some of these shortcomings can be remedied by *pluralism*, or group-based politics. As interests and needs emerge in society, citizens form new groups to pressure elected and appointed government officials. James Madison, in Federalist 10, argued that as long as no single faction becomes too dominant, individual liberty can survive group-based politics. In this view, *interest groups* act as a glue between individuals seeking to change public policy and government decision makers who control it. Interest groups form to pressure government to do or act a certain way. The American Federation of Teachers (an employee union), the Thomas B. Fordham Institute (a think tank), the Business Roundtable (an industry association), and the National Association for the Education of Young Children (a special population advocacy group) all try to influence government policy to benefit their membership or ideology. The number of interest groups in the United States has skyrocketed since the 1970s; more than 20,000 interest groups now lobby in Washington, D.C.[41] As national and state spending on education has increased, educational lobbying groups have likewise proliferated. These groups help translate the public's desires to government organizations when elections are not sufficient, as explored in Chapter 5.

Defenders of pluralist democracy claim that these interest groups function better than elected representatives to control policy. The U.S. Congress, state legislatures, and, one suspects, school boards, do not have adequate time, personnel, or desire to watch everything that the U.S. Department of Education or a state department of education does. Instead, elected representatives wait for complaints, "fire alarms," from interest groups who think policy needs to be changed.[42] Voters may not be able to remember a candidate's position on school choice, but members of an interest group will. Voters may not be able to attend every meeting of the state legislature's committee on education, but staff from an interest group can. Interest groups can watch elected representatives and let officials know when they step out of line, so members of the union, or conservatives, or businesses, or parents do not have to.

Although pluralism can represent the interests of many citizens who would not have the time or inclination to participate in elections or sit through public hearings, it does not comport well with inclusion in the democratic process. Critics of pluralism have shown that groups do not form readily, and that the groups that do form tend to overrepresent well-off interests in society.[43]

Defenders of pluralism suggest that interest groups form readily or at least have the *potential* to form readily—so politicians should be wary of alienating some portion of the electorate because they *might* form an interest group to cause trouble at the next election—but others argue that actual evidence for this is weak. Beginning with Mancur Olson, critics have shown that most people would not join a group unless the benefits to them were greater than the costs of participation.[44] So if preventing the school board from closing a neighborhood school means attending a year's worth of school board meetings, Olson would predict that few, if any, parents will spend the time. If the state department of education were cutting funding for full-day kindergarten, even fewer of the affected parents would be willing to call the state superintendent or visit the state capital. And federal policy changes might attract the least effort, simply because the costs of effective participation are so great. Compounding the problem is that if a group defending a person's interest *did* exist, that person would not have the motivation to join, because he or she would receive the benefits anyway. Why should a busy parent call the state superintendent to bolster support for full-day kindergarten if the National Association for the Education of Young Children (NAEYC) is already doing something similar?

Critics point to a second flaw in pluralism. Existing interest groups represent better-funded, better-informed, and more elite interests.[45] Groups that do exist for less active groups, such as recent immigrants or poor urban families, have fewer resources to spend lobbying policymakers. And most interest groups favor existing government programs rather than new ones.[46] Although better-organized groups can nudge policymakers toward their preferences, interest groups are not particularly successful at pushing major policy changes.[47] The combined bias toward the better-off and the status quo does not give all citizens equal treatment or an equal voice.

American educational policy is no different. The arena is filled by group interests, but because virtually all educational policy relies on teachers to actually *do* what it calls for, state and district teachers' unions are the most influential. Although some states, usually in the South, do not permit teachers' "unions," teachers' associations play a similar role.[48] In states with unions, school boards have to bargain with the union to set teacher pay and working hours and days. If the school board and the union are hostile to each other, it will be difficult to convince teachers to adopt some educational initiative of the board. That hostility may extend to state or national programs, too.

For example, one of the major components of the NCLB is standardized testing of third through eighth graders and of tenth to twelfth graders in reading and math. Schools have to show that their students are proficient based on a state standard. Teachers and others have been very critical of the law, and teachers have spent more time talking about how to take the test rather than on the material students are supposed to learn.[49] Penalties levied on a district for failing to show improvement in aggregate test scores can be severe—including firing all school staff. As a result, the National Education Association (NEA) and American Federation of Teachers (AFT), both discussed in Chapter 5, have taken a stand against these and other elements of the law, and states have made it easier for students to appear "proficient" on the exams.[50] In light of these negative responses, U.S. Secretary of Education Arne Duncan offered $4 billion to states through the "Race to the Top" program as a reward for improvement. The U.S. Department of Education has awarded states this money *after* they show that local teachers' unions and associations are supportive. The two states that won initial grants from the U.S. Department of Education showed substantial buy-in from both districts and unions—100 percent in Delaware and 93 percent in Tennessee.[51]

Chapter 5 explores the growth and effectiveness of American teachers' unions as the most influential interest groups in American education, especially in local school districts. Unions are focused on pay, benefits, and workplace conditions for their members, but in education, workplace conditions necessarily include what and how teachers teach. The role of unions has become a highly charged issue, and since 2010 state lawmakers in Wisconsin, Ohio, Massachusetts, Florida, New Jersey, and elsewhere have taken steps to restrict their influence, bringing contentious protests to state capitals around the country. There is no doubt unions encourage participation by their members, and Chapter 5 suggests how that participation influences American educational policy.

If democracy is to be inclusive, equal, and participatory, democracies need voters and policymakers who are well-informed and judicious. Policymakers face the dilemma of creating consensus about *what* America's future voters should know.

Understanding

Participating in elections to make decisions about representatives and policy does not require any particular knowledge of "the issues." The democratic norm of understanding may also be democracy's weakest link, as most American voters have very low levels of political information, from naming the vice president to explaining how a high tax on imports might affect the price of American products, employment, or other countries' behavior.[52] This lack of information is compounded by bad memory. It appears that voters forget half of the political information they hear within one week, and 75 percent within three weeks.[53]

At first glance, this stunning amnesia would seem damning to the democratic project and even to educational policies like No Child Left Behind, which assume parents will be attentive to school performance and curriculum. Large numbers of voters might just as well be voting randomly. Political scientists have shown that voters who are well-informed make different choices than those who are not, and if all voters were well-informed, election outcomes might differ.[54] Ignorance of *specific* information appears to cause otherwise well-informed voters to make the wrong political choices. One study found that voters who had high levels of political knowledge (such as which political party was more conservative and which party controlled Congress at the time of the study) did not know that the Reagan administration reduced its enforcement of some environmental regulations in the 1980s. These voters were 18 percent less likely to support their own policy preferences of increasing spending on environmental enforcement.[55]

Yet just as stunningly, Americans' individual ignorance of politicians and policy effects does *not* prevent them from electing the same candidates they would have with full information and supporting the "right" policy proposals at the ballot box most of the time.[56] Voters do forget the specific political information that they hear, but they remember their *opinion* of the information, sometimes called a *consideration* or a "shortcut."[57] Voters keep an unconscious running tally of considerations about a political candidate (or policy issue) as they learn new information. Then, when they're asked to vote, they can make a decision based on the candidate's "score," even though they cannot remember any details about the person. So long as voters are paying some attention to politics or a particular policy area, they make reasonable judgments if there are a limited number of options (as in most elections for public office). Some evidence suggests that parents making decisions about where to send their children to school can make similarly reasonable decisions based on "marginal" information.[58]

When options are plentiful, as they are in public policy, citizens' lack of understanding can severely hamper decision making. Political theorists have long wondered about how "democracy" can function when the "demos" (people) do not have enough information to make policy. The framers of the Constitution feared the mob rule of uninformed but incited citizens, so they created a Senate and president who would not be directly elected. Others have suggested that democracy is not actually an aggregation of the people's will but an election contest to make decisions on behalf of the people.[59] Still others see bureaucracies of experts, such as a department of energy or college of education, as more or less representative of what is best for some citizens.[60] Low-information citizens, policy experts, teachers, administrators, and the elected representatives who oversee American educational policy disagree (and fight) over *who* should shape children's education. For example, this battle rages over who should write educational standards, explored in Chapter 6. Who knows what is best for a child's education, teachers or the experts and legislators who write state educational standards? Where can parents participate? How can schools measure whether children are informed? The core question is who has enough expertise to do what is right for a child, and whether the democratic process produces a good or a harmful remedy.

For example, the NCLB dealt squarely with where expertise about quality schooling should lie—outside the classroom. Proponents of the law believed that existing policy gave too much discretion to teachers and school administrators and argued that schools had little incentive to serve students with low academic achievement or behavioral problems. Federal educational policy since the 1960s had tried to address low academic performance by increasing federal spending on low-performing, low-income children, but by the late 1990s, evidence seemed to show that high spending on education did not mean high graduation rates or high scores on national achievement tests.[61] If spending in the schools could not help students, the argument went, federal policy should empower those outside the school. NCLB's public reporting of schools "in need of improvement" (because of low scores on tests) was meant to ensure that the temptation to ignore low-performing students had a visible, politically expensive, cost. Public accountability was meant to boost community awareness of school performance. In return, educational expertise would be left to parents by emphasizing school choice and to state departments of education through the creation of state standards and administration of testing.[62] Thus, the law has great faith that parents better understand the educational needs of their children than the teacher professionals who are hired by school administrators based on credentials.

Critics have vociferously opposed this view of informed parents. Although teachers' unions such as the National Education Association (NEA) and the American Federation of Teachers (AFT) did not deny that parents had legitimate concerns about the quality of education, particularly in urban districts, they argued that increasing funding for teacher training and retention would be far more effective than testing or school choice. The AFT complained that NCLB ignored "quality instruction" and urged lawmakers to redesign the law to be "teacher-driven [and] focused on student needs" and give teachers wide latitude over how the law would be implemented.[63] The NEA argued in court that NCLB did not provide enough federal money to fulfill its testing requirement or provide technical expertise about testing to schools or teachers (*School District of Pontiac v. Spellings* [2005]). In essence, the teachers' unions protested that the law undercut teachers' professionalism because they would not be consulted meaningfully about assessment tests and would have less time to tailor the school day to individual students. One principal told a researcher that "teachers are more nervous about how students do on tests and spend more time on test related items and less on creative, mind-expanding activities. They have less time to help develop the total student emotionally, physically, and academically."[64] Critics suggest that voters and their elected representatives do not have sufficient understanding to make well-informed decisions about elements of American educational policy.

The tests and accountability that NCLB and previous federal legislation inspired were meant to promote a common, basic understanding of American history, democracy, and government and to ensure that schools were providing equal opportunity to all children. Chapter 6 investigates how state and federal policymakers have urged schools and districts to increase their rigor through the use of graduation requirements, academic content standards, and standardized tests. Although the effects of these policies on children's education are hotly debated, the move to increase accountability has helped policymakers and the public know where students, schools, and teachers have gaps in understanding.

Self-Rule

Although self-rule is the cornerstone of democracy, democracies face the dilemma of giving as many people as possible the ability to make meaningful decisions about how their government should act *without* impinging on the rights of others. Policymakers incorporating citizens' self-rule into public policy must answer first, who should have the ability to make decisions, and second, how many people should be affected by those decisions. From an individual's point of view, the most restrictive version of self-rule would treat the person as a single vote among many but still bind that person to the result, as in an election. For example, some states have amended their constitutions through elections to dictate that legislators spend a certain sum on public education: California's Proposition 98 and Colorado's Amendment 23 are examples. The amendment process gives all state voters the right to make the decision jointly in an election and binds all state residents to the outcome. This approach to self-rule fits best with the norm of equality, because *all* residents are treated the same regardless of how they vote. The norm of inclusion is most at risk because individuals may have no recourse if the majority fails to respect minority group rights. At the other end of the spectrum, the strongest form of self-rule gives an individual control over government policy for his or her own situation only. Education voucher programs, which give parents tax-funded vouchers to use for a child's education at public or private schools—as in Milwaukee, Wisconsin, or Cleveland, Ohio—give *one* person the right to decide what educational policy should be, but only for his or her children. Lawmakers have also permitted parents to choose between public school districts or public charter schools. In the main, educational policymakers have encouraged self-rule using multiple, special-purpose governments—school districts—and more recently through public school choice.

The democratic norm of self-rule is most apparent when citizens engage in the politics of a public policy directly, and in American education that means they engage in school district politics. As discussed in Chapter 2, there are 13,628 regular school districts in the United States, ranging from 1,032 in Texas to just one in Hawaii (see table 2.2). Although their legal responsibilities differ from state to state, school districts offer citizens an obvious way to interact with educational policy, whether by selecting board members, speaking at board meetings, or raising taxes at the polls. In sum, school districts can fulfill self-rule through elections. School districts serve this norm well in that, excepting Hawaii, the districts are closer to the people they serve than are state or federal governments.

But elections are as flawed in translating the "will of the people" into government activity as they have been in encouraging meaningful participation. Economist Kenneth Arrow found that no system of elections could always be logical *and* fair.[65] In a democracy, a fair system of self-rule would ask voters to select among everyone's policy desires, but presenting everyone's desires would mean that voters would face a vast number of choices. A logical system would ensure that the winning choice is preferred by more voters than are losing choices, but any election in which voters were presented with more than two choices could easily result in the "winner" having a minority of votes.

For example, school districts in many states hold elections to set the tax rate for school support. In the 1950s and 1960s voters in Florida could write in their preferred tax rate on the ballot if they did not like the rate requested by the district. This made the election fair, because every voter had an equal opportunity to express his or her preference directly. But the system also meant that no single tax rate would garner a majority of votes. Most voters selected a rate other than the one that won.[66] Imagine an election system with three school board candidates running for one seat (so "everyone's" preferences are represented). Assume one candidate receives 28 percent of the vote, a second receives 35 percent, and a third 37 percent. The third candidate will win despite 63 percent of the electorate voting for the two losers. In both cases, the election outcomes were unfair to a majority of voters. There was no "majority" winner, and the majority was not self-governing.[67] (Even American presidential races, in which there are two dominant partisan contenders, show this flaw. Since the Civil War, thirteen presidential elections have yielded winners who garnered less than half of the total popular vote, among them George W. Bush, Bill Clinton, Richard Nixon, and John Kennedy.)

Elections in school districts may improve the chances of voters for self-rule, but even without elections, school districts serve another kind of self-rule, called Tiebout choice. Federalism allows citizens to choose among similar *governments* with roughly the same responsibilities. If one government does not provide the level of services a citizen wants, levies taxes that are too high, or appears unresponsive, in theory the person can leave to find a more suitable place to live. Such choice is most likely to work when there are many, small jurisdictions that have differing levels of service—a characteristic of many school districts—and when it is relatively easy to move. This process suggests that the public's satisfaction will be highest when residents have the option to pick a government that is reasonably close to their preferences on taxing and spending, so long as there are no major barriers to moving.[68] This form of self-rule requires a trade-off with equity: having different levels of school services or spending is a prime source of educational inequality.

Unlike voter rule through elections, citizens employing Tiebout choice do not send government policymakers signals about a specific direction for policy, but do so indirectly through population trends. School district administrators are keenly aware of these signals as they watch local birth rates and annual student attendance, which drive state and federal funding, and they do try to cater to the wishes of the local population. For example, the mass movement of young families to the suburbs and later the exurbs has strained both rural and urban districts as enrollments have declined. When Detroit lost 36 percent of its students and Minneapolis lost 28 percent between 2000 and 2008, both districts tried to respond by reshaping their educational programs in an attempt to keep students still in the district.[69] Proponents of Tiebout choice suggest that it disciplines local governments by keeping them attentive to their residents and neighboring governments.[70]

Tiebout choice is a slow process, because it occurs as citizens choose to move their homes, but some educational policymakers have tried to duplicate the discipline and voter satisfaction that Tiebout choice may bring to school districts through school choice. School choice means that parents can choose a school for their child (other than the assigned public school) without paying any money other than their existing taxes. Over 1 million students have participated in some form of school choice in recent years.[71] They attend magnet schools, charter schools, voucher schools, or just a school outside the district in which they live. There are two ways to think about how school choice shapes educational policy.

The first is by encouraging schools to cater to the desires of a particular group of students. Think of schools as like a business establishment, such as a restaurant. A person might pick a restaurant because of its price ("I'm on a $5 budget"), its location ("I don't have a car"), its service ("I only have thirty minutes"), its menu ("I'd like sauerkraut and bratwurst today"), its reputation ("I always like the meals I get there"), or its atmosphere ("I want a candlelit dinner"). Restaurants go out of business if they do not find a group of loyal patrons who return again and again. They have to reshape their product until they find a successful menu and atmosphere. Economists call restaurant services *experience goods*, because people cannot evaluate the service until they actually eat there—although they could seek the opinions of friends.

Schools are also experience goods. A parent might pick a school because of its price ("I cannot afford parochial school"), its location ("it's close to my work"), its curriculum ("it specializes in math and science"), its reputation ("95 percent of students are proficient in reading"), or its atmosphere ("the school just *feels* happy"). Desirable schools attract more interest, and less desirable schools struggle even without a formal program of school choice.[72] The school attendance zone that a house is in is the most important factor in setting the price of the property, even if the home buyer has no children.[73] School districts may respond to these "market pressures" by offering special-interest charter schools, like an engineering- or arts-focus school, or by upgrading sports facilities. This can bring students from neighboring districts directly or influence where people build and buy houses.[74] Through these forms of choice, parents show what they want from local educators.

If school districts respond by emphasizing the desires of diverse groups of residents, school choice might also improve parent participation in local school politics. School choice requires someone to make a choice, as in an election, but unlike an election, the consequences of the choice are real and immediate: a child goes to the school the parent chose. Choice gives parents control over government policy, but for only their children. This increases the likelihood that parents and students will have a stronger bond to the educational system and a much greater propensity to be involved in the educational process at that school. Charter schools in particular can incorporate much more parental, teacher, and even student feedback into what is taught and how it is taught.[75] Thus school choice can enhance the norm of participation.

Chapter 7 discusses how American policymakers have shaped school choice through voucher programs, charter schools, and open enrollment between school districts. It also discusses the implications of choice on democracy and educational performance. Although it does seem that choice improves parent satisfaction, whether it improves education itself is an open question.

Conclusion

For many, American educational policy cannot satisfactorily balance the tensions among democratic norms. If equality is highly valued, then curriculum standards in all schools should be as uniform as possible—or perhaps schools with needy populations should have additional teachers or more funding. If majority rule is paramount, then local public opinion expressed through frequent, contested elections should govern most aspects of school policy—or maybe a national majority should dictate what students should learn.

There is no obvious way to address these tensions, but the unique federal structure of American education serves as a release valve for pressure that builds among the norms. Educational policy can simultaneously follow local desires (on contentious curriculum), state values (school funding), or national priorities (desegregation). When policymakers draft choices for school leaders or members of Congress to consider, they can weigh which democratic norms are most important, or most salient, for their constituents. This book traces the path that policymakers have followed to find an imperfect but workable balance among democratic norms.

This chapter has given an overview of five norms that characterize healthy, modern democracies. First, inclusion suggests that democracies try to incorporate the views of as many of their citizens as possible; in education, that means offering education to as many different children as possible. Second, equality means that democracies treat citizens as similarly as possible without regard to their background, income, or status; in education, equality can mean equality of opportunity or outcome. Equal opportunity suggests that classrooms and curriculum be the same for children at the same level, whereas equal outcome means that children will have the same knowledge at the end of their formal education. Third, democracies encourage participation by citizens in governance. American education has many opportunities for citizens to provide input, from school board meetings to running for local office, but this book focuses on interest groups, especially teachers' unions, and their influence on educational policy locally and nationally. Fourth, democracies require citizens to be able to understand political issues to make intelligent choices when participating in the democratic process; indeed, democracies are uniquely dependent on an educated population to make good public policy. Educational policy incorporates the norm of understanding when policymakers design curriculum standards and some form of accountability into the education system. Finally, democracies promise that decisions are made "by the people" through self-rule. Self-rule can be expansive, giving a single person the ability to choose government policy for himself or herself, or it can be confined to the electoral process. Both Tiebout choice and school choice programs allow citizens to make decisions about the appropriate level of education for their children.

Suggested Readings

Dahl, Robert A. 1982. *Dilemmas of Pluralist Democracy.* New Haven, CT: Yale University Press.

Delli Carpini, Michael X., and Scott Keeter. 1996. *What Americans Know About Politics and Why It Matters.* New Haven, CT: Yale University Press.

Gamoran, Adam, and Daniel A. Long. 2006. "Equality of Educational Opportunity: A 40-Year Retrospective." WCER Working Paper 2006–9. Madison: Wisconsin Center for Education Research.

Hirsch, E. D., Jr. 2009. *The Making of Americans: Democracy and Our Schools.* New Haven, CT: Yale University Press.

Olson, Mancur. 1965. *The Logic of Collective Action.* New York: Schocken Books.

Ostrom, Elinor. 1990. *Governing the Commons: The Evolution of Institutions for Collective Action.* New York: Cambridge University Press.

Ringquist, Eric, Jeff Worsham, and Marc Allen Eisner. 2003. "Salience, Complexity, and the Legislative Direction of Regulatory Bureaucracies." *Journal of Public Administration Research and Theory* 13 (2): 141–164.

2

....

Structuring Democracy in American Education

AMERICAN EDUCATION is one of the most federal policies that American policymakers handle, because the national, state, and local governments all
have some say in how policymakers answer the four policy questions introduced in Chapter 1. American federalism allows the country's diversity to
tailor national policy to circumstances in local schools, but it also frustrates
reformers, who see children in poverty-laden schools, parents fleeing urban
schools for the suburbs, or gifted and talented students left to languish without challenging curriculum.

This chapter introduces education *governance*, or how political
institutions work together to make public policy. In a federal system, some
decisions are made and implemented by one level of government, some are
made by one and implemented by another, and still others are made jointly
by multiple levels. Frustrated policymakers have to face the uniquely
fragmented system of government in which multiple governing bodies all
have the *same* responsibilities—a fusion of functions but a division of
power.[1] The great difficulty for making coherent public policy is that each
governing body is elected (or appointed) by different groups of voters, who
may have very diverse wishes. School boards are elected by voters most
interested in the politics of local education, but Congress is populated with
members elected based on promises of economic growth, protecting the

environment, or saving Social Security. The U.S. Department of Education is the highest-level educational policy organization in the United States, but it has very little policymaking power compared to state governments. This chapter discusses each of the major policy players in educational policy and highlights the diversity of American schools and districts.

"The most important duty of the state should not be overseen by an unwieldy department with splintered accountability," Ohio Governor Ted Strickland told legislators in his state-of-the-state address in February 2008. As the state's top elected official, he argued that voters would expect *him* to enhance the state's academic achievement, crack down on its charter school program, and boost aid to Ohio's ailing big-city schools. He wanted power to directly appoint the state superintendent and to demote the nineteen members of the state school board from policymakers to mere advisors.

Strickland's proposal was born from experience. During her decade-long tenure, State Superintendent Susan Tave Zelman had been pushing strong, top-down accountability programs that department officials claimed were "a rigorous example for NCLB."[2] These clashed with Strickland's goals, but Zelman would not change. In 2008 he roasted her as "an academician, a psychometrician, [and] a statistician"—but not an educator.[3] Strickland's advisors charged that Zelman's Department of Education was "inordinately slow" and administered charter school policy that was "a train-wreck waiting to happen."[4] Yet Strickland could not do much about it—the state superintendent was beyond his reach. Only the state board of education could fire her.

The Ohio General Assembly nixed Strickland's request, but he was not alone in wanting direct control over state educational policy. Many governors have worn the mantle of "education governor," especially in the South, since the early twentieth century. With few exceptions, though, that title usually meant making rosy speeches about education but leaving the details to state departments of education.[5] In 1981 Wisconsin Governor Lee Dreyfus told the state's superintendent, "Make me the best education governor ever, OK?"[6]

By the 1990s, however, governors had become serious about intervening in educational policy. In 1991 Ohio Governor George Voinovich blasted the state's Department of Education in an attempt to take some of its power for himself. In 1993 Michigan Governor John Engler junked the state's existing school finance system and forced voters to choose between *no* state funding and *his* funding plan.[7] Wisconsin Governor Tommy Thompson cut $2.79 billion out of the state Department of Instruction's $2.8 billion budget in 1995. He then promised to create a new, separate Department of Education accountable to *him*, not the state superintendent.[8] In 2003 New Mexico Governor Bill Richardson successfully stripped the state's board of education of policy-making powers.[9] In 2006 Washington Governor Christine Gregoire used new powers to appoint half of the state board of education herself.[10] And in 2008 Maryland Governor Martin O'Malley demanded the appointed state superintendent step down to make way for someone he chose (she refused).[11] In 2009 U.S. Secretary of Education Arne Duncan lauded the strong role played by governors: "Governors . . . challenged all of us to make education more than a political talking point or an empty slogan."[12] Strickland was only one of a crowd.

Power grabs? Maybe—but these governors saw the matter differently. It is true that *they* wanted to reshape educational policy, but without exception, these governors echoed Tommy Thompson's sentiment: giving governors control over educational policy would "give power back to the parents, the teachers, and the taxpayers of Wisconsin."[13] Although each governor had different priorities, they all saw themselves as agents of self-rule. In their view, educational bureaucracy, school districts, and interest groups could distort the will of the people.

Governing American Education

No matter how innovative a policymaker's idea is, or how strong interest group support is, or even how overwhelming the majority will is, all policy decisions are made through political *institutions*. How well a state's institutions work together is called *governance*. Institutions include the U.S. Congress and Department of Education; the fifty state governors, state superintendents, and legislatures; and the tens of thousands of local school board members and district superintendents. The apportionment of responsibility among them varies from state to state, but understanding how they work together is crucial for understanding how well a federal public policy could be implemented in schools.[14] Are school districts responsible for major educational policy decisions, or, as asserted in one state supreme court's opinion, is such local control only a "cliché"?[15] Does the state department of education control curriculum and teacher promotion policy, or is that left to school districts? Should the states or the federal government decide what children learn, and when? These formal institutions are enmeshed with *policy subsystems*, or informal networks of interest groups, researchers, governmental policy specialists, and legislators who support a particular constellation of public policy. Such public–private cooperation can help legislators decide among competing policy options, because they can increase buy-in from teachers or other stakeholders, provide evidence to support the policy's theory of action, and provide political support in the legislative process. Or they can hinder reforms because received wisdom within the system suggests that some policy "cannot" work or is somehow inappropriate. These subsystems exist in both state and national governments and to a lesser extent in school districts.

The quality of governance in educational policy may thwart *any* of the norms of democracy, and navigating the diverse governments of the United States is a thorn in the flesh for educational reformers—although whether that is a bad thing depends on what policymakers think is good policy. In large countries like the United States, it is likely that some citizens will be unhappy with decisions made by a distant government or by citizens in another part of the country. To minimize these disputes, James Madison, one of the framers of the U.S. Constitution, suggested that the national and state governments share functions and powers. For Madison, multiple governments with the same responsibilities would prevent any single government from becoming too powerful (because other governments would resist) and improve the possibility for self-rule.[16] It may be that people in Massachusetts prefer higher state spending on education than do those in Colorado; having independent state governments increases the chance that voters in those states will have their own preferences met. In Federalist No. 10, Madison argued that minority rights, interests, and policy ideas would be protected if it were difficult for majorities to form and change legislation. Nationally, the U.S. Constitution protects minorities by separating powers among three branches; and the U.S. Senate allows a minority of one to stop legislation, at least temporarily, through the filibuster, but outside Washington, D.C., American *federalism* enhances these barriers, as one level of government works at cross-purposes with another.

Three examples will illustrate the dilemma of seeking reform in a federal system. First, when national, federal courts first ordered schools to desegregate in the 1950s, it took almost twenty years for all major school districts to even begin to comply (see Chapter 3). Second, some governors began pushing higher academic standards in the late 1970s and early 1980s, but many chafed when the *federal* government tried to create national academic standards in 1994. They and others successfully thwarted that effort (see Chapter 6). Third, in 2011, when it became apparent that Wisconsin Governor Scott Walker would successfully limit teachers' collective bargaining to wages only in his state, many school districts rushed to approve new contracts with local unions before the law went into effect (see Chapter 5). In each case, one level of government prevented policymakers at another level from making the changes they wanted, when they wanted. The following section presents a brief overview of the educational responsibilities of the four primary layers of American educational governance discussed throughout this book: federal, state, school district, and school. The appendix presents a timeline of some of the events discussed.

Federal Institutions

For much of American history, the federal government in Washington, D.C., limited direct involvement in educational policy, and to date, its influence is limited to offering federal money in return for states and districts enacting various public policies voluntarily. States and districts *could* ignore federal legislation and refuse federal funding. No state has ever done so, although some legislators have threatened to do so. The U.S. Constitution does not give Congress the authority to regulate education, but courts have ruled that *fiscal federalism*, in which one level of government complies with another in return for funds, is appropriate. The U.S. Congress currently appropriates about $47.7 billion annually for K–12 education, approximately 8.2 percent of all education revenues (see figure 2.1).[17] It was not always this way; the federal government had no practical role in K–12 education until 1917, when Congress provided limited funding for vocational education. Some additional math and science funding was added in 1958, but it was the 1965 Elementary and Secondary Education Act (ESEA) that announced the entry of the federal government into the classroom (covered in more depth in Chapter 3). Federal policy is made in the U.S. Congress primarily in two committees, the House Committee on Education and Labor and the Senate Committee on Health, Education, Labor and Pensions. These two committees draft legislation that specifies the requirements for receiving federal money. Through major educational legislation like ESEA, Congress has structured how districts provide education to special-needs students, how

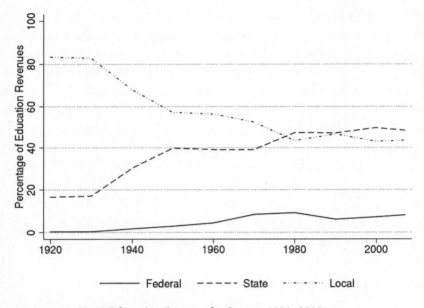

FIGURE 2.1   K–12 Education Revenue by Source, 1920–2008

Source: National Center for Education Statistics (2011), table 180.

frequently state tests are administered, and how many high school sports must be provided for girls and boys. Current U.S. Secretary of Education Arne Duncan has suggested that he will push to increase federal aid to schools, thereby increasing federal influence.[18] Along with Congress, the federal courts have played some role in educational policymaking, chiefly in desegregation efforts, special-needs education, religion, and sex equity issues.

The primary federal bureaucracy responsible for educational policy is the U.S. Department of Education, created as the Office of Education in 1867. Then, as now, its purpose was to collect statistics on teachers and schools and to ensure that state governments were using federal monies appropriately. In 1867 that money was for land-grant colleges, but now it is for ESEA, higher education, disability education funding, and other federal legislation. The agency began to gain policy influence as a compliance office in the early 1970s—ensuring that districts spent federal money on appropriate children—but only began to actively advocate major state policy changes in the 1980s under Secretary of Education William Bennett. He maintained a "wall chart" of educational statistics to cajole states into

---

BOX 2.1   Selected Educational Interest Groups, Think Tanks, and
Research Organizations

American Association of
  People with Disabilities
American Enterprise Institute
American Federation of Teachers
American Institutes for Research
The Arc of the United States
Association of School Business Officials
Brookings Institution
Center for American Progress
Center for Education Reform
Council of Chief State School Officers
Economic Policy Institute

Heritage Foundation
Learning Disabilities Association
  of America
Mathematica
National Association for the Education
  of Young Children
National Association of State Boards
  of Education
National Education Association
Progressive Policy Institute
RAND Corporation
Thomas B. Fordham Institute

Note: This list is not comprehensive. There are hundreds of associations
that lobby on behalf of educational interests.

---

improving academic standards, and later the department housed a research
arm that has become the Institute for Education Sciences. The Department
of Education is charged with writing rules for states, districts, and other
providers of education who implement their own public policies, but they
must comply with federal goals.

Both staff at the Department of Education and members of Congress
cooperate with members of think tanks and interest groups in the policy
subsystem, who are eager to influence federal legislation. These groups
lobby federal personnel in the hope that legislation will treat particular
groups of students, employees, parents, or taxpayers favorably (see Chapter
5). Interest groups and think tanks also raise public awareness of educational issues, or they may serve to communicate the needs of a particular
group to the government. In the main, members of Congress listen carefully,
because these groups often have more expertise in a particular policy area
than do members of Congress. For example, the National Education Association (NEA), one of two major American teachers' unions, has produced
estimates and studies about teacher employment and pay for decades, and
the U.S. Department of Education uses NEA data as a primary source of

information. If the NEA argues that some piece of federal legislation will harm teachers, members of Congress are likely to consider the association's arguments carefully, even if they do not adopt the NEA's position. There are certain major educational interest groups, but the sheer number of groups at the federal level prevents any one of them from being too influential.[19] Box 2.1 (page 35) lists the major educational interest groups.

State Institutions

State governments control the lion's share of educational policy. State laws dictate what courses schools must provide, the number of days a school must be open in a year, who may participate in athletics, whether teachers may unionize (and whether they may strike), and whether students can choose which public school they attend. Even with increasing federal control of state standards, states still write those standards and decide what score will pass a state test. In doing so, states have shown James Madison to be right: they have pushed back against the federal government by lowering proficiency standards.[20]

When policymakers propose structures for governing public policy, they make explicit choices about distributing political power among voters, legislators, bureaucrats, and the governor.[21] Every state (except Hawaii) has local school districts that give voters some measure of control over school decisions, although school boards have lost much of their political clout. In many states, school boards once controlled teacher qualifications and academic curriculum, and both policies undergird the quality of schools. But since governors have taken an active interest in education beginning in the 1970s, state legislators and governors have wrested these decisions away from districts. An increase in state and federal school funding has also weakened *the* major attraction of many school districts for homeowners: "We spend more on our education."[22] Although school spending is nowhere near equal across districts, local districts no longer control the majority of spending.

State lawmakers face two basic institutional questions about state educational governance: Should there be an elected or appointed state board of education? and Should a state superintendent be elected, appointed by the board, or appointed by the governor? The spectrum of answers policymakers have offered appears in table 2.1. Most states involve their governors at some level, but many also check their power with independently elected officials.

TABLE 2.1   State Educational Governance Structures

	State Board Elected	*State Board Appointed*	*No State Board*
State Superintendent Elected	None	AZ, CA, GA, ID, IN, MT, NC, ND, OK, OR, SC, WA*, WY (13)	WI
State Superintendent Appointed	AL, CO, KS, LA, MI, NE, *NM*, NV, OH*, *TX*, UT (11)	AK, AR, *CT*, *DE*, FL, HI, *IA*, IL, KY, MA*, MD, *ME*, MO, MS, *NH*, *NJ*, NY, *PA*, RI, *SD*, *TN*, *VA*, VT, WV (24)	*MN*

States with governor-appointed state school superintendents are *italic* (12). All other appointed chiefs are board-appointed (26). States with part-appointed, part-elected boards are indicated by an asterisk (*). Most appointed boards are appointed by the governor, although some are appointed by legislatures.

Source: National Association of State Boards of Education (2011).

How well educational governance works is influenced by formal institutions as well. State superintendents and state school boards may be appointed or elected. Unlike either legislatures or voters, governors have clear, strong preferences in public policy. Governors cannot attend to every policy area all the time, so they prefer to have like-minded people at the helm of various agencies. Appointees also allow the governor to take credit for successes. ("In the last four years, *my* policies have boosted the graduation rate" sounds much more convincing as an election stump speech than "I support *the board's* graduation policies.") Of course appointees also shield governors from blame—governors can fire appointees if they do not live up to expectations and claim that they will find a better candidate more in tune with their own preferences. Critics argue that appointees are more likely to use *political* judgment than sound *policy* judgment. Appointees are not *supposed* to be politicians, because they are buffered from voters, but they must stay in the good graces of the governor.

Governors argue that appointees allow voters to make a clear connection between public policy and the governor. If voters are unhappy with the state graduation test pushed by an appointed state superintendent, they can punish the governor at the next election. If the state superintendent is hired by a board, voters might be able to turn out state board members (if *they* are elected), but that might not affect the state superintendent. Of course if the state superintendent is elected statewide, the voters have more clout. However, it is possible that few voters will pay attention to elections for state superintendent. As discussed in Chapter 1, elections are not robust expressions of self-rule. Too few voters turn out on election day, and most elections do not allow voters to choose public policies. Many states hold school elections at a different time than general elections (April is a common month). That means that the blanket election coverage that typically dominates November elections is missing, and turnout hovers in the low teens. But even where education officials do run in November elections, few voters cast ballots. The race between Barack Obama and John McCain in 2008 drew one of the highest turnouts in the last fifty years, but only 38 percent of Ohio voters selected *any* candidate for the *seven* state school board seats.

Wisconsin's Thompson argued that low turnout made the state's *elected* state superintendent a pawn of the "educational establishment," the state's largest teachers' union. Similarly, in 1999 Governor Roy Barnes of Georgia argued that his state's elected superintendent was hiding data from the public to protect herself and "interest groups" who supported her.[23] He successfully took away many of the state superintendent's policy powers and vested them in his own "Office of Educational Accountability." Whether interest groups can swing an election in their favor or not, democratic self-rule is undercut by low-turnout elections. Both of these governors made the argument that the voters who turned out to elect the state superintendent were *different* voters than the general public. Both argued that the voters' choice of governor was better informed and more representative—that is, the governor's decisions would be fulfilling the norm of self-rule for *more* voters. Gubernatorial appointees would be more accountable to voters than elected specialists.

Supporters of independently elected education officials argue that education is not really a "bargainable" policy. State attorneys general are elected separately from governors to take away one avenue of corruption. Governors have a much harder time persecuting their political foes when the attorney general is accountable to voters rather than the governor. Likewise, independently elected superintendents or state school board members should not be motivated by fear of the governor. Should education or prisons receive more funding? The governor might have to make that choice, but an elected superintendent only has one answer: the schools. Voters can select *how* the superintendent or board defends the schools, but they know that their choice will fight for a core constitutional responsibility. (Unlike the federal constitution, many state constitutions explicitly guarantee education to residents. See Chapter 4.)

The division of state authority can create constitutional crises when the governor and his fellow state officials disagree. A despairing Wisconsin state superintendent, John Benson, faced with losing $2.79 billion, tried and failed to convince the legislature that he had *equal* power to that of Governor Thompson. The legislature didn't buy the theory. "You can't do anything! The governor thinks he's God!" the senate majority leader told him.[24] The senator was right—but legal trouble loomed. The state attorney general, also independently elected, refused to defend the governor in court, and Thompson had to hire an outside lawyer. The Wisconsin Supreme Court decided that the state education department's budget was subject to the legislature, and the governor could not eviscerate it. Although Benson could not equal the governor's budget powers or command of state government generally, voters knew he was the top advocate for the state's education program.

Granting the governor appointment power creates a dilemma for democratic norms. A strong governor is more visible than state school board members, but eliminating elections weakens the norm of participation. Even though elections for state superintendents draw few voters, it is likely that those voters have a higher interest in state educational policy. Their views might not be representative of voters as a whole, but they *are* representative of voters who are best informed on the issue.[25] ("Timenka has taken four classes with Professor Spurgeon—you should ask her about his courses.") But ceding one of the most expensive state policy areas to a minority of voters also risks undercutting the norms of inclusion and self-rule. Perhaps school costs are out of line with how much state voters value education versus low taxes, quality roads, an efficient criminal justice system, or land conservation. Gubernatorial appointees can make unpopular changes in the policy area that elected officials cannot.

Like the federal government, states have legislatures that write funding formulas and give authority to state bureaucracy. However, many state legislators have less time and fewer staff to process information about legislation than the U.S. Congress has. (In the U.S. Senate, for example, each senator has one staff member devoted to only educational policy; in some states, a legislator may have just one staff member.) Thus legislators are more dependent on interest groups, think tanks, and state bureaucracy for reliable information and policy ideas than are members of Congress.[26] Departments of education write state rules and may distribute state funding to districts. Their capacities vary dramatically across the United States: in Iowa the state education department has a small budget and advertises that it exists to serve district needs, but in Georgia the state department can specify classroom practice.[27]

Local Institutions

Federalism extends to the local level also, and school districts fulfill this role in educational policy (see table 2.2). In most states school districts are responsible for constructing buildings, hiring and paying teachers, and funding about half of the costs of schooling.[28] Most of those funds come from local property taxes, but school districts might not have the ability to set the tax rate or determine how the money is spent, because the school funding level is set by state law (see Chapter 4). Ninety-six percent of school districts are governed by elected school board.[29] Districts may choose curriculum and sometimes how that curriculum will be taught. School boards can be attentive to the wishes of citizens simply because active voters can show up at public meetings if they are dissatisfied, although it is more likely that school boards are "captured" by small groups of very active parents or teachers.[30] In theory, school district governance ensures that educational policy is tailored to voters in that district.

Despite the democratic potential of school boards, critics have long assaulted the existence of school boards. In the late nineteenth century political reformers framed education as a public policy that was too important to be left to regular "politics." Then, allowing an elected board to control education would lead to local political ward chiefs determining school quality, partisan retaliation, or religious indoctrination of pupils. Now, critics argue that school boards have been "captured" by politically motivated educational interest groups and teachers' unions.[31] For example, figure 2.2 shows cartoonist Thomas Nast's view of textbook changes ordered by New York City's commissioner of public works, William M. "Boss" Tweed in 1871. Tweed was a fabulously successful politician because he and his associates were driven by electoral math rather than educational considerations. The textbooks were published by a media company whose newspapers published

TABLE 2.2   Number of Regular School Districts by State, 2008–2009

State	Districts	Students	State	Districts	Students
Texas	1,032	4,728,202	Georgia	180	1,660,643
California	958	6,100,700	New Hampshire	180	197,131
Illinois	869	2,101,198	Colorado	178	825,242
New York	696	2,721,522	Kentucky	174	679,901
Ohio	615	1,672,054	Connecticut	169	538,756
New Jersey	603	1,368,811	South Dakota	156	123,558
Michigan	551	1,510,716	Mississippi	152	491,651
Oklahoma	532	653,592	Tennessee	140	972,549
Missouri	523	897,385	Virginia	134	1,231,205
Pennsylvania	500	1,682,891	Alabama	133	748,889
Wisconsin	425	864,898	Idaho	116	266,707
Montana	417	141,693	North Carolina	115	1,444,409
Iowa	361	491,255	New Mexico	89	331,436
Minnesota	337	798,508	South Carolina	85	715,590
Kansas	316	474,026	Louisiana	69	651,930
Washington	295	1,034,698	Florida	67	2,627,390
Indiana	294	1,026,053	West Virginia	55	281,828
Vermont	291	89,999	Alaska	53	131,265
Nebraska	253	294,948	Wyoming	48	87,913
Maine	246	188,694	Utah	41	548,397
Arkansas	244	474,897	Rhode Island	32	130,623
Massachusetts	244	792,874	Maryland	24	848,252
Arizona	224	958,968	Delaware	19	117,628
Oregon	190	558,960	Nevada	17	423,859
North Dakota	185	94,997	Hawaii	1	180,196

Source: National Center for Education Statistics (2010a).

scathing attacks on Tweed's alleged graft and corruption (including Nast's cartoons; note the reference to "honest" government). Tweed punished the company by banning its textbooks. In the end, Tweed and many of his associates were convicted of rampant election fraud and graft. Political bosses' meddling in education convinced political reformers in the 1870s and Progressive reformers in the early twentieth century that appointed personnel would be a significant improvement over general-purpose government. They would enhance pupils' chances for democratic understanding.

Yet elected school boards have their defenders. Proponents suggest that they help the local community influence education democratically. For

FIGURE 2.2   Thomas Nast: "Sowing the Seed, with an Eye to the Harvest"
Source: Paine (1904), 159.

example, socially contentious issues regularly come up at school board meetings. The Dover, Pennsylvania, district school board adopted a statement in October 2004, noting that Darwinian evolution was "not a fact." Although students still covered the subject in ninth grade, the school board drew national media attention, and the six (of nine) board members who voted to adopt the policy lost the subsequent board election.[32] Many school districts also struggle with how to present homosexuality in sex education courses (and how to present sex education in general); school boards tend to follow local opinion. Some districts, especially in the South, do not cover it at all; other districts, especially on the West Coast and in the Northeast, tend to spend several days on the topic.[33] In 2005 the Montgomery County, Maryland, school board introduced a comprehensive sex education curriculum that was the product of a twenty-seven-member community board, in an effort to reflect the wishes of the parents and community groups in the district. A handful of community critics, however, convinced a federal judge to issue an injunction against the curriculum. They charged that the curriculum violated the First Amendment's Establishment Clause (because the curriculum attempted to interpret passages from the Bible) and presented only one view of sexual orientation.[34] The district later adopted a much-reduced version of the curriculum that was "viewpoint neutral."[35] The Dover and Montgomery County cases show that school boards do respond to community desires, even when those desires cause conflict.

Nevertheless, critics of school boards suggest that they are anachronisms of a more participatory time when Americans were more rooted to location. Elections for school boards are frequently held at odd times that make it likely only the most invested citizens—and school employees—will vote. In 2002 only 4 percent of registered voters had cast ballots to elect Dover's six board members; this number is not abnormal.[36] Attentive groups can greatly influence policy, especially teachers' unions. Some 31 percent of school boards report that unions are "very active" in elections, to good effect: almost 76 percent of union-supported candidates win.[37] Teachers' unions have a vested interest in the outcome of board races, of course, because the board sets pay, benefits, and working conditions for teachers, so it is in the unions' interests to have friendly employers (see Chapter 5). Critics also suggest that school boards are more concerned about preserving funding than in improving academic outcomes of schooling.[38] Some large cities have experimented with appointed school boards or giving mayors direct control of school systems, notably Baltimore, Chicago, New York City, and Washington, D.C. Yet these are exceptions. Despite a century of attacks, elected school boards have survived in almost every school district in the United States.

School Institutions

The lowest level of governance is the school itself. Teachers and principals, the front-line workers, are charged with carrying out policies decided by other levels of government, and their cooperation is crucial for the implemented policy to resemble what policymakers want (see Chapter 6 for a discussion of this loose coupling). Because some research has found that schools with a strong sense of mission and a coherent school culture improve student learning, some schools offer explicit opportunities for teachers and principals to make decisions about hiring and teacher placement; this is called *school-based management*.[39] Depending on state law, public charter schools take school-based management further, often giving the school the right to choose its own curriculum as well (see Chapter 7).[40]

Conclusion

Does giving governors more control over education actually increase educational efficiency or the representation of interests *not* associated with traditional public school advocates? Or do governors simply want the power to push through reforms of their own, whether those are introducing vouchers, cracking down on charters, cutting property taxes, or imposing state-run fiscal accountability on school districts? Do school districts help local communities resolve the democratic dilemma of education, or are they financially inefficient, unrepresentative local elites? Policymakers seeking dramatic policy changes have to navigate the very difficult waters of educational governance. Special-purpose school boards and strong-willed governors can easily work at cross-purposes to state legislators' best intentions, and even the attraction of federal money cannot guarantee that teachers on the front line themselves will readily adopt new programs. Thus, when the U.S. Supreme Court ordered desegregation "with all deliberate speed" in *Brown v. Board of Education* (1954), it was faced not with the massive resistance that some white Southerners threatened, but fragmented educational governance that made speedy implementation impossible (see Chapter 3). Later, when No Child Left Behind (2002) required states to test students for academic proficiency, states could raise or lower the bar for passing state tests, frustrating reformers (see Chapter 8). The roadblocks—and protections—of federalism persist.

Suggested Readings

Berkman, Michael B., and Eric Plutzer. 2005. *Ten Thousand Democracies: Politics and Public Opinion in America's School Districts.* Washington, DC: Georgetown University Press.

Elmore, Richard F. 1996. "Getting to Scale with Good Educational Practice." *Harvard Educational Review* 66 (1, Spring): 1–27.

Henig, Jeffrey R. 2009. "Mayors, Governors, and Presidents: The New Education Executive and the End of Educational Exceptionalism." *Peabody Journal of Education* 84 (3, August): 283–299.

Hess, Frederick M. 2008. "Looking for Leadership: Assessing the Case for Mayoral Control of Urban Schools." *American Journal of Education* 114 (2): 219–245.

Manna, Paul. 2006. *School's In: Federalism and the National Education Agenda*. Washington, DC: Georgetown University Press.

3

. . . .

Including Americans

THE DEMOCRATIC NORM of *inclusion* has dominated American educational policy since the 1950s, especially at the federal level. Efforts to increase inclusion in educational policy have taken two distinct paths. The first, founded on court decisions in the 1950s, 1960s, and 1970s, emphasized racial desegregation. The second spent federal money on civil rights and antipoverty programs. Since the initial court decisions about race, policymakers have extended inclusion to sex and children with special needs. Yet inclusion sits uncomfortably with other democratic norms. Neither self-rule nor participation has much place for citizens who are not in the majority, because both norms seek power for specific individuals or groups, whereas inclusion values *all* comers. Policymakers trying to model democratic understanding through careful research may find that inclusion thwarts other policy values like community loyalty or efficient spending.

This chapter introduces problem definition, path dependency, and limitations on policy evaluation. *Problem definition* is among the most difficult aspects of designing public policy. Although it helps policymakers answer the first policy question—Is there a problem?—directly, the definition of a problem limits how policymakers answer the other three questions. For example, this chapter considers whether American democracy should address racial segregation as the core policy problem, or whether policymakers should target instead the problem of low academic achievement among African Americans and Latinos. Decisions made in the mid-twentieth century pushed policymakers toward racial integration, which constrained state and federal efforts to improve academic achievement later. This is an example of *path dependency*, in which previous policy decisions limit the options available for policymakers later. Finally, this chapter suggests that a clear problem definition helps legislators and the public perform *policy evaluation* later. If policymakers define the source of the problem, an evaluator can measure how much of the original problem still exists. For example, if racial segregation became a public policy problem in the 1950s, evaluators in 2011 can measure how segregated American schools still are.

Since the 1950s American educational policy has become deeply entwined with race politics, affecting school vouchers, academic achievement, school funding, and teachers' unions.[1] This chapter explores the two major policy responses to the norm of inclusion: federal desegregation orders and federal spending on education through the 1965 Elementary and Secondary Education Act (ESEA). These responses complemented each other in the 1960s, but court decisions and a lack of political will since then have eliminated desegregation orders as effective policy instruments. Few policymakers now view segregation alone as the top educational policy problem, and the problem definition has expanded to include the availability of school finances, teacher training, school quality, and above all, student academic achievement.

Sometime during the night of February 5, 1970, dynamite destroyed twenty-four of Denver, Colorado's, school buses and damaged fifteen more—almost one-third of its fleet. On February 21 an antibusing school board member found a firebomb in his front room; three days later Wilfred Keyes's porch was blown up.[2]

Keyes, an African American, had sued the Denver Public School district in 1969, claiming that the district did not spend the same cash on schools in heavily black neighborhoods as on those in white neighborhoods and that it deliberately kept blacks out of mostly white schools in northeast Denver.[3] Denver's leaders prided themselves on the city's reputation for an inclusive political culture, so Keyes's charges stung. Could Denver in 1969 really be like Little Rock, Arkansas, was in 1957?[4]

The charges hurt more because the school board, with apparently strong community support, had adopted a busing program in 1968 to ensure that all children had an "integrated experience." The board redrew school attendance zones and called for busing 2,790 out of 93,000 children to different schools to improve the racial balance in the district.[5]

But community support was not as strong as the board thought it was. In the May 1969 school board elections, the controversy over busing energized candidates on both sides of the issue. Opponents of the policy won the election better than two-to-one, and they promptly terminated the entire integration plan. Keyes and seven others sued in federal court. Then the bombings began.[6]

Busing children to achieve racial integration in the schools—an attempt to build democratic inclusion—inflamed both whites and blacks. Blacks questioned inclusion: Weren't they capable of educating themselves? Why weren't African American teachers and principals good enough for white children? Whites asked: Don't black children drag down academic achievement? Weren't inner-city schools havens for crime? Both asked: Why does my child have to travel an hour on a bus to go to first grade?[7]

The Problem: What's Race Got to Do with It?

For Keyes, racial segregation was the problem, but for others, keeping children close to home or maintaining racial pride was the core policy problem. The problem definitions give public policies their shape and direction. They indicate who or what causes an undesirable situation, limit the policy instruments government policymakers consider, and suggest how they might evaluate the proposed public policy.

Problem definitions help policymakers limit their options. For example, in 2009 and 2010, 4,200 Toyota car owners alleged that their cars sped up on their own. At least 58 of these occurrences led to high-speed crashes. The car owners blamed Toyota's car design (the "problem"); Toyota and the National Highway Traffic Safety Administration argued that driver error was actually to blame. If the problem was that drivers were, in fact, pushing the gas pedal instead of the brakes, then it did not make sense to sue Toyota. If Toyota's design was at fault, then some government action might be in order.[8]

The Toyota case shows how *cause* is crucial to problem definition. Defining causes has always bedeviled educational policymakers, but especially so since the federal government made its foray into K–12 education. Without knowing the major causes of a problem, policymakers cannot realistically propose governmental activity to solve it. How much is segregation caused by law (de jure), and how much is it caused by people deciding to live near others of the same ethnicity or race (de facto, or residential segregation)? How much of a student's low academic achievement is a result of poverty, cultural biases against school success, a lack of school spending, and poorly qualified teachers? The most difficult challenge for a policymaker is weighing these factors to design appropriate policy instruments—without conflicting with other policies or creating unintended negative consequences.

Problem definition is also a political process, meaning that "causes" are likely to be defined by crisis events, interest groups, and ambitious policymakers as much as by dispassionate analyses of a policy area.[9] For example, when the Soviet Union beat the United States into space by launching the *Sputnik* satellite in 1957, members of Congress panicked, thinking that American math and science education was deficient. Congress quickly allocated federal funds for math and science education—even though at best, boosting high school math and science in 1958 and 1959 would do nothing to improve American rocketry until much later. Second, American desegregation efforts began through the careful legal efforts of the National Association for the Advancement of Colored People (NAACP) and later the Southern Christian Leadership Conference (SCLC), rather than by policymakers deciding that the wide gap between white and nonwhite student achievement was a public policy problem. Politicians and groups who want a particular government action are also likely to create a problem definition that lends itself to the solution they already prefer.[10] For example, a major interest group for the learning disabled, The Arc of the United States, borrowed the language of civil rights to lobby federal legislators to force school districts to integrate special-needs children into their regular academic programs through the Education for All Handicapped Children Act (1975) and the Individuals with Disabilities Education Act (1990).

Policymakers have only incomplete information, so they have to muddle through with the best political sense they have. Deciding on a cause can help policymakers suggest what government can, and cannot, do about a problem. For example, although high levels of poverty correlate with poor academic performance and other social problems, the causes of poverty are not well understood.[11] Some policymakers might suggest that poverty results from the lack of stable employment opportunities, so providing broad-based employment programs is something clearly in the domain of public policy.[12] If poverty is caused more directly by cultural norms than by economic opportunity, however, policymakers are left with little in their toolboxes.[13] Likewise, if school segregation is the result of school district administrators drawing lines to ensure most Latinos attend one school while whites attend another, policymakers have a straightforward solution: change the law. But if segregation results from whites choosing to minimize their children's interactions with African American children in school by moving out of a school district, democratic governments have few options.

Incomplete information limits policy choices, but the choices that policymakers can recommend today are also narrowed by government policy decisions made last year and a century ago, even if the original policy no longer works well. This is *path dependency*.[14] A good example of path dependency is summer break. Almost all schools in the United States continue to give students three months off from school in the summer, a remnant from the country's agrarian past. Sports camps, college prep courses, and family vacations now fill these months, even though research shows that summer vacation is extremely detrimental to learning. The average student loses one to three months of school learning in the summer, especially in math and spelling, but the difference is most pronounced between whites and Asians on the one hand and African Americans and Latinos on the other.[15] Yet the plethora of summer activities and the vast number of people who expect the time off has made "switching costs" extremely high. In this context, switching costs could include the loss of summer jobs for teens, depressed tourism revenue, increased school building costs for air conditioning and janitorial services, and higher pay for teachers and administrators to compensate for a change in schedule.

Another example of path dependency in educational policy is the wide use of "Carnegie units." Each unit is 120 hours of instruction in one subject in a year. In 1906 the Carnegie Foundation for the Advancement of Teaching successfully persuaded colleges to adopt these units to standardize the admissions process. Colleges could then demand, say, "four Carnegie units in high school English" for admission and not have to investigate the educational practices of every student's high school. The units were convenient for colleges and high schools, and they were quickly adopted by virtually every high school in America (if your high school had grade-point averages, it used Carnegie units).

Path dependency helps policymakers understand that changes to institutionalized policies are likely to occur only after critical junctures, like major social disruptions (war, terrorist attacks), political shifts (a sudden one-party dominance), or demographic changes (a rapid growth in immigration).[16] Even though the Carnegie Foundation has disowned the unit bearing its name, federal government commissions have harshly criticized the units, and a century of empirical research has questioned their academic usefulness, they remain the basic units.[17] The Carnegie unit has become *institutionalized*. New reforms must be framed around old institutions.

The critical juncture for the norm of inclusion was *Brown v. Board of Education* (1954). After a half-century of other efforts, the NAACP's Thurgood Marshall persuaded the U.S. Supreme Court that sending blacks to separate schools created a steep psychological barrier to a child's life chances. The justices held that such separation generated "a feeling of inferiority . . . that may affect their hearts and minds in a way unlikely ever to be undone" (494). They called education a "right" and said it must be offered "to all on equal terms" (493). Thus the Supreme Court held that racial segregation fundamentally undercut the ability of African Americans to participate in American democracy. They could not fully appreciate other democratic norms so long as public facilities, especially schools, were segregated.

This decision was a dramatic break from prior policy. Not only was segregation widespread and legal (since *Plessy v. Ferguson* [1896]), but the federal government had had almost no involvement in education. Only 3.5 percent of all elementary and secondary education revenues came from the federal government in 1950 (versus 9.6 percent in 2009). *Brown* and subsequent court decisions filled in that blank canvas by announcing that the federal government would intervene in one of the most basic functions of local government: building, staffing, and maintaining schools. Court decisions over the next twenty-five years sharpened the federal focus on racial inclusion at the expense of other norms.

Despite this policy path, the race-based focus of federal policy has significantly weakened. Indeed, some scholars argue that American children are as segregated by race now as they were in the 1950s, calling into question whether the vast sums of time and money spent on inclusion could be better spent enhancing other democratic norms, such as participation or self-rule.[18] For example, in *Missouri v. Jenkins* (1995), Supreme Court Justice Clarence Thomas wrote:

> Given that desegregation has not produced the predicted leaps forward in black educational achievement, there is no reason to think that black students

cannot learn as well when surrounded by members of their own race as when they are in an integrated environment. . . . [B]lack schools can function as the center and symbol of black communities, and provide examples of independent black leadership, success, and achievement. (121–122)

Thomas's opinion suggested that the public policies meant to address democratic inclusion were not actually fixing the core policy problem. His view was that federal policy was supposed to improve "black leadership, success, and achievement," not necessarily inclusion. For him, inclusion was an ineffective means, not the ultimate policy goal. Thomas's view was not shared by federal policymakers in the 1960s or even by fellow justices at that time—he wrote an opinion concurring with the court's majority, but it was not joined by any of his colleagues—but elements of it are found in the No Child Left Behind Act of 2001(NCLB). Similarly, in 2011 the federal judge overseeing desegregation efforts in Little Rock, Arkansas, ordered the state to stop funding the effort because the districts did not seem to be actively desegregating any longer. He described the system of carrots and sticks the state had been using, but he then observed that state funding had become "an impediment to true desegregation. . . . The districts are wise mules that have learned how to eat the carrot and sit down on the job."[19] Desegregation efforts had simply become a budget line-item.

Once policymakers narrow down a policy problem that it is politically and judicially feasible to address, they can recommend appropriate policy instruments. Governments use policy instruments to make citizens do something. They can be punitive, like fines or prison, or persuasive, like tax breaks or educational programs such as Drug Abuse Resistance Education, or D.A.R.E. Most educational policy instruments are tied to funding. For example, No Child Left Behind requires schools and school districts to make adequate yearly progress toward universal proficiency in state standards. If schools or districts do not meet that goal, the law specifies increasingly tough sanctions, including firing all school personnel. States do not have to comply with the law's requirements, but they cannot receive any federal funding if they do not.

Federal funding has been a core policy instrument since the 1940s, and state and local governments, schools, and individuals have all benefited from the money. These programs provide federal money on the condition that the recipient do some particular thing. Federal Pell Grants for college, for example, give students "free" money for college, but the money must be used for higher education. Most federal educational spending comes in the form of *categorical grants*. A school or district receives a large sum of money to spend on a particular program or category of student. ESEA, for example, has provided billions of dollars to states, schools, and districts for classes and (later) whole schools with low-income students. Although ESEA was meant to encourage districts to boost spending on low-income students, the money was also used to prod districts toward compliance with federal desegregation efforts. The 1964 Civil Rights Act forbade any federal money being used for segregated programs. ESEA proved to be more motivational to Southern school districts than court decisions were, but the power of the money was that it was clearly targeted at certain students.[20]

At times, local and state politicians complain about too much federal intervention, and they are often referring to programs funded with categorical grants, because local officials have very little discretion in how the money is spent. In response to this criticism, the federal government also uses *block grants*. Like categorical grants, block grants must be spent on a particular policy area, but usually *without* specifying *how* the money should be spent. In the 1980s President Ronald Reagan temporarily succeeded in converting large chunks of ESEA money into block grants, known as "Chapter 2 grants." Block grants allow greater local discretion and participation, but may undercut federal attempts at strengthening inclusion if local officials do not share the policy preferences of federal program officers.

In both desegregation and academic achievement, policymakers have contested the definition of the policy problem, making progress on democratic inclusion difficult.

Healing Hearts Through Desegregation . . .

How could African Americans (and later Hispanics) be included in public education? The contention that education is a gateway for meaningful participation in a democracy, as the court argued in *Brown*, seems relatively uncontroversial. The Court tried to avoid controversy by giving policymakers almost unlimited discretion over *how* its policy goal would be carried out. The court's deferential approach did not directly challenge self-rule, but its problem definition led to widespread "cheating" (a manifestation of negative *unintended consequences*, or people changing their behavior in unpredictable ways in response to a policy). The problem was too vague, too broad, and impossible to track.

The problem of race and education seemed straightforward to Chief Justice Earl Warren. Providing separate school facilities by law for whites and blacks caused a feeling of inferiority among blacks—they were not able to tap into community resources (and local self-rule) in the same way whites were. Although Southern states were scrambling to increase spending on "black schools" to avoid desegregation, the difference between spending on blacks and whites was immense.[21] In 1950 eight Southern states spent 80 cents or less on black children for every dollar spent on white children. Mississippi spent only 31 cents on blacks for every dollar spent on whites.[22] Requiring local governments to provide just one set of schools would ensure that, on balance, all children would mingle in the same classrooms, and blacks could overcome centuries of formerly legal discrimination.

Policymakers and justices could easily find the cause and the most promising policy remedy. Because segregation was caused by the law, a uniquely governmental policy instrument, the court was well within its normal jurisdiction to dictate changes to the law. But *Brown* became murky on how the policy should be evaluated. One interpretation of *Brown*'s problem definition suggested that dual school systems were the target; another view suggested that the lack of common, integrated educational experiences was. The justices were aware of the possibility of a strong backlash—Chief Justice Earl Warren told his colleagues the decision should be "unemotional, and, above all, non-accusatory"—so the Court suggested no concrete public policy.[23] Indeed, when the court issued a second *Brown* opinion in 1955, it included the vague dictum that district courts should order desegregation "with all deliberate speed." In other words, lower-level courts were to decide the what, when, and how of public policy.

Perhaps the most damaging amendment to *Brown*'s problem definition was a decision in 1955 by federal district court judge John Parker. *Brown* implied that desegregation could undo "damage to hearts and minds," but Parker demurred. Parker followed the first problem definition, that dual schools were the core problem. In *Briggs v. Elliott* (1955) he argued that "the Constitution . . . does not require integration" (777). Following his lead, many Southern judges only ordered integration for students who actually sued. Had this pattern continued, integration would have happened only a few children at a time.[24]

Opponents of desegregation took full advantage of the opening, strengthened by American federalism. Judges in one district could not mandate changes in others. States and districts, especially in the South, were quite able to comply with the law's letter but equally able to thwart its spirit. Others simply refused. In 1958 Virginia Governor Lindsey Almond Jr. threatened to sue district superintendents who *did* desegregate schools.

By 1968 it was apparent that simply abolishing official segregation was not going to desegregate schools. The Supreme Court forcefully dismissed Judge John Parker's interpretation of *Brown* in two cases, *Green v. New Kent County* (1968) and *Swann v. Charlotte-Mecklenburg* (1971). "The time for 'deliberate speed' has run out," wrote Justice Brennan in *Green*. The Court held that inclusion trumped individualism and self-rule. Desegregation meant that *all* schools were to be *fully* integrated.

The court took individualism to task in *Green*. The New Kent County, Virginia, school administrators, knowing many whites would be angry, had created a "free choice" plan. The plan let parents choose whether to send their children to the formerly white or formerly black schools in the district, subject to space. All of the district's white parents chose the formerly white-only school, as did 119 blacks, leaving the district with almost complete racial separation, just like before. The difference now was that school officials had not assigned whites and blacks; the parents had done it themselves. The district's plan was a transparent attempt to thwart *Brown*, and the justices called its bluff. Desegregation plans had to actually desegregate the schools, even if individuals would not do it voluntarily. "We've moved from brown to green," Earl Warren told a colleague. "Hallelujah!"[25]

Swann extended this attack on self-rule and individual choice in 1971. The city of Charlotte, North Carolina, had merged with the surrounding county in 1960. The city held the districts' African American population, and the county was mostly white. Using "neighborhood schools" so children could be close to home left the district almost entirely segregated. Blacks and whites did not live in the same neighborhoods, a condition called *de facto segregation* or *residential segregation*. A federal judge ordered immediate desegregation *and*, unlike the *Brown* court, he specified *how* it was to be done. The most controversial part of the proposal was busing across town to ensure that all schools had the same ratio of black to white students. When the case reached the high court, the justices upheld the judge's remedy, overruling concerns over local decisions about school placement and attendance. If the district could not desegregate schools by redrawing attendance lines, it would have to bus. Unlike later busing plans in other cities, Charlotte's generated strong community support. When President Reagan visited the city a decade later in 1984 and denounced busing as an untoward federal intrusion on self-rule, the crowd replied with boos.[26]

For the courts, then, the policy problem was the existence of segregation itself rather than leadership, success, or achievement. In the court's thinking, blacks could not improve their academic achievement unless they could enjoy the benefits enjoyed by whites in newer schools with better equipment and better-trained teachers. For whites, attending school with blacks would increase racial tolerance. Desegregation itself would improve the life chances of African Americans.[27]

. . . Or Healing Minds Through Academic Achievement?

Brown announced the entry of the federal government into desegregation, but within ten years policymakers had identified a second policy problem. Black children did not seem to succeed in education as well as white children even in the same schools. If inclusiveness was meant to improve learning and thus students' ability to meaningfully participate in democracy, simple desegregation did not seem to be sufficient.

Early explanations for the *achievement gap*—those used by policymakers to design the federal government's first major foray into K–12 education, ESEA—were that poverty and unequal school funding accounted for much of the disparity.[28] The extreme inequality in Southern funding provided a straightforward political argument. Indeed, the wide disparities between school facilities had been one of the key motivators for the NAACP's anti-segregation court cases in the 1940s and 1950s. At the same time, others suggested that poverty itself was not to blame, but rather a "culture of poverty" that actively discouraged academics.[29]

Members of Congress in the 1960s recognized the empirical problem, but legislators had little grasp of how federal dollars could be spent to improve the lot of African Americans and other groups. Section 402 of the Civil Rights Act of 1964 authorized a national study to help policymakers learn how federal policy could expand equal educational opportunity. Many assumed that the report would support the Supreme Court's definition of the problem—that the unequal educational achievement resulted from unequal school resources. Blacks, Latinos, and others did worse at school because they attended worse schools.

The result was the Coleman Report. James S. Coleman, a professor at Johns Hopkins, and six colleagues undertook possibly the largest social science study in the twentieth century (see box 3.1). The study, officially titled *Equality of Educational Opportunity* (EEO), surveyed more than 570,000 students, 67,000 teachers, and 4,000 principals in the fall of 1965.[30] Its purpose was to estimate the effect of schools on student learning and especially academic achievement.[31] Although the report would not make policy suggestions to Congress, it would provide concrete evidence of what variables the government could manipulate.

While Coleman and his colleagues were still at the drafting board, Congress pressed ahead using the Court's *theory of action* that better school resources would lead to better student learning. On April 11, 1965, President Johnson signed the landmark federal education legislation, the Elementary and Secondary Education Act, which provided schools with substantial federal money to spend on poor students.

On July 2, 1966, Coleman released *Equality of Educational Opportunity*. It confirmed, empirically, that African Americans and most other minorities (but not those from East Asia) did worse academically than whites. Much worse—black children scored ten points lower on four of five standardized tests, or one full standard deviation. Further, contrary to the Court's belief, Coleman found that "variation in the facilities and curriculums of the school account for relatively little variation in pupil achievement."[32] Or, pundit-style, "schools don't matter." This finding was a damning blow to the theory behind the ESEA.

The Coleman Report did not undercut desegregation efforts themselves, however. Coleman and his colleagues found that, despite the apparent irrelevance of schools, African Americans did better when they were in school with college-bound whites. (Those same college-bound whites suffered no "penalty" in a school of non-college-bound blacks.)[33] Thus the racial composition of a school, rather than its programs, seemed to be a driver of nonwhite achievement.

Why did Congress push ahead with federal action without waiting for the report? For one thing, President Lyndon Johnson believed that the schools available to the poor were a civil rights travesty. Conservatives—and Daniel Patrick Moynihan, a liberal member of Johnson's administration—argued that culture was partly responsible for poverty. Johnson partly agreed but

BOX 3.1   James S. Coleman

Swapping stories after dinner with fellow graduate students about high school cliques drew sociologist James S. Coleman (1926–1995) to study schools. His high school had "destroy[ed]" his own interest in school; the only boys who mattered were "first-string varsity football players." His first major study, *The Adolescent Society* (1961), confirmed what he suspected: student culture valued sports and social success above academics. Although Coleman placed some blame at the feet of teachers and administrators for creating impersonal institutions, his study shaped his basic view on the interaction between governments and individuals. Individuals are shaped by peer groups more than by formal institutions.

Equality of Educational Opportunity (1966), widely known as the Coleman Report, reinforced this belief. With his coauthors, he argued that school spending on facilities, textbooks, and salaries had much less effect on academic achievement than a student's family and peers did. The report fueled the drive to integrate schools and also challenged a core assumption of much American educational policy and teachers' unions: that school spending correlated with educational achievement. The Coleman Report was unique in its dramatic impact on American public policy, but Coleman thought of it as a "detour." He was more interested in social systems than achievement.

But Coleman saw himself as realistic about social systems. Although he defended his report's implication that racial integration could help African American achievement, he also showed that unless the interests of whites in public schools were accommodated, they would undercut desegregation. *Trends in School Desegregation* (1976) found that whites left school districts that had busing faster than those that did not. In an attempt to desegregate "now," government policy had worsened segregation. In response, the NAACP's general council derided Coleman as a "first-class fraud." The president of the American Sociological Association sought to expel him for his "flammable propaganda." Yet he stood firm, and his findings were cut from the same cloth as the dissenters from *Milliken v. Bradley*: segregation was a problem of city and suburb. Coleman never shied from controversy, and a decade later he was elected the ASA's president.

Coleman's third major report again found that school culture builds academics. In *High School Achievement: Public, Catholic, and Private Schools Compared* (1982) and a follow-up in 1987, Coleman and his coauthors found that schools with a strong, communal culture—especially Catholic schools—produced more academic learning than those without. From his own high school days on, Coleman believed that social capital was the cornerstone of learning.

Source: Marsden (2005); Peterson (2010); "James Coleman" (1995).

quickly turned the federal spotlight elsewhere.[34] Poverty, he said, came from "our failure to give our fellow citizens a fair chance to develop their own capacities in a lack of education and training."[35] Johnson argued that the promise of civil rights would remain a hollow one without major federal intervention in education. ESEA gave Johnson his wish even as the plan was pushed out ahead of Coleman's report.

A second reason was that Johnson had record-breaking Democratic majorities in Congress in 1964 and 1965. ESEA was not the first attempt by legislators to create a federal role for schools. Democrats had been trying to boost federal spending in education since the 1940s, but deep-rooted opposition to federal meddling in race issues and local control had stymied their efforts. Further complicating matters was that American Catholics, who were bedrock supporters of the Democratic Party, would not support any federal program that *did not* support parochial Catholic schools. The National Education Association (NEA) and American Federation of Teachers (AFT) would not support any program that *did*. The large Democratic majority helped the president out-vote opponents in Congress, and the Johnson administration also hit on a winning political strategy for fence-sitting members of Congress. Instead of shipping money to schools, why not tie the money to children? Framing the *to whom* policy question this way was political genius. Like the teachers' union that claimed "what teachers want is what children need" (see Chapter 5), ESEA supporters could torpedo opponents' arguments with the line: "It's about our children's future." Civil rights guarantee individuals the right to participate, and Johnson linked education to civil rights. ESEA money would be available to both public and private schools. This also meant federal money would be sent to hundreds of congressional districts, not just to those with high concentrations of low-income children. Congressmen could brag about bringing home the federal bacon in their next reelection campaigns.[36]

Democrats did not succeed in passing general, unrestricted federal aid to schools. Johnson and others thought that it would bolster discriminatory practices in some school districts. Instead, policymakers wrote the law to strengthen schools' commitment to low-income and minority-group children. The core of this focus is found in a section of the ESEA known as Title I (read "Title One"). The targeted nature of the law would have far-reaching consequences for local democracy. The categorical grants in Title I tried to ensure that districts targeted the money to the neediest students, but it also meant that *what* a district could do was subject not to local or state, but to federal regulations. Local voters (self-rule) and teachers' unions (pluralism) had no say in who those students were and only a little say in how the money was spent.

Here, as in so many other educational policy areas, American federalism thwarted initial federal expectations. Originally ESEA did not grant the U.S. Office of Education much ability to monitor the programs. Even if it had, the office had long been a mediocre, report-writing agency, ill-suited to badgering slow-moving school districts for data, let alone for compliance with federal goals. Some districts used Title I money for its intended purposes, but others did not. Memphis, Tennessee, upgraded its central mainframe; Milwaukee, Wisconsin, used the cash to pay swimming coaches.[37] Districts quietly ignored the targeted nature of Title I. At first, then, when the federal government sought to "borrow strength" from the states, ESEA failed to reach its targeted population.[38] One observer noted that, "when Title I was implemented, it produced not *a* Title I program, but something more like 30 thousand separate and different Title I programs."[39]

Congress moved quickly to crack down on this evasion of federal intent. Anecdotes about school districts misappropriating Title I monies became systematic evidence in the early 1970s.[40] The law was changed to give the Office of Education, and later the U.S. Department of Education, power to withhold federal funds. States and schools came into line, and Title I services were carefully restricted to the appropriate students. Controlling for inflation, ESEA provided 62 percent *more* money per Title I child in 1978 than it had in 1966, even though the total appropriation was virtually the same. Title I funds were finally being sent to the right students.[41]

Combined with increasing federal court control of racial integration and busing, self-rule took a back seat to mandatory inclusiveness. Low-income and poor children would be given extra funding regardless of local desires. This theme also dominated school funding arguments in the states (see Chapter 4). Pluralism, however, thrived. Virtually each new category of needy student prompted a new interest group to defend it and extend the money that Congress appropriated.[42]

Evaluating Federal Action

Since *Brown v. Board of Education*, American policymakers have tried to maximize inclusion for disadvantaged students with two quite different policy solutions. (See box 3.2 for major federal legislation.) The first solution,

---

BOX 3.2   Major Federal K–12 Education Legislation

1867   **U.S. Office of Education created.** This data-collecting agency was originally in the Department of the Interior. In 1953 it was added to the Department of Health, Education, and Welfare. It was reorganized in 1972 and replaced by the Department of Education in 1980.

1917   **Smith-Hughes Act (65–347).** Authorized direct federal funding for high school vocational education programs. Prohibited any money from being spent on academic education.

1958   **National Defense Education Act (85–864).** Provided federal funding to improve math, science, and foreign language instruction in public and private schools. One clause forbade the federal government to control the curriculum, however.

1964   **Civil Rights Act (88–352).** Title VI prohibited any federal money from going to segregated schools.

1965   **Elementary and Secondary Education Act (89–10).** Provided direct federal aid for low-income students in public and private schools. Allowed schools to hire staff, purchase classroom equipment, and improve teaching. Almost 94 percent of public school districts received aid after passage. Reauthorized in 1968, 1972, 1978, 1983, 1989, 1994, 1999, and 2002.

1972   **Education Amendments (92–318).** Title IX prohibited sex discrimination in schools, including sports.

1975   **Education for All Handicapped Children Act (94–142).** Expanded an ESEA program. Required public schools to educate special-needs children with all other children whenever possible in the "least restrictive environment" (sometimes called "mainstreaming"). Also required public schools to create "Individualized Education Programs" (IEPs) for special-needs students. In 1990 Congress reauthorized it as the Individuals with Disabilities Education Act (IDEA).

1978   **Education Amendments (95–561).** For the first time, provided federal money for (but did not require) states to create programs to improve *academic achievement* in basic skills.

1979   **Department of Education Organization Act (96–88).** Created a presidential cabinet-level agency to improve educational accountability and the efficiency of federal educational policy. It administers ESEA and most other federal education programs. President Ronald Reagan targeted the department for elimination, but he failed.

1981   **Education Consolidation and Improvement Act (97–35).** A major redesign of ESEA funding. Congress gave states much wider latitude in spending the money, but it cut federal funding by 20 percent.

1993 National Assessment of Educational Progress Authorization (103–33). Authorized the NAEP to compare state academic performance (rather than just "national" performance). States may choose to participate or not.

1994 Goals 2000: Education America Act (103–227). Called for national voluntary standards and academic assessments, but created a National Education Standards and Improvement Council to approve those standards. Also promoted public school choice. Major shift in federal policy from financial inputs to academic outputs.

1994 Improving America's Schools Act (103–382). Reauthorized ESEA, but focused the Act on academic performance rather than low-income students. Required states to develop content or performance standards and describe "adequate yearly progress" for schools and districts. If schools didn't meet adequate yearly progress, states had to propose corrective action for the school or district.

2002 No Child Left Behind Act (107–110). Reauthorized ESEA, but put teeth in the previous version's performance standards. Required states to use annual, statewide tests for all children in public schools in third to eighth grades. Required states to participate in NAEP to ensure that state standards were rigorous. Required all students to be proficient by 2014. Also required public report cards on schools and districts.

2009 American Recovery and Reinvestment Act (111–5). Provided $97.4 billion to states for educational programs through the U.S. Department of Education. Primarily used to avoid layoffs, although the funds were to be used "to improve student achievement . . . [and to] help students of all backgrounds achieve high standards" (U.S. Department of Education 2009).

Note: The numbers in parentheses are the Public Law reference.

---

desegregation, tried to overcome psychological barriers to participation in American democracy and thereby provide *equal* educational opportunities. For most schools, the federal incentives to desegregate were sticks rather than carrots, because primarily direct judicial administration of school districts and busing left little leeway for local self-rule. The second approach, direct federal educational spending, used carrots instead. ESEA's policymakers thought school districts were ignoring entire categories of students, but especially low-income and racial or ethnic minorities. Policymakers hoped to improve school opportunity by providing *extra* educational opportunity for these groups. Eventually, policymakers used ESEA to pressure districts to produce academic results as well.

How well have these policies worked? A well-thought-out problem definition makes future evaluation of a program much easier. Analysts can see what the policy was supposed to address and then evaluate whether the problem is better or worse than when Congress or the state legislature first enacted the policy. One of the drawbacks to evaluating the results of desegregation and ESEA until 1994 is that neither had a theory of action that tied the *inputs* (racial composition and school spending) to short-term *outputs* (grades, graduation, or college attendance) or long-term *outcomes* (lifetime earnings, staying out of prison) (see Chapter 4). Judges overseeing desegregation efforts focused almost exclusively on the racial balance within schools. Until 2001 legislators used ESEA to focus exclusively on providing additional inputs, cash and training, to targeted students. Thus any evaluation of these policies is unfair from one perspective—policymakers could not agree how the inputs produced better outcomes, so they had policies just target inputs.

Educational policy is not the only policy area that targets inputs. Most government policy relies on controlling inputs on the assumption that Americans will respond to incentives. National defense, highway spending, and antipoverty programs tend to focus on providing funds for a service rather than solving a particular problem. For example, the 2009 American Recovery and Reinvestment Act (often called the "stimulus bill") provided $787 billion to encourage state and local government spending and private-sector hiring. Its theory was that providing money (an input) to public and private employers would encourage Americans to spend more to pull the national economy out of a recession. Although the Obama administration did produce estimates of "jobs saved or created" by the Act, the numbers were not really meant to evaluate the policy—the output was not supposed to be jobs but economic activity. (Some of the stimulus bill's liberal critics argued that the government *should* have just hired people directly, like President Franklin Roosevelt did with the Works Progress Administration in the 1930s.) The lack of tightly linked output measures has left policymakers to debate whether the Act "worked."[43]

Inputs are not the whole story. No college gives diplomas to students who sign up for classes but never study, write papers, or pass their final exams. As desegregation efforts and ESEA plodded forward, both proponents and critics were eager to show that American children were learning more—or not. If the outputs of federal policy showed substantial academic improvement or democratic participation by targeted students, then citizens

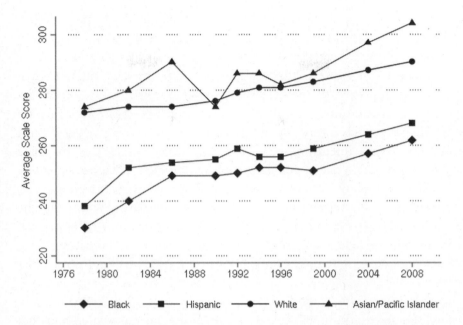

FIGURE 3.1   National Assessment of Educational Progress Average Mathematics Scale Scores by Race, 1976–2008

Note: The sample size for Asian/Pacific Islanders is smaller than for the other demographic groups, so the averages have larger standard errors.

Source: U.S. Department of Education (2011c).

might be willing to rank the norm of inclusion over self-rule and pluralism. If federal activity has not improved inclusion, then citizens and policymakers could demand that self-rule and pluralism again shape answers to these policy questions.

The outputs are discouraging by one measure. Figure 3.1 shows scores on the National Assessment of Educational Progress (NAEP) for 1976 to 2008 by racial categories. The federal government created NAEP in 1969 to track students' educational abilities across the country using the same test, an output measure. In part the exam was meant to measure how well the country provided equal educational opportunities to different racial and ethnic groups. The exam revealed systematically what most policymakers only knew from anecdotes and scattered academic studies: black and Latino students persistently scored one full grade level behind their white and Asian counterparts. Low-income students did a bit better; they scored about one-half of a grade level lower than their wealthier peers.[44] This achievement gap is stubborn, and it has come to dominate almost every contemporary discussion of educational policy and democratic inclusion.

None of these data tie directly to desegregation or ESEA before NCLB. Both policies were focused on giving students opportunities, but even when they had opportunity, the outputs did not improve. Unfortunately for proponents of democratic inclusion, both policies targeted those school districts in which money or integration should have made the biggest difference. The difficulty of narrowing the achievement gap is all the more alarming given the target population of these policies. What happened?

There are many ways that public policy can go awry, including poor communication, resistance to change from people charged with doing the work, and rivalry between government agencies. The implementation of ESEA and the federal government's desegregation efforts illustrate three basic flaws of public policy. As a public policy, ESEA demonstrates the problem of *incomplete information*, a situation that sociologists say grows from "uncertain technology" (see Chapter 6). Despite many advances in research on education, the actual learning process is not well understood. Legislators knew this in 1965 when they enacted ESEA the first time and made reasonable guesses about what might work, but a half-century later ESEA's proponents still struggle to pin down "what works." Critics of desegregation might argue that it, too, suffered from unproven assumptions about education (racial integration would improve learning and self-worth), at least in 1954. But the government's desegregation efforts illustrate the dilemma of implementing a policy with *unclear goals* in the face of unintended consequences.

Incomplete Information

Incomplete information bedevils many public policies. Policymakers do not have a convincing theory of action—they do not know what causes what, though they may have hunches. The Johnson administration's War on Poverty is a classic case. Policymakers in the 1960s (as now) did not know what caused poverty, but they thought government activity could somehow help. Daniel Patrick Moynihan was blunt: "The Government did not know what it was doing. It had a theory. Or rather a set of theories."[45] As a result, the rate of poverty in the United States did not change appreciably despite investing millions of federal dollars. Sometimes policymakers recognize their limits and design policy to overcome the problem. In the 1980s and 1990s, the federal government moved away from its decades-old antipoverty program, Aid to Families with Dependent Children (AFDC), because some observers argued that the program actually encouraged dependence on government assistance. Policymakers did not have a clear idea how to change the program, so the federal government allowed several states to experiment with radically different welfare programs. In the mid-1990s Congress looked at the state programs and adopted Wisconsin's W-2 program, with few changes.[46] The number of people on the new federal Temporary Assistance to Needy Families (TANF) dropped precipitously. (There is a dispute about whether there were actually fewer poor or simply fewer taking government aid.) Nevertheless, federalism allowed national-level policymakers to reduce the cost of incomplete information.

ESEA also illustrates information problems. Because the bill was originally designed to spread federal money to as many parts of the country as possible to make it politically palatable, policymakers could not be too specific about identifying causes of educational inequality. They would have eliminated many school districts—and the support of members of Congress who represented them. Aside from this political limitation, however, ESEA also suffered from the lack of a coherent theory of action.

No one really knew *how* to improve educational opportunity; that was what James Coleman was supposed to tell them. When his report argued that schools had only a small effect compared to a student's family situation, ESEA's attempts appeared misplaced. How could it help low-income and minority-group children? In the mid-1960s there was little educational research on the issue, and Congress was not waiting for Coleman to finish his study. Although rebuffing teachers' unions' calls for general financial support, policymakers adopted the basic strategy that money matters. ESEA would focus on educational inputs, especially cash, but it encouraged districts to spend the money on teacher training, social services, library assistance, and other programs that were thought might improve the environment of the school. Obviously government spending is easy for policymakers to manipulate and measure. What was not included, and what became contentious later, was any consistent way to measure whether low-income and minority-group children actually did better in schools that were assisted by federal funding. That is, ESEA was designed with virtually no way to assess the outputs of the policy, let alone its outcomes. Think of it this way: You are in a class where the professor gives quizzes and assigns papers but never returns anything. You have no idea how you are doing until the grade shows up on your transcript.

A taxpayer backlash and the conservative political ascendancy in the late 1970s turned the spotlight on results. The impact did not seem commensurate with the amount of money spent. A report released by the U.S. Department of Education in 1983, *A Nation at Risk*, presaged the sea change from inputs to outputs (see Chapter 6). It suggested that poor academic performance in the United States might undercut the country's economic competitiveness. Many states began increasing course-taking requirements in the late 1970s and early 1980s, but it was only in the 1980s that state legislators fell over themselves to demonstrate how their states were beacons of academic *excellence*, not inclusion or equality. For example, Georgia's 1985 state budget was emblazoned with "The Year of Education." Many states began testing students for academic competency, though without penalty for low scores. The U.S. Department of Education went public with a "wall chart" of state education statistics to pressure academic laggards. Journalists began a new weekly newspaper, *Education Week*, to cover the fray.

This flurry of activity squeezed local districts but did not fundamentally affect federal spending priorities. Until the 1990s the democratic norms of self-rule and pluralism had friends in high places. Conservatives like President Ronald Reagan argued that if the national government measured local school performance, the national government would claim the right to set those performance standards. This was an affront to self-rule. On the other hand, liberal interest groups like the NEA and AFT had successfully kept output measures out of ESEA. The teachers' unions feared that measuring school performance might lead to evaluating teachers on the same grounds (and a form of this has come to pass; see Chapter 5). They saw this as a threat to teachers' status as autonomous professionals. Such a policy would undercut their privileged position as dominant, pluralist interest groups.[47]

But a bipartisan chorus emerging from American states threatened that bargain in the late 1980s. The low level of federal involvement in the day-to-day work of education left the states free to experiment, much as they would later do with welfare. When they did, however, many residents and legislators became disillusioned with the results of spending on education. (Many states were subject to school finance lawsuits in the 1980s; see Chapter 4. Although fewer than half were successful, lawmakers began to question the wisdom of "blind"—input—spending.) This chorus included Lamar Alexander (R-Tenn.; future U.S. secretary of education), George W. Bush (R-Tex.), Bill Clinton (D-Ark.), Joe Frank Harris (D-Ga.), Tommy Thompson (R-Wis.), and George Voinovich (R-Ohio). These governors wanted education to produce economic results, not just educational expenditures.

In 1987, for example, the Georgia Department of Education (GADOE) adopted a controversial exam that would determine whether students could pass to the next grade, beginning in kindergarten. Teachers revolted, using many of the angry criticisms opponents of NCLB would use later. GADOE considered tossing the exam, but state legislators threatened to ax funding if it was *not* adopted. The chair of the education committee complained, "They told me at the time that they had piloted this for two years and interviewed over 4,000 teachers and everything's ready—and then the first year we had the test and all of a sudden everything's wrong."[48] Ohio had a similar experience, and by 2005 an Ohio Department of Education official could boast that his state's accountability requirements for state aid were more extensive than NCLB. "We out-NCLB-ed NCLB before it even existed," he recalled.[49] Indeed, Ohio's performance exams were deeply implicated with the state's school finance lawsuit in the 1990s. In return for more state funding, Governor Voinovich and the state superintendent demanded results. It was no coincidence that one of the chief deal-makers behind NCLB, Republican Rep. John Boehner, was a prominent Ohio congressman.

The shift to performance meant trouble for ESEA, as it was written before 1994. It had not been designed to produce academic results, only academic opportunity. Incomplete information could stymie the evaluation of results. What should be measured? What did performance look like? How could the public know that changes in academic results came from spending on education? All of these concerns had percolated into the discussion surrounding the 1994 reauthorization of ESEA (renamed the Improving America's Schools Act, or IASA), but with little effect. The law introduced academic accountability and required states to develop academic standards, but it left states to define both what "accountability" meant and what "standards" should cover. Although IASA represented a major shift in focus, it did not have teeth. A 1994 piece of federal education legislation, Goals 2000, encouraged states to adopt standards, but did not require them to do so.

That changed in 2001 when federal educational policy reached another critical juncture.[50] The No Child Left Behind Act required output accountability for the first time. *Accountability* means that policy stakeholders, like legislators, teachers, parents, and children, can see how well a public policy works. Like IASA, the law required states to adopt academic standards, but unlike IASA, it required states to create exams to measure students' performance. (In reality, most states purchased exams from one of the ten major educational testing companies in the United States.) Schools would have to test at least 95 percent of their students annually from third to eighth grades and once in high school. Although students could not be evaluated on their performance, their schools were.

NCLB's results focus was ambitious. By 2014 every public school student in the United States was to be "proficient" as measured by state standards. Between 2003 and 2014, schools had to make adequate yearly progress (AYP) toward that goal. If they did not, the law provided a number of sanctions against the school, including providing school choice, district-paid tutoring, and school reconstitution (firing of the entire staff). (IASA introduced AYP, but it allowed considerably more flexibility in its remedies.) Although states successfully pressured the U.S. Department of Education to allow more exceptions to its testing policy for special-needs children, NCLB's testing is the law's most pervasive feature.

The warnings of Reagan and the unions, though, were on target. State government had been eroding local control with state standards; now NCLB forced changes in the classroom, too. School district administrators, principals, and teachers bristled under NCLB.[51] The NEA tried to thwart NCLB's corrective actions through collective bargaining, going so far as to suggest that teacher contracts state that the school district would not enforce anything from NCLB that would have "an adverse impact on any bargaining unit member."[52] Later the NEA and nine school districts filed a lawsuit claiming that the law was underfunded. NEA was partly concerned that NCLB's requirements would force districts to shift their limited finances away from salaries and benefits. They lost in federal district court but appealed. The U.S. Supreme Court declined to hear the case in 2010, leaving the original district decision in place.[53] Teachers reported that they were forced to "teach to the test" by devoting more time to math and reading, at the expense of other subjects (especially science and the arts).[54] Administrators persistently worry about their schools or districts being identified as "in need of improvement." That identification triggers one of the corrective actions; in 2006, some 17 percent of all public schools were so identified, even some in upscale suburbs.[55] Some scholars complained that NCLB's measures did not reflect what districts actually did.[56] Conservative politicians, too, were alarmed, although few took action against it. Utah passed bills and resolutions that specifically require the state to ignore provisions of NCLB that conflict with state law.[57] Most states simply cannot forgo millions of federal school dollars.

NCLB tilted the scales away from local control and pluralism, but how was it supposed to improve democratic inclusion? Policymakers argued that the low academic results after thirty-five years of spending meant schools were systematically ignoring the neediest students. President George W. Bush argued that schools had "just shuffled [children] through the system" under previous Title I legislation, and this was not just presidential rhetoric.[58] Even interest groups whose members *benefited* from Title I thought ESEA was broken. One policymaker recalled that "the teachers unions were saying 'everything is fine, just give us more money,' but increasing numbers of African Americans and Latinos were saying 'we want out of these schools.'"[59]

Both the president and civil rights interest groups were right. Many schools *had* been assigning low-performing students—especially African Americans—to special-education programs at a rate much greater than whites. Although labeling students this way did bring in extra federal dollars, it also freed schools from demanding the same level of learning. It was easier to call low-performing students "learning disabled" and take them out of the regular classroom.[60] Bush and others saw that states with tough accountability standards in the late 1990s had seen appreciable gains in learning for low-income and nonwhite children.[61] NCLB policymakers sought to duplicate that success nationally. *Brown* had promised blacks and others that American public education would give them access to democratic discourse, but across schools and districts, students were receiving very different levels of education. NCLB's defenders argued that the law's tight timeline and near-universal testing requirement would force schools to focus academic efforts on the neediest students—or else.

By the time NCLB came due for reauthorization in 2007, policy analysts could begin to see whether NCLB's output focus had forced schools to target low-performing students and therefore had improved democratic inclusion. (The law has a reauthorization provision that requires the act to be passed again every seven years to force it to be evaluated. As of 2011, however, reauthorization was still stalled due to a stalemate between the president and Congress.) The results were mixed.

For government policymakers committed to inclusion, the combination of required state participation in NAEP and state-designed proficiency standards proved to be a gold mine. Even critics of NCLB who shared a commitment to inclusion found solace in the laser focus the law placed on the academic chasm between ethnic and racial groups.[62] Policymakers could use NAEP data to ferret out states that were setting low academic standards. For example, Alabama claimed 77 percent of its fourth graders were proficient in reading in 2003, but only 22 percent were so by NAEP's definition. In Iowa, the state said 1.1 percent more were proficient, but NAEP scores showed a 0.7 percent *decline*. Because every state has a different definition of "proficient," it is not necessarily problematic that NAEP's version of proficient is not the same as the states'. But it is problematic when a state shows an increase but NAEP shows a decline, or when the state's conclusions are vastly different than NAEP's—something is amiss.[63]

Critics of schools in the 1990s wanted school-level change, and NCLB appears to have given them just that. Some policy analysts found that teachers and administrators deliberately targeted students who were close to meeting state proficiency standards but not there yet.[64] Public theme-based, limited-enrollment charter schools, which increased in the 1990s, seem to have uniquely addressed these concerns, as their classrooms seem to be particularly successful at moving low-performing students closer to proficiency (see discussion of charter schools in Chapter 7).[65]

Yet ESEA's fundamental problem of incomplete information has prevented the desired results. NCLB's policymakers were aware that they did not really know what worked to boost the academic achievement of American children, but they thought that high-profile accountability would light a fire under schools to find out what did. It has not worked that way. Math scores have shown a steady improvement (see figure 3.1), but they have only continued a trend present before NCLB. Reading scores have stagnated. Perhaps more troubling for proponents of inclusion is that African Americans and Latinos continue to score almost as far behind their white and Asian counterparts as they did before NCLB was enacted. The achievement gap has not noticeably narrowed.[66] Improving democratic inclusion by overriding self-rule and pluralism has so far eluded policymakers.

Unclear Goals

Racial desegregation exposed a rift between policymakers over the goal of this public policy. Some argued that ending legal racial segregation should be the goal of government policy, but others argued that only racial integration could overcome the substantial economic and academic divide between white and nonwhite students. This argument appeared starkly in the 1970s as the courts considered school busing as a remedy for segregated schools.

In *Milliken v. Bradley*, Verda Bradley, a black parent in the Detroit, Michigan, school district, alleged that the city maintained segregated and underfunded schools. Judge Steven Roth agreed and held that the school board and state were responsible, though as much by acts of omission as by deliberate segregation. For example, the school board drew school attendance zones with a north–south line. But Detroit's population *also* split roughly down a north–south line: blacks on one side, whites on the other. The school board could have simply drawn the line east–west to decrease segregation. The board did not deliberately bus white students to white schools, but it did not try to improve the racial balance of its schools, either.[67]

Roth did not stop with a busing order—at least not the kind ordered by judges and upheld by the Supreme Court in Charlotte, North Carolina, or Denver. These districts bused crosstown, but always within the district. Instead, Roth argued that Detroit *could not* be desegregated. White families had decamped for Detroit's suburbs in large numbers in the 1950s and 1960s. By the time Judge Roth heard *Milliken*, the demographic trends suggested there would not be enough whites in the district to make "desegregation" meaningful. In 1960–1961, 54 percent of Detroit's schoolchildren were white; by 1970–1971, only 35 percent were. (In 2009–2010, only 2.5 percent were.)

Roth ordered busing between the suburbs and Detroit. He said school districts were "simply matters of political convenience."[68] The proposal he approved involved fifty-three suburbs; 310,000 students would be bused.

White flight was particularly difficult to combat in the North because of multiple, small school districts. Southern states often had county-wide school districts, so moving out of the district usually meant moving away altogether. In Northern states, moving out of the district *could* mean leaving town, but more often it meant moving a few miles. Some cities even had multiple school districts. Though a boon to school choice (see Chapter 7), multiple, small school districts meant that in-district busing had a much smaller population to integrate, and a much higher chance that the population was homogeneous.

Population changes were not the only trouble in Detroit, however. Detroit's case illustrated that the South's strategy of officially prohibiting comingling was not the only way to produce separate facilities. Indeed, many Southern politicians complained bitterly that the federal government held a double standard. After busing was ordered in Charlotte, Georgia Governor Jimmy Carter said that "the North is still going free."[69] Northern governments did not crack down on other acts that contributed to segregation, including real estate agents who "redlined" neighborhoods, banks that would refuse loans for homes in parts of the city, and covenants and housing codes designed to keep one part of the city white and another part black.

In 1974 the Supreme Court voided Roth's order. Detroit could be ordered to remedy its segregated facilities, but the surrounding suburbs had no hand in the operation of Detroit public schools. The surrounding districts could not be compelled to participate. "No single tradition in public education is more deeply rooted than local control over the operation of schools," wrote Chief Justice Warren Burger in *Milliken v. Bradley*.[70]

The combination of *Swann* (permitting busing) and *Milliken* (preventing busing into the suburbs) doomed the federal government's ability to integrate schools. Busing worked in the South because the districts were big; but in the North, whites reacted by leaving the cities.[71] Integration needed whites to boost academic opportunity, so the theory went, but they were leaving because of decaying schools, increasing urban crime, and changing racial demographics. Busing was required to overcome urban segregation, yet busing was explosively unpopular, as the case of Denver showed. All of these factors combined to create a strong incentive for whites to leave. Whites could get away from crumbling schools by leaving for the suburbs, and *Milliken* ensured they'd be safe there.

White flight is an example of unintended consequences. Policymakers cannot know the future, and sometimes the targets of public policy change their behavior in response to policy changes. For example, raising the cigarette tax in Massachusetts to discourage smoking is not very effective, because low-tax New Hampshire is less than an hour away. Smokers can easily thwart Massachusetts legislators' intent. Likewise, Northern cities with many small school districts gave whites a choice of where their children went to school without requiring much change in the family's lifestyle. Parents could still work at the same place and socialize with the same friends; they just had to move across the street or to the next small suburb. Roth tried to make white flight unappealing by removing the easy exit from cities.

Judge Stephen Roth's order and the Supreme Court's reaction revealed the fundamental disagreement over what "desegregation" meant, both an unclear goal and an instance of imperfect communication. Some policymakers took the goal of desegregation to be that legal discrimination should end.[72] Constitutionally and economically this made sense. Did Detroit segregate its schools through official, government actions? Yes. Did its suburbs? By the early 1970s, the Supreme Court did not think so. The court moved even farther in the 1990s when it took the view that once "past discrimination" had been eliminated, court control of district desegregation policies should end. Democratic inclusion could not be forced by the courts.[73]

Others argued that *Brown*'s theory of action demanded more than ending official discrimination. If black children received some democratic benefit from being in the same classrooms as white children, then the federal goal requires positive action. Schools should be integrated and diverse *regardless* of the immediately surrounding population. (Legislators believed that the experience was valuable in itself, just like the federal government providing billions of dollars of grants and loans to college students *even if* they do not finish college.) Gary Orfield, a prominent proponent of this view, argues that, "the old goal of getting black students access to white institutions . . . is no longer adequate. . . . [Diverse classrooms] can foster the kind of collaborative equal-status learning that produces the best educational and human relations outcomes"[74] (see box 3.3). This goal, adopted by Roth, enshrines democratic inclusion as a pathway to other democratic values.

The dispute about the true goal of desegregation has made the policy difficult to evaluate. Federal desegregation efforts have seriously depreciated self-rule and pluralism, but from one viewpoint, those efforts justify the end of improving democratic practice. To others, meager academic results and continued racial disparities after sixty years of the public policy raise questions about whether the time, money, and protests spent on desegregation have harmed democracy. Could not learning have been improved some other, more efficient way?

BOX 3.3   Gary Orfield

"Don't get involved in politics or causes," a professor told Gary Orfield when he was a student at the University of Chicago in the mid-1960s. He resolutely ignored that advice and spent the next fifty years "working under fire" as a champion of racial integration in schools, especially after it fell out of political favor. "I had no idea that the next 40 years would see no liberal administrations, and that in terms of civil rights, as Julian Bond has said, we would have one party that was 'shameless' and another party that was 'spineless,'" he said. Orfield thought President Lyndon Johnson's administration had barely begun to address entrenched racial segregation.

Orfield left an academic job in 1973 to work at the U.S. Commission on Civil Rights and at the Brookings Institution, a think tank in Washington, D.C. After the U.S. Supreme Court ordered busing in *Swann v. Charlotte-Mecklenburg* (1971), he conducted closed-door interviews with a handful of school districts in the throes of the busing controversy. The interviews became the basis for *Must We Bus? Segregated Schools and National Policy* (1978)—but they also thrust Orfield into the center of dozens of civil rights lawsuits, including one decided by the Supreme Court in 2006.

After Orfield returned to academia in 1977, he produced a stream of highly critical reports on American education and housing policy. He took on vouchers, charter schools, accountability testing, and special education, claiming that they could inflame racial inequality. He praised busing and magnet schools. Despite his success in court and in publishing, Orfield felt he was a voice crying in the wilderness. "I learned that, with rare exceptions, the institutions that were engaged in issues of minority rights and opportunities had almost no research capacity, and government agencies had almost no interest in looking at racial inequality," he said.

But Orfield again ignored received wisdom. In 1996 he and a Harvard University colleague founded the Civil Rights Project, a research and policy program. In 2007 it moved to the University of California, Los Angeles. "We have to . . . come to depend more deeply on creating a successful multiracial society," he said. The project continues Orfield's goals and trains students to look at race in American education.

Source: Orfield (2010b).

Proponents of inclusion for its own sake point to studies finding long-term outcome benefits. Researchers found that adults who had attended court-ordered integrated schools in Seattle, Washington, and Louisville, Kentucky, had very positive experiences. Whatever the academic merit of the program, virtually all of their interviewees said that school diversity helped them in racially diverse workplaces.[75] Other researchers suggest that diverse schools help white children with languages other than English and to develop empathy for students in other life situations.[76]

Others point to academic benefits of integration—even if the achievement gap persists. Although improving academic achievement was not an original goal of desegregation, educational opportunity is difficult to separate from achievement—there is not much opportunity for a high school dropout to go to college. The Coleman Report suggested that students picked up their aspirations from other students, and policymakers used the report to argue that integrating African Americans into white-majority schools would help blacks' own educational aspirations.[77] Two policy scholars argue:

> Even if America miraculously succeeded in rendering every school racially integrated, the new problem—the problem of differential academic performance—would not melt away. The most fundamental problem is an achievement gap, not gerrymandered attendance boundaries.[78]

Recent evidence on this *compositional effect* is mixed. Some scholars suggest that predominantly low-income and nonwhite schools are organized differently than middle-class-dominated schools. The actual demographics of the student body do not affect learning as much as teachers with low expectations and less challenging courses do.[79] Others suggest that academic achievement does not follow desegregation at all, although learning is not hurt by it, either.[80]

Critics of integration argue that African American and Latino children have not seen the gains promised. They argue that the means (desegregation) have replaced the real goal, improved learning and life chances.

A handful of critics have suggested a return to some form of single-race schooling. Like the black community school board discussed in Chapter 5, some racial and ethnic groups have felt that integrated schooling has undercut their own cultural heritage.[81] At the prompting of an African American legislator, Nebraska passed legislation in 2006 to split Omaha into three largely race-based school districts. The legislator argued that the division would give black and Hispanic parents more control over education, but subsequent lawsuits prompted the state legislature to repeal the law in 2007.[82]

Others suggest that policymakers' focus on financial disparities to remedy the effects of segregation is misplaced. Indeed, some well-funded school districts continue to exhibit weak academic performance and continued disciplinary problems.[83] In response to a desegregation lawsuit, a judge gave

Kansas City, Missouri, an almost blank check to attract white students into the district. The district spent $2 billion between 1985 and 1997, built fifteen schools, and renovated fifty-four others. The district spent more per pupil than any other urban district in the United States (accounting for cost of living differences). But the district's test scores continued to be far below the state's averages, and student absenteeism was rampant.[84] Instead, policymakers might consider nonschool effects, such as a child's home environment and the value parents put on education.[85] Selling parents on the value of education is a much different policy than building new schools or busing children across town.

Yet proponents and critics agree on one educational variable that is fully within the government's purview: quality teachers. As discussed in Chapter 5, high-quality teachers are more important to student learning and behavior than any other in-school variable. One reason for the achievement gap appears to be that teachers have lower expectations for their African American and Latino students.[86] Other research suggests that students respond differently to teachers of their own race or ethnicity.[87] NCLB included some requirements for teachers but provided relatively little money to help upgrade the teacher workforce.

All public policy is made in a political atmosphere. No evaluation can settle dilemmas over political values. But unclear goals, such as those that have troubled desegregation, make evaluation difficult and open the policy to the charge that policymakers are ignoring evidence. Has desegregation been effective? There is no doubt that its implementation has disappointed even its most ardent supporters. Overall, schools are less integrated than they were in the 1980s, and academic achievement has not followed in those that are integrated.

Conclusion

This chapter outlined the difficulties that policymakers have when they try to define a policy problem. Even when politicians and the public agree that a situation may be an issue, they may not believe public action is appropriate, justified, or useful. Has the federal government's unprecedented intervention in local politics in the name of democratic inclusion bolstered democracy? Has it fulfilled its own goals?

The pursuit of democratic inclusion has overshadowed all of the other democratic values in educational policy for sixty years. The value of inclusion still shapes school choice, educational finance, teachers' union relations, and other educational policies. But the weak results of both ESEA and integration have diminished the dominance of inclusion. Clearly, both policies *have* helped some students in some schools. But neither policy has lived up to the promise that thrilled early policymakers. If policymakers cannot show a convincing theory of action or a consistent goal, Americans can reasonably demand that other democratic values return to the policy debate.

And they have. Beginning with the 1994 reauthorization of ESEA, federal policymakers have turned away from a single-minded focus on improving inclusion and have tentatively embraced academic goals as well. In 2001 NCLB promoted equal outputs and school choice. In 2009, despite large Democratic majorities in Congress and a decisive presidential victory, President Barack Obama showed no signs of returning ESEA to its roots as it came up for reauthorization again. In a January 24, 2011, forum hosted by the U.S. Department of Education, Secretary of Education Arne Duncan argued that ESEA should focus on international competitiveness, increasing parental engagement, broadening standards to include more areas, and improving the law's provisions for rural schools. Some of these initiatives would certainly benefit the low-income, nonwhite students for whom Congress originally designed ESEA, but the administration's proposal highlights academic achievement and career readiness.[88] ESEA heralded the earnest entry of the federal government into educational policy, but the federal government displaced democratic inclusion with equity and self-rule.

Suggested Readings

The Civil Rights Project. http://www.civilrightsproject.ucla.edu/.

Clotfelter, Charles T. 2004. *After* Brown*: The Rise and Retreat of School Desegregation*. Princeton, NJ: Princeton University Press.

Guthrie, James W., and Matthew G. Springer. 2004. "Returning to Square One: From *Plessy* to *Brown* and Back to *Plessy*." *Peabody Journal of Education* 79 (2): 5–32.

Jencks, Christopher L., and Meredith Phillips, eds. 1998. *The Black-White Test Score Gap*. Washington, DC: Brookings Institution Press.

Manna, Paul. 2011. *Collision Course: Federal Education Policy Meets State and Local Realities*. Washington, DC: CQ Press.

Moynihan, Daniel Patrick. 1965. *The Negro Family: The Case for National Action.* Washington, DC: Office of Planning and Research, U.S. Department of Labor.

National Assessment of Educational Progress. http://nces.ed.gov/nations reportcard/.

Peterson, Paul, and Barry Rabe. 1983. "The Role of Interest Groups in the Formation of Educational Policy." *Teachers College Record* 83 (3, Spring): 708–772.

Pierson, Paul E. 1995. *Dismantling the Welfare State?* New York: Cambridge University Press.

Stone, Deborah A. 1989. "Causal Stories and the Formation of Policy Agendas." *Political Science Quarterly* 104 (2, Summer): 281–300.

Wilson, William Julius. 1987. *The Truly Disadvantaged.* Chicago: University of Chicago Press.

4

....

When Equity Is
Not Adequate

THE DEMOCRATIC NORM of *equality* in modern democracies suggests that all citizens should be treated equally by the law and that they should have an equal chance to participate in decision making. This chapter demonstrates how the norm is contested in American school finance. In this context, policymakers debate whether equal spending or equal educational outcomes fulfill the norm best. Spending an equal amount of money on each student in a state seems equal, but only if the students themselves have equal needs, which is unlikely. As Chapter 3 discussed, some advocates for racial integration argue that low-income and some nonwhite students should receive additional funding to help compensate for lower average academic achievement. Further, requiring equal per-pupil spending across a state can thwart self-rule, because voters in some school districts might value K–12 education more than those in another district do. Yet policymakers who propose replacing this simple definition of equality have found no widely acceptable alternative and, as this chapter shows, all definitions of financial equality have found their way into court.

This chapter discusses policy inputs, outputs, and outcomes in more depth and provides a basic overview of the dilemmas in American school finance. Inequity between school districts in terms of spending was recognized as a public policy problem in the 1920s, and states have experimented with a number of means to balance equality with self-rule. Often self-rule is represented by preserving a local property tax, but property in one town may be worth far more than similarly situated property in another, which compounds the dilemma. Most contemporary school finance policy tries to limit these inequities by using funding from the state government to complement local revenues. At a minimum, state policymakers try to provide *horizontal equity*, or treating equals equally, and some components of *vertical equity*, or treating unequals fairly. For example, states maximizing horizontal equity might use flat grants, which disburse the same amount of money per student to schools in the state. All schools are treated as if they provided the same services, and so they should be assisted with the same state aid. Advocates for vertical equity suggest that additional funds are needed to provide some students with the same education. But neither approach is without drawbacks.

Although this chapter uses a long-running Ohio school finance court case as an example, Ohio is by no means unique. Lawmakers in states as diverse as California and New Hampshire have wrestled with how to make school spending equitable while still responding to other democratic norms.

Perry County, Ohio, sits in the beautiful Appalachian Mountains in southeastern Ohio. In the 1880s the county had the world's largest coal mines—and, as in many other coal communities of the time, explosive bargaining between the miners and the mine's owners. In 1884 striking miners pushed oil-soaked lumber on train cars deep into the New Straitsville mine, igniting tons of coal. That fire is still burning more than 125 years later. The mine closed, sending the industry into steep decline.[1]

Ohio lawmakers started a similar, century-long conflict in 1847, when they rejected uniform educational funding in favor of district-based educational spending. Although Ohio legislators had permitted school districts to levy property taxes for local schools in 1821, few actually did so. Instead, they relied on tuition and the limited income from school property given to the state by Congress. In response, the General Assembly made the taxes compulsory and instituted a county-wide tax in 1825.[2]

The pressure to keep the tax low was immense. Ohio businesses and other property owners in cities worked hard to keep that tax as low as possible or just conveniently uncollected.[3] The county-wide nature of the tax also hurt Ohio's burgeoning city schools in midcentury as voters outside the cities kept rates down and had less-valuable property. This was a win-win situation for residents outside of town: multiplying a low percentage by a low value yields a low tax. But schools were strapped for cash until a minister in Akron, Ohio, suggested that *cities* be the school district, that schools be entirely funded by property taxes rather than by a tuition-tax combination, and that the tax rate be decided by an elected school board. The Ohio General Assembly solved the problem when it adopted the "Akron School system" statewide in 1847. The system solved cities' immediate need for money for schools and ensured that all children could attend even if their parents could not pay. The system also placed a strong emphasis on self-rule.[4] Ohio was chiseled into hundreds of school districts, enshrining rural-urban inequality in state law. The law did not acknowledge that many districts, especially rural ones, had poorer residents and lower property values. These districts would have to impose a higher tax rate to yield the same revenue, which was a proposition many of them found electorally distasteful. The divergence was present in the nineteenth century, but more people lived outside the cities then. More people could provide more revenue, so the discrepancy was not as obvious because rural districts could raise more dollars overall. As Americans and Ohioans became overwhelmingly urban in the twentieth century, the differences became stark.

Perry County's school districts were rural, disadvantaged districts, then as now. As are many other coal-producing counties, Perry County is home to higher-than-average poverty rates and below-average levels of education. Only 7 percent of residents have a bachelor's degree or higher (21 percent of all Ohioans do), and the median household income is 15 percent below the Ohio average. One county district, Northern Local, collected $4,903 in revenue per child in 1995, some 16 percent less than the average Ohio district, and 70 percent less than the highest regular district (ironically, that district is also called the Perry Local school district—but it is in another county). Proponents of self-rule might argue that this reflects the value the community places on education, relative to other government spending in the county, but proponents of equality would argue that even if the current taxes reflect the residents' priorities, the children in the school system would be at a severe disadvantage if they ever left the area.

In 1991 the Northern Local School District in Perry County sued the state of Ohio for the glaring inequity among Ohio's school districts. The district alleged that Ohio's school funding system was "immoral and inequitable."[5] Observers of Ohio's school code argued that trying to understand its provisions might cause "brain damage."[6] And no prominent newspaper in the state supported the existing system.

The state agreed on virtually every point. Except the remedy.

Both sides agreed on the first question of public policy: Is there a problem? Yes. They disagreed on when, for whom, and how the state of Ohio should intervene.

Both sides wanted Ohio schoolchildren to receive a good education wherever they lived. The plaintiffs wanted better funding; the state wanted better academic performance. In a press release issued during the litigation, State Superintendent John Goff was explicit: "If we just talk about money, we can never resolve the school-improvement debate. *We have to talk about results*."[7] Which value should be equal?

This dispute is not unique to Ohio. Forty-three other states have been targets of lawsuits claiming that school funding was illegally or unconstitutionally unequal. (As of 2011, Delaware, Hawaii, Iowa, Mississippi, Nevada, and Utah have never had a case heard on this subject.) Districts, parents, lawmakers, and courts struggle to balance financial equity with self-rule and other democratic values.

The debate between equity and self-rule is not about what exists now, the status quo, and every other relevant policy. Few school finance scholars today are advocating a return to the "rate tax," essentially per-child tuition, for public schools, although many school districts relied on that tax in the nineteenth century. Nor is there serious, widespread discussion of repealing mandatory school attendance laws, which were extremely controversial when legislatures first enacted them.

Instead, the school finance policymakers are constrained by choices made earlier. Their options are constrained by path dependency, discussed in Chapter 3. Because of these previous choices, debates about educational equity have been framed around educational production, spending, and states and school districts rather than educational provision, outcomes, and individual students. Policymakers in the nineteenth century used property taxes for education, and the courts have repeatedly suggested that spending is one way to remedy racial discrimination. Policymakers now start their analyses by comparing new proposals to these old, well-established institutions. The dilemma has not been resolved, but contemporary policy favors self-rule over equity in school finances (but equity over self-rule for curriculum, as discussed in Chapter 6). This chapter explains why policymakers made these choices and how these choices have effectively closed off other reforms.

The Problem: Provision or Production?

All policies begin with a problem: Can government intervention solve problems of educational inequity? As in Ohio, observers can easily find differences in education, but do those differences create a meaningful, measurable inequality? Policymakers, and especially the courts, debate whether contemporary democratic norms support the equal *provision* or the equal *production* of education.[8]

The difference between provision and production is subtle. The public *provision* of education is a government guarantee that some level of education is available. All states have compulsory attendance laws that require students to attend some form of school until a certain age—most states specify sixteen or eighteen. School need not be funded by taxpayers, although it may be. Milwaukee, Wisconsin, and Cleveland, Ohio, have publicly funded voucher programs that permit parents to choose to send their children to public or private schools, and these programs still fulfill the state function of providing education. Some states have additional rules to define what a "school" is, especially for home-based schooling. In this case, the state is complementing provision with regulation.

The public *production* of education means that government employees teach students. Production requires fees or taxation to be levied to pay for it and some form of public accountability. (Public accountability can be direct, through a school board or state legislature, or it can be indirect, such as when schools post how many students pass a state reading test or SAT scores. Residents of the district could use this information to infer the quality of the local public school.) Traditional public schools, which 90 percent of American schoolchildren attend, are government "produced."

Equalizing the provision of education appears to be easier than equalizing production. All state constitutions except Mississippi's guarantee residents that the state will provide an education. The traditional legal view held that as long as education was required and some form of schooling was provided by taxes, state and local governments had fulfilled their constitutional responsibility. In *Milliken v. Bradley* (1974), the U.S. Supreme Court preferred local provision of schooling over equal production. The Court argued that "local autonomy has long been thought essential both to the maintenance of community concern and support for public schools and to quality of the educational process" (741). From this point of view, decisions about funding, attendance policy, and curriculum should be made as close to the classroom as possible. Further, measuring whether education is provided is simple. Are schools available for all students in the state? Wisconsin, for example, has statutory funding to compensate sparsely populated rural districts that might not otherwise be able to provide any public schools.[9]

The debate slowly shifted from provision to production in the early twentieth century. School reformers seized upon differences in school spending and quality to argue that equal provision was meaningless without some kind of equal production as well. These reformers urged state lawmakers and education departments to impose a variety of standards on both facilities and school subjects, especially in high schools. For example, a 1908 school fire in Ohio that killed 160 children and teachers prompted the state to impose uniform school building standards.[10] In the first decade of the twentieth century, the University of Wisconsin required high schools to offer a common, basic core of academic courses. If a school did not, the university would not admit that school's graduates.[11] More ominously, the Georgia Department of Education created a Division of Negro Education in 1911. Over vigorous objections from white-controlled county school boards, the division boosted funding and standards for the state's African American schools. Although government officials in the Department of Education did not try to desegregate schools (which would have preempted the later thinking of the U.S. Supreme Court), they knew competent, skilled blacks were vital to rebuilding Georgia's struggling industries.[12]

By the 1950s these reformers had succeeded. The last major legal debate between equal provision and production was *Brown v. Board of Education* (1954). It was a critical juncture in race politics in American education (see Chapter 3), but it also nearly settled the debate between production and provision. The Supreme Court famously argued that even absolutely equal provision of education to whites and blacks was "inherently unequal" because the education itself, the product, could not be the same if schools were operated by different people, with different curricula, at different sites. In its decision, the Court made reference to the Equal Protection Clause of the Fourteenth Amendment of the Constitution—a clause that would become the centerpiece for future court cases challenging unequal production of education. Arguments over equal provision continue on a smaller scale, especially about students who are English-language learners and those with developmental disabilities, but there are no major contemporary challenges to the public provision of education.

Brown effectively prevented policymakers from taking a different policy path. For example, they could not explore Milton Friedman's proposal to supply publicly funded vouchers to parents on a wide scale because a version of it had been used to circumvent desegregation.[13] For Friedman, the voucher system would maximize individual freedom and require schools to accommodate the desires of individuals; government production of education would have to compete on an equal footing with private production of education. In this scenario, government would have to expend more resources to equalize provision but do little for production.[14] When voucher programs reappeared in the late 1980s as a viable though controversial policy, lawmakers designed them as an "escape hatch" out of troubled public schools—and just for the poor (see Chapter 7).[15]

The *Brown* decision closed the door on policy arguments over equal provision: equal publicly produced education would exist for all Americans. But it did not answer the basic question that has troubled policymakers since then: What are the "equal terms" of production?

Measuring Policy Effectiveness: Inputs, Outputs, and Outcomes

It only takes a few school visits to realize that the production of education is not equal.[16] The schools in Perry County, Ohio, were obviously different than those in wealthier districts, even though they all provided education. In some districts, students study Chaucer, Malory, and Spenser in English classes, while in others students may scarcely have a textbook. Some students excel with great teachers even in "bad" schools, while others "lose" learning even in "good" schools.[17] Another observer might notice that African American students consistently score lower on standardized tests (19 to 40 points lower on a scale of 0 to 500).[18] Still another would note that high school dropouts earn about $300,000 less over their lifetimes than someone with a diploma (and more than $1 million less than a college graduate).[19]

Each of these measures of equality—curriculum, spending, test scores, and lifetime earnings—suggests different policy proposals, and each suggests a different "problem" that government might address. Policy problems are usually difficult to measure directly, so good measures are indicators that can be plausibly linked to the actual problem. A lawmaker should not be concerned about raising the state's SAT scores, but rather about the underlying problem of academic achievement among high schoolers considering college. For example, the Carnegie unit, introduced in Chapter 3, is a good indicator of the subjects a student took but a very poor indicator of what that student learned. Academic grades are a better indicator, but they combine academic achievement (Sam scored 100 percent on all of his chemistry quizzes) and student behavior (Katie turned in all of her work late).[20] Measures can be categorized as input measures, output measures, and outcome measures (see table 4.1).

Input measures include booklists, credit hours, teacher pay, and teacher certification. In the 1980s, policymakers who were concerned about the "rising tide of mediocrity" in American schools (as identified by *Nation at Risk* in 1983) convinced lawmakers to require students to take more academic courses to graduate. For school finance, input measures include teacher pay, capital spending (buildings), and administrative costs. Input measures are almost always easy to measure; for financial measures, the school district budget is the first and last stop. The difficulty of input measures is that they are only tangentially related to a desired policy output. Simply increasing teacher pay is rarely the actual policy objective (though this may be the actual goal for some interest groups; see Chapter 5). Instead, policymakers expect that higher pay will attract teachers with better academic skills, keep teachers in difficult schools, or attract teachers of subjects that few can teach (typically high school sciences).[21] In school finance, teacher pay may be linked to a basic level of educational quality, despite its weak links to outputs or outcomes.

Grades, dropout rates, and test scores are examples of *output measures*. Outputs may be easy to measure, because they usually involve a concrete event like a test or enrolling for a year of school. Output measures may be more closely linked to policy goals than input measures, and they often serve as shortcuts for an underlying problem in policy discussions. For example, discussion of the "race test-score gap" between children of different racial and ethnic backgrounds is not usually argument about test scores themselves (the output) but about apparent inequality in education.[22] Policymakers often assume that outputs are tightly linked to solving a policy problem, as did State Superintendent John Goff when he saw academic results, not financing, as evidence of "thorough and efficient" education. Proponents of "merit pay" suggest that teachers who can raise the output of student performance in their classrooms should be paid more.[23] But these are *assumptions* that have supporting, but not conclusive, evidence. Just as with inputs, policymakers have to be careful to disentangle the cause of

TABLE 4.1   Input Measures, Output Measures, and Outcome Measures

Inputs	The easiest to measure because they often are available before a policy intervention begins. Inputs can indicate government priorities in the present or suggest a policy problem.	• *Teacher salaries* • *Students who enrolled in kindergarten without prekindergarten* • *School districts with high course requirements for graduation* • *Time spent on instruction in a classroom*
Outputs	Short-term results from a policy intervention, often measured as soon as the policy is implemented. These should be logically tied to the policy.	• *Graduation rate* • *Job placement* • *Teacher performance changes from merit pay* • *Achievement test scores*
Outcomes	Long-term results of public policy. Outcomes are what policymakers claim policies produce, but they are rarely evaluated in practice because some results do not become apparent until long after a policy intervention.	• *Total lifetime earnings for high school versus college graduates* • *Incarceration rate for dropouts* • *Alumni donations* • *Transferability of academic learning to nonacademic settings*

outputs. If one student's score on a state standardized test is "below basic" (the lowest level), does that mean her most recent teacher or the school is at fault? Probably not, but what if *most* students score below basic? Is the quality of the school's teachers the cause, or is it the low socioeconomic status of the neighborhood? The outputs should be carefully specified.

Outcomes are difficult to measure, but they are what policymakers really want. Does attending a well-funded suburban school improve a student's prospects for a successful career, even if the student does not come from a well-off home?[24] Does requiring a student to stay in school until twelfth grade to receive a diploma actually improve that child's life?[25] Do quality kindergarten classes improve the student's health and future income?[26] Does the federal Head Start program reduce the incidence of adult poverty?[27]

These questions suggest why outcomes are difficult. Outcomes are not known until long after a person participates in a public policy. The *time horizon* for a kindergarten study may be twenty or thirty years, so that a five-year-old has time to make consequential life choices, like attending college, marrying, having children, and choosing a career. The length of time also means that isolating a single public policy as a cause is exceedingly difficult. A 2010 study of people who were kindergarteners in an experimental small-class-size program in Tennessee (the Student/Teacher Achievement Ratio, or STAR, program) from 1985 to 1989 found very positive effects versus similar people who had not been in the smaller classes.[28] But does a kindergartner earn $1,000 more a month at age thirty because of his top-notch kindergarten teacher, or because he came from a supportive family, worked hard in high school and college, and married well?

Although policy outcomes are the gold standard for policy analysis, legislators cannot wait for them. They are in a catch-22: politicians need to show voters that they are "doing something" about education, but they cannot measure policy outcomes unless they enact public policy now. They *can* see if other American states have already experimented with a policy— one of the benefits of a federal system of government. In the early 1990s legislators in many states looked at evaluations of the Tennessee STAR program, liked what they saw, and provided extra school funding to enable their own states' districts to provide smaller classes.

Generally, input measures are the easiest to address and outcome measures the most difficult, but policymakers must account for the uncertainty that plagues all measures of educational policy. Deciding how to measure the problem goes a long way toward suggesting what government can do about it, if anything. Measurement involves a unit of analysis (dollars or test scores?) and a level of analysis (per pupil, per school, or per district?). The answers to these questions may lead policymakers to different policy recommendations. For example, a policymaker using the results of state achievement tests to mete out dollars might suggest better curriculum, more instruction, or different teachers when he finds districts have significantly different average scores. An analyst using classroom spending might suggest that legislators supplement local instructional spending with state funds so that districts have access to the same per-student funds for teachers—and extra spending, say on new football equipment, is not considered at all.

In *McInnis v. Shapiro* (1968), the first modern educational finance case, a federal district court noted that there was no way for the court to know what a student "needed" in education because students had widely varying skills, interests, and aptitudes. Both the court and the party suing for financial reform conceded that local control—the democratic norm of self-rule—would be better able to understand the needs of local children than a constitutional mandate (so long as those needs included racially integrated education, where the courts were especially resistant to self-rule in the late 1960s). The justices wrote, "The desirability of a certain degree of local experimentation and local autonomy in education . . . indicates the impracticability of a single, simple formula."[29]

The process of learning is not very well understood, at least in a classroom setting. It is easiest to see this in fights over school curriculum (see Chapter 6). There is little evidence that learning to read with phonics is clearly superior to whole-language or that learning math with blocks is better than memorizing multiplication tables. As a result, policymakers have struggled with measuring the needs of education.[30]

More broadly, some policymakers argue that the equal production of education is impossible, because government cannot control a child's surroundings outside school. In 1966 the Coleman Report indicated that a student's family and neighborhood had a stronger influence on that student's chances in school than the school did.[31] So students with college-educated parents are much more likely to be successful in school than those without. And even within the school, it is difficult to make production equal. One of the most important factors in a student's experience is the teacher, but teachers are not all the same (as students are keenly aware!). The worst teachers can actually lead students to lose a half-year of learning, and students in the best teachers' classrooms—with the same material—actually learn more than a year's worth.[32] The uncertainty also leaves political avenues wide open for debate. As discussed in Chapter 5, pluralism is in full play over educational measurement. For example, do teachers make what they are worth? There is no definitive answer to the question, because it implies a value judgment, that is, a political judgment. It depends on the analysts' conception of what counts as "work" and the value of public employee unions.[33]

To find the "equal terms" of education requires that policymakers decide what they can make equal. They *should* focus on equal outcomes, but those may be impossible to measure until long after today's children are out of school. They *may* look at equalizing outputs, but the uncertain nature of education means that public policy may not be able to affect the causes of the output. Instead, while advocates of financial reform acknowledge the limitations of input analysis, they argue that equalizing inputs is the most feasible option for equalizing education. Many inputs do have one almost irresistible, unique characteristic: they can be manipulated directly through legislation. And anything that a legislature requires costs money. Thus, school spending has become a shorthand measure of educational equity and adequacy.

From Financial Equity to Adequacy

By the 1950s the NAACP, an interest group for African Americans, had successfully sued to end racially segregated schooling on the grounds that education produced in separate facilities could not be equal. In addition to some social science research, the justices relied on the Equal Protection Clause of the Fourteenth Amendment of the U.S. Constitution, which requires that citizens be given equal treatment unless there is a compelling state interest to discriminate based on a person's group membership and there is no other, less discriminatory way to accomplish the goals of the law. This interpretation has been the core argument for policymakers who advocate the equality of production. If courts were to accept this argument, the Constitution would require something like equal per-pupil spending in each school district.

Yet the Equal Protection Clause itself has provided inconsistent outcomes. Despite *Brown*, federal courts have not been willing to use it to give all students the same level of education. Instead, they have suggested that unequal school spending is not necessarily unconstitutional and that Americans do not have a federal right to education, though state constitutions may grant that right. Others, including school finance reform advocates, contend that some needy students require *extra* spending, so they have tried to turn attention away from spending (inputs) to the outputs of education.

Why have courts not been willing to find the obvious disparities between districts unconstitutional? Courts have been very willing to use the Equal Protection Clause to strike down legislation that treats people differently based solely on their race, national origin, religion, and sometimes citizenship status. These are called *suspect classes* (as in, "I suspect something is wrong in this law."). If a plaintiff can show that unequal treatment by the government is based on a suspect class, the courts will apply strict scrutiny to the law. If the government could somehow show that there is a compelling state interest in treating races differently, the law would be upheld. That has happened only once, in *Korematsu v. U.S.* (1944), when the U.S. government moved Japanese Americans into camps in the West on the premise that they might aid Japan, a wartime enemy. In short, a court that uses strict scrutiny almost certainly will deliver a verdict against the government.

Two court cases decided in the early 1970s forced reformers to abandon the federal court system and the Fourteenth Amendment and look for help in the fifty states' own constitutions. These were the California state case *Serrano v. Priest* (1971) and the federal case *Rodriguez v. San Antonio* (1973). Plaintiffs sued in California and Texas, respectively, arguing that these states discriminated against students because different districts spent differently *only* because of different district wealth. Thus, in their argument, district wealth was a suspect class. The California Supreme Court agreed in *Serrano*. In *Rodriguez*, the U.S. Supreme Court did not.

Gaping disparities between school districts do create obviously unequal educational programs. Using the Ohio example cited previously in this chapter, a child in Perry County, Ohio, could not count on attending an AP calculus course, have a well-funded football team, or even expect reliable heating in the winter. The plaintiffs in *Rodriguez* had used arguments similar to those in *Serrano* to claim that Texas's wide disparities resulted from property wealth, but the Supreme Court found both tenets of the equal protection argument wanting. The majority argued that the dilemma between self-rule and equality was best settled in favor of self-rule. Justice Lewis F. Powell wrote, "The Justices of this Court lack . . . the familiarity with local problems so necessary to the making of wise decisions with respect to the raising and disposition of public revenues."[34] Again, the Court tipped the balance in favor of self-rule over equity.

First, the Court wrote that district wealth was not a suspect class, so it would not apply strict scrutiny. All of the accepted suspect classes are based on *individual* characteristics: race, sex, homeland, faith. But the core financial argument was that states did not spend enough on a *group* of students. Further, district wealth was a condition of political geography, because a student's family could move, and the condition would no longer exist for the student. More troubling for the majority was that a correlation between property wealth and school spending did not work in the "right" way. (Urban districts with more residents did not necessarily spend less than suburbs did.)

The problem of linking district wealth and equity is that virtually all states use property taxes to fund public schools. Property taxes depend on

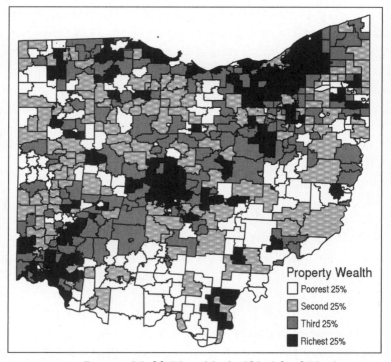

FIGURE 4.1   Property Wealth Disparities in Ohio School Districts, 2009

Note: Districts are ordered by revenue raised by 1 mill of property tax per pupil.
Source: Ohio Department of Education (2011).

property wealth, and wealth is not distributed equally among school districts. (Wealth is owning something of value; income is like a paycheck. Retirees may be wealthy—they may have a second home in Florida, own a boat, and have a retirement account—even though they have no income from a job.) Factories tend to be worth more and cluster near cities; farms less so. Coal mines are not found in every county. The trouble emerges when property wealth is mapped onto poverty. Families with lower incomes tend to live in districts with higher (though not the highest) property wealth, because the poor tend to live in cities that have high-value industrial bases.

An illustration from Ohio appears in figure 4.1, which shows the distribution of property value in 2009. The darkest school districts are those with the highest property value (per pupil), and the lightest are the poorest. (All of the wealthiest districts are in major metropolitan areas.) The highest-value school district is Danbury, near Toledo, with property values of $721,611 *per pupil*, but its median income is $30,033. The lowest-value

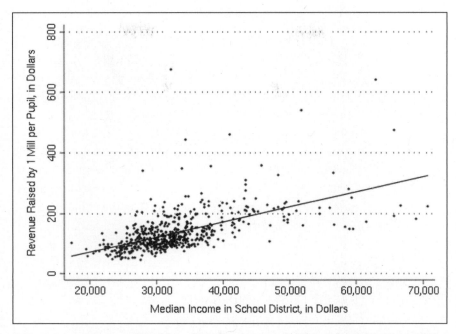

FIGURE 4.2   Property Wealth and Median Income in Ohio School Districts, 2009

Source: Ohio Department of Education (2011).

district is Huntington, with property values of $48,033 per pupil and a median income of $26,549.[35] Figure 4.2 shows the wide disparity between these districts. Each black dot represents one school district. The x-axis represents the data shown in the map. That number answers the question, "How much money will the district net by raising property taxes 0.1 percent?" The Olentangy district, near Columbus, can expect to raise $224 per pupil if it increases property taxes by 1 mill (0.1 percent). The Trimble district, near Athens, can only expect to raise $47 per pupil. This means that poorer school districts have to raise taxes much higher to bring in the same amount of money. This would not be much of an issue if school district expenses were correspondingly less, but they are not.

For some school finance reformers, that is troubling enough, but property wealth does not correlate well with individuals' incomes. In the graph, the y-axis represents median income in the district, and the line represents a best-fit line of these data. If the correlation between wealth and income was good, most school districts would lie close to the line, but there are many outliers. For example, the Beechwood district has a median income of $51,742 and can expect $538 per pupil. The Kenston district has a median income of $51,504 but can expect only $239 per pupil. The Pickerington district, with a median income of $47,041, can raise only $107 per pupil. Limitations like these prompted the Court to dismiss the alleged class as "large, diverse, and amorphous."[36] So in federal courts, educational spending could not be subject to strict scrutiny.

Advocates tried another line of attack—maybe wealth was not a suspect class, but surely education was a "fundamental right" of Americans, just like free speech, free association, or the implied right to move from one state to another. If the courts accepted this idea, advocates knew they would be likely to win, as the courts have been very willing to overturn laws that interfere with fundamental rights of participation in American democracy.

Even though education was even more unequal and unavailable in early America, Americans have long associated education with high-quality democracy. Thomas Jefferson argued that, "If a nation expects to be ignorant and free, in a state of civilization, it expects what never was and never will be."[37] Congress explicitly agreed in the Northwest Ordinance of 1787, approving language that said "knowledge [is] necessary for good government . . . [so] schools and the means of education shall forever be encouraged" (Art. 3). In the twentieth century Congress linked education to national defense in the National Defense Education Act of 1958. *Brown* suggested that education was a basic element of a successful democracy. Governors, legislators, and business owners often link education to economic growth, as did Georgia's bureau for African American education, described previously. In 2010 the Common Core State Standards Initiative continued this theme: "With American students fully prepared for the future, our communities will be best positioned to compete successfully in the global economy."[38] The plaintiff in *Rodriguez* noted that the right to vote and participate in democracy would be "hollow privilege[s]" without a basic education to read and understand political arguments.[39]

This second appeal to the Fourteenth Amendment also failed, even though the Court heartily agreed that education was critical for a well-functioning democracy. The Court made the distinction that the government could *promote* but could not *guarantee* high-quality democracy. The majority argued that the Constitution did not "guarantee the citizenry the most effective speech or the most informed electoral choice" that education might provide.[40] Instead, the Court argued that if education was a fundamental right, future justices would have trouble finding any social benefit that was *not* protected by the Constitution.

What the Court did say was that education should be undergirded by a vibrant, participatory, local democracy—and that meant localities should be able to spend more (or less) than other districts: "No area of social concern stands to profit more from . . . a diversity of approaches than does public education."[41] That answer angered proponents of equalization, but the belief was hardly unique to this decision; the *McInnis* decision in 1968 had also invoked local self-rule.[42] After *Rodriguez*, advocates turned away from the federal courts and looked to the states for leadership.

Rodriguez closed the federal courts for school finance lawsuits, but *Serrano* opened the door to states. After the Supreme Court's decision opposed the California Supreme Court's, the *Serrano* case returned to court. The state of California argued that its school finance system was not unconstitutional because of the court's finding in *Rodriguez*. The state supreme court turned down this argument in a subsequent legal challenge. Each state has its own constitution, and the federal courts cannot interpret these constitutions. The California court held that even if the federal Constitution did not contain a right to education, the California Constitution did. If the federal government did not want to treat district wealth as a suspect class, California law could. Thus the state court, using the *state* constitution, required California's finance system to provide equal funding across districts. This ruling only applied to California, but the strategy reverberated in states as diverse as Arizona, New Jersey, New York, West Virginia, and Wyoming. Lawsuits in these states argued that state constitutions required equal protection and therefore equal funding. Courts agreed in seven cases out of twenty-two.[43] Again, local self-rule proved to be a stumbling block to those seeking equality.

However, the two most important state cases, one in New Jersey and one in California, demonstrated the risks of arguing for fiscal equity. In 1973 the New Jersey Supreme Court decided *Robinson v. Cahill* against the state. New Jersey's funding system was unconstitutional in the court's view because unequal school spending violated the state constitution's requirement of a "thorough and efficient" school system. The court used spending because it was the only measure available. Although this decision validated the state-constitutional approach to financial equity, it also prompted a severe backlash from the legislature. Three years after the decision, the legislature had done nothing, and the state court shut down the entire school system in the summer until it acted. It did, yet New Jersey state government has returned to its supreme court on the issue twenty times since 1973, most recently in 2011 (the cases are heard under the name *Abbott v. Burke*). The legislature and interest groups (chiefly a group called the Education Law Center) are clearly at odds over what equity means.

California's second *Serrano v. Priest* (1976) case appeared to be a stunning, thorough victory for those reformers who desired absolute equity. As it had in the first *Serrano* case, the state supreme court applied the fiscal neutrality standard.[44] This standard (sometimes called Proposition I) held that the quality of education must not be a function of district wealth. The court ordered California to spend equal amounts throughout the state. It did so by restructuring the state's property taxes. But in 1978 California entrepreneur Howard Jarvis and others successfully convinced voters to reject that change and severely curtail property tax collections, causing a steep drop in educational funding (see box 4.1). By 2007 California's spending per pupil was twenty-eighth in the nation, without accounting for regional differences in expenses.[45] Accounting for those differences, California spends less per pupil than forty-five other states.[46] Funding *was* now equal, but uniformly low.

The strong response from legislatures and taxpayers led to a leveling down in states where funding was equalized along the lines of California. Having an equally poorly funded educational system did not meet the reformers' desire for a quality education. Thus they switched strategies and argued that state constitutions required *adequate* education—a strategy that has widened the focus beyond finance to state standards and student performance.

Adequate education has no uniform definition, and courts have come up with various interpretations of what a "good-enough" education should be. Usually, courts and policymakers suggest that an adequate education is one that permits a student to meet state educational standards. Some courts have been much more specific, including New Jersey, Kentucky (in *Rose v. Council for Better Education* [1989]), and New York (*Council for Fiscal Equity v. State* [2003]). These courts have required things as diverse as kindergarten for three- and four-year-olds, specific curricular reforms, school-to-work programs, and state-funded building construction and repair. Kentucky's case was one of the earliest using an adequacy argument and is notable because the court advanced its own definition of adequacy, shown in box 4.2.

BOX 4.1   Howard Jarvis and Proposition 13

California's 1978 Proposition 13, which sharply curtailed property tax collections, was the brainchild of Howard Jarvis (1903–1986). Until his retirement in 1962, Jarvis was a successful industrialist in southern California. Although he had shown some interest in the state's Republican Party when younger, he thrust himself into the political process within months of his retirement. He ran for the Republican nomination for U.S. Senate in 1962 and lost; he then ran as an independent and garnered 9,963 votes out of 5.6 million cast. Governor Ronald Reagan encouraged him to run (unsuccessfully) for the State Board of Equalization in 1970. He also lost a race for mayor of Los Angeles in 1977.

Jarvis was not much more successful outside electoral politics. He became chairman of a Los Angeles–based group, the United Organizations of Taxpayers, in 1962, which spearheaded three unsuccessful antitax ballot drives between 1968 and 1977. Despite his group's repeated inability to place tax limitation measures on the California ballot, the UOT gave Jarvis statewide and, briefly, national prominence. By the late 1970s he was a frequent guest on talk radio, and the *Los Angeles Times* called him "the chief spokesman for a large group of disgruntled California property owners." He later appeared on the cover of *Time* magazine.

By the late 1970s a combination of spiraling property taxes and severe state budget problems gave Jarvis an opening. With the assistance of large commercial property owners, he and a like-minded organizer in Northern California collected 1,263,698 valid signatures to put Prop 13 on the ballot. In June 1978, 65 percent of voters agreed, and California became home to one of the most restrictive tax limitation measures in the United States. Almost immediately afterward, Jarvis organized the California Tax Reduction Movement to sponsor similar tax-limiting initiatives.

The organization is now the Howard Jarvis Taxpayers Association. Although HJTA has had mixed success, the group claims it has reduced tax collections by $528 billion since 1978.

Source: Smith (1999); Howard Jarvis Taxpayers Association, http://hjta.org.

The difficulty in establishing what an adequate education is raises many questions about democratic governance. Financial equity is a consistent standard; it favors democratic equality over democratic self-rule. Adequacy has no natural standard because it does not provide an answer to who should define what children should learn.

If policymakers favor understanding over equity, they might suggest that judges, education professionals and experts, and state bureaucrats are the best suited to draft a list of expectations. Presumably these persons have

---

BOX 4.2   *Rose* Adequacy Standards

Education is adequate if "each and every child" has sufficient

1. Oral and written communication skills to enable the student to function in a complex and rapidly changing civilization.

2. Knowledge of economic, social, and political systems to enable the student to make informed choices.

3. Understanding of governmental processes to enable the student to understand the issues that affect his or her community, state, and nation.

4. Self-knowledge and knowledge of his or her mental and physical well-being.

5. Grounding in the arts to enable each student to appreciate his or her cultural and historical heritage.

6. Training and preparation for advanced training in either academic or vocational fields so as to enable each child to choose and pursue life work intelligently.

7. Academic or vocational skills to enable public school students to compete favorable with their counterparts in surrounding states, in academics or in the job market.

Source: Rose v. Council for Basic Education (1989), 579–580.

---

studied effective education, know the limits of the state's capabilities, and have observed teaching and learning in classrooms. Their recommendations may not specify horizontal equity but may recognize that the education of some students, particularly those with disabilities or low academic performance, may cost more than that of others.

Policymakers could also favor self-rule and participation. This approach could place control for "adequate" education in the hands of local districts and their voters or state legislatures. State legislatures could design standards that all students would have to meet. Although adequacy defined this way might not recommend as much special help for disadvantaged students, state legislatures are far more likely to support funding for changes to schools. Both the New Jersey cases and Ohio's Perry County case (*DeRolph v. Ohio* [1997 to 2003]) demonstrate the political difficulty of using experts to push unwilling legislatures toward changing state educational programs. Yet in practice, states—both courts and legislatures—have relied on experts rather than majority rule. These experts define what students should know and recommend what implementing the programs might cost. Experts may be a panel of educators and administrators, economists, or outside consultants.

In *DeRolph v. Ohio*, the state hired Augenblick Associates to construct an "adequate" level of spending. John Augenblick used what is called a *successful schools model* to create an estimate. In brief, this approach examines data from existing districts to find those with desirable outputs, such as a 90 percent graduation rate and high scores on state achievement tests. Those districts are further analyzed to determine how much they spend, given the population each school serves.

In Ohio's case, Augenblick used teacher salaries, pupil-to-teacher ratio, dropout rate, and the passage rate on the state's ninth- and twelfth-grade proficiency tests, among other variables.[47] He suggested $4,350 per pupil be given in state aid. Although that figure was an increase for many districts, the Ohio School Boards Association worked to defeat the formula.[48] Why? Changing Ohio's financial system along the lines of Augenblick's recommendation would create losers—districts that already spent more than $4,350 felt undercut. Others thought the formula was irrational because it would give some low-spending wealthy districts *more* state aid, so Augenblick's figure disappeared from political consideration.[49] The Ohio General Assembly provided funding of $3,851 per pupil. That increased state educational spending $1.4 billion; in a return trip to the state supreme court, the justices required $1.2 billion more. The state balked, and in the final decision in *DeRolph*, the court said it would not enforce its decision or hear any more challenges. The majority also concluded that the repeat trips to the court amounted to an "ill-disguised attempt" to thwart democratic accountability through the legislature.[50]

Adequacy is far more politically contentious than equity. Part of the difficulty is that equity speaks to a deeply democratic value, but adequacy claims justify spending different amounts on different students, and doing so with little local input.

Inequity and Its Remedies

In a promotional video released in 2001 by the Ohio Coalition for Equity and Adequacy of School Funding, the primary party in *DeRolph v. Ohio* is emphatic: thunderclouds gather as lightning splits the Capitol dome in Columbus, Ohio.[51] The state supreme court is explicit: Ohio's educational finance system is unconstitutional, is inequitable to children, and enslaves districts to debt. In bold letters: The time is now! Another bolt of lightning strikes the dome.

Interest groups and politicians (when running for office) rarely define what equality looks like. It does not mean exactly equal spending in most proposals. Few groups want to offend local control advocates—indeed, many equal financing advocates are staunch defenders of local control. Most of the coalition's members were school districts whose school boards were intent on not surrendering more power to the state. Further, virtually all policy scholars recognize that it costs more to educate some students than others, such as English-language learners, the developmentally disabled, and children with behavioral problems. So a rational policymaker realizes that some districts will have to spend more per student than others. But how much extra should these districts get? That is a question of vertical equity, treating unequals fairly, and is fraught with empirical and political difficulties. Most analysis tries to factor in differences in wealth (usually property), educational needs, and educational costs.

Another approach, much simpler, assumes that all districts should provide the same services. Thus every district should receive the same funding per student as every other district. This is known as horizontal equity. Although this implies that all students and all districts are the same, this philosophy fits well with other educational policies, like common statewide educational standards and teacher certification programs. It is also much easier to design a school finance formula to provide horizontal equity.

Although early proponents of equalization relied on horizontal equity, contemporary financial reformers, such as the Ohio Coalition for Equity and Adequacy, focus on vertical equity. Each of the components of vertical equity has its own measurement difficulties.

Wealth

The most straightforward component of vertical equity is wealth. Some 40 percent of American education is supported by local taxes, most of which are property taxes. Although this percentage has declined steadily over time, it remains the single most important cause of different educational spending among school districts.[52] Historically, state governments have used a combination of four major policy proposals to minimize the effects of different property wealth.

First, states use *flat grant* programs. The state provides a fixed sum per child to each district. In 1900 thirty-eight (of forty-five) states used these, but no state has relied only on flat grants since 1975.[53] Flat grants are not equalizers, but their proponents argue that the sum provided by the state is somehow enough to provide a minimum education while preserving maximum local control (at least for mid- to higher-wealth districts).

Flat grants were not meant to equalize spending, and reformers quickly moved to show that wealthy districts could easily spend far above the state minimum, while property-poor districts could spend little above the state grant. In response two analysts, George D. Strayer and Robert M. Haig, recommended that New York State adopt a *foundation program* in 1923. Like the flat grant, this program assumes that the state should provide funding for a minimum level of education. Like grants, the state sets minimum per-pupil funding. Unlike grants, foundation programs require districts to levy a property tax at a certain level (as a percentage of property value). If that tax rate generates less than the minimum value, the state will make up the difference. If the tax rate provides more than the minimum value, the state will not provide any financial aid. (This is mostly true; some states combine a flat grant program with a foundation program, so that even wealthy districts receive some state aid.) About forty states use foundations as their primary state aid program.[54]

In most states, school boards and voters want to raise more money than required for state aid and keep the extra revenues. Of course that means that foundation programs do not really provide financial equity, although they may ensure that the poorest districts can provide a reasonable education, if the foundation is high enough. Legislatures in a handful of states, including Montana, Texas, Utah, and Wyoming, have valued equity over district self-rule, and they require districts that raise revenues above the foundation level to send the extra money to the state. These are called "Robin Hood" or *recapture provisions*, and they tend to be politically tenuous because wealthy districts are clear losers. Although the Texas Supreme Court ordered changes to that state's school finance system, the justices invalidated part of its Robin Hood legislation because money taken from 134 wealthy districts (13 percent of Texas districts) created an unconstitutional (in Texas) statewide property tax.[55]

A third widespread formula is called *power equalization* or sometimes *guaranteed tax base* programs.[56] Power equalization programs improve on foundation programs by emphasizing federalism and local self-rule. Unlike the foundation program, which requires a certain tax rate, power equalization lets each district determine how much funding it should receive. The state legislature creates a schedule of tax rates and corresponding guaranteed revenue. For example, if the district levies a ten mill tax (1 percent of property value), the state might send $2,000 per student to the district. If the tax does not raise that much revenue due to low property wealth, the state will make up the difference. At twenty mills, the state might guarantee $4,000, and so on. This approach combines self-rule—because the district can choose the rate—with a reward for valuing education. (A college analogy: If a student takes six credit hours, she receives no financial aid at a local college. If she takes nine credit hours, the college guarantees 75 percent financial aid, but if she takes twelve to eighteen credit hours, she receives 100 percent financial aid. As her educational effort increases, the financial reward increases.)

The final formula for improving vertical equity between different districts is *full state funding*. Only Hawaii uses this formally, because there is only one school district, but other states, like New Mexico and Florida, have come close because they guarantee high per-pupil spending even if local districts cannot raise sufficient funds themselves. Voters in any given district cannot value education more (or less) than the value given to it by the state legislature. That is, full state funding sacrifices self-rule for equality.

Full state funding also comes with increased state supervision of local educational programs. The Ohio Supreme Court ruled that the state should stop pretending districts had control over their own educational programs. The state should pay districts as if they had to provide a state-mandated educational system. Although this line of argument undercuts self-rule, national teachers' and districts' interest groups have raised the same argument against federal legislation.[57] In 2005 the state of Connecticut sued the federal government over the implementation of No Child Left Behind (NCLB). The state alleged that doing what the law required cost far more than what the federal government provided, although Connecticut continues to fulfill NCLB's requirements.[58]

Need

Some students cost more to educate, whether they require special building accommodations, specially trained teachers, or special curriculum materials. The need component of vertical equity tries to accommodate different districts for the different populations they serve. Most states do this by defining a "standard" student, for whom a district would receive 100 percent of the state share of per-pupil funding (meaning that, if the state provides $5,000 per student, the district would receive $5,000 for this student). A standard student is often an average student in upper elementary grades. Students in high school would be weighted more (say 110 percent) because they take classes that require more expensive equipment (chemistry, vocational education, marching band). Developmentally disabled and English-language learners typically receive a higher weight because they need special instruction in addition to their regular classes. In Florida districts may receive up to 1,000 percent of state funding for students who cannot physically attend school.

The great difficulty is that there is no consistent empirical evidence about appropriate financing weights.[59] States use weights from zero to double, and state legislatures may choose a politically feasible weight rather than a percentage drawn from what research there is.[60] Treating different groups of students differently also creates a strong temptation for districts to cheat. Administrators may overclassify students as needy in order to receive more funds and avoid other state regulations.[61]

Cost

The final component of vertical equity is cost. Different parts of the country cost more to live in (like New York or Los Angeles) than others (like Jonesboro, Arkansas, or Iowa City, Iowa).[62] These variations occur within states, too, especially between urban and rural areas.

Cost may be divided into two parts. First is simply the cost of supplies, utilities, and building materials. These tend to be lowest in suburban areas (urban areas face high land costs and rural areas face high transportation costs). The far more important variation, though, is in salaries. Salaries consume three-quarters of the average school district budget, and some school districts have to pay significantly more to attract and retain teachers.[63] Paying teachers differently within the same state is extremely contentious, as discussed in Chapter 5, and it is a significant disequalizing factor among school districts.

Conclusion

Ohio's decade-long finance case illustrates the political and technical difficulties of balancing self-rule with equity. Ohio's school districts knew they had higher costs than they felt they could handle, and they knew that districts around the state had vastly different financial resources. But they, and Ohio's supreme court, could not agree on a remedy that all parties considered fair or adequate.

Some of the dispute in Ohio and elsewhere was political—Republican legislatures and governors butted heads with Democratic teachers' union leaders—but the deeper problem lay in the definition of the purpose of public education. The Ohio Coalition argued that the best measure of educational quality was the inputs, namely school spending. This view is taken by many scholars and has been accepted by most state courts as a measurable way to address murky concepts. If Perry County spent less money on education than another Ohio school district, it could not be providing an education of equal quality.

Superintendent John Goff represented another side. Is not education supposed to be about what students are learning in school, the outputs? Or even how successful they are in life, the outcomes? Framing the finance debate in terms of outputs makes financing far more challenging. Except in extreme cases, there is little evidence that spending alone affects what students learn in school.[64] Targeted spending may do so, but all of the formulas discussed in this chapter assume that a whole district needs a base of general revenue.

Consider the spending on the federal Head Start program discussed in Chapter 1. Evaluations of that program show mixed results. Tennessee's STAR program showed results in academic achievement in early grades, though not in later grades. New Jersey's revised school finance system has provided substantial extra funding to the poorest districts in the state, yet their academic performance is only slightly improved.[65]

Initially, Perry County won its case without winning. In its 2003 decision, the Ohio Supreme Court said the system was unconstitutional, but that it would not require the state legislature to do anything about it. The justices also refused to hear any more litigation on the matter. But Governor Ted Strickland, a Democrat, proposed a fundamental overhaul in his budget for the 2010–2011 fiscal year that reduced districts' reliance on local property taxes and calculated school aid using a need-based formula. The plan won support from the Ohio Coalition for Equity and Adequacy in Education and passed with bipartisan support in 2009, only to be repealed in 2011 by a Republican legislature.[66] Other governors and other legislators will favor different approaches to equity and adequacy.

The dilemma of balancing equity, adequacy, and self-rule comes down to a question of values. Legislatures and courts can easily make spending equal, and they may attempt to create an "adequate" spending level. But the weak linkage with academic outputs leaves room for critics (like Friedman, Hanushek, and Sugarman) to suggest that self-rule might satisfy democratic values better than financial equity.

Suggested Readings

Coons, John E., William H. Clune, and Stephen D. Sugarman. 1970. *Private Wealth and Public Education*. Cambridge, MA: Harvard University Press.

Duncombe, William. 2006. "Responding to the Charge of Alchemy: Strategies for Evaluating the Reliability and Validity of Costing-Out Research." *Journal of Educational Finance* 32 (2, Fall): 137–169.

Friedman, Milton. 1955. "The Role of Government in Education." In *Economics and the Public Interest*, edited by Robert A. Solow, 123–144. New Brunswick, NJ: Rutgers Press.

Gamoran, Adam. 2001. "American Schooling and Educational Inequality: A Forecast for the 21st Century." *Sociology of Education* 74 (Extra): 135–153.

Hanushek, Eric A., and Julie A. Somers. 2001. "Schooling, Inequality, and the Impact of Government." In *The Causes and Consequences of Increasing Inequality*, edited by Finis Welch, 169–199. Chicago: University of Chicago Press.

Kozol, Jonathan. 1991. *Savage Inequalities*. New York: Crown Publishers.

Reynolds, Laurie. 2007. "Uniformity of Taxation and the Preservation of Local Control in School Finance Reform." *University of California Davis Law Review* 40 (5): 1835–1895.

5

....

Participation and the Picket Line

THE NORM OF *participation* means that citizens expect their democratic government to welcome their taking part in the policymaking process. As Chapter 1 showed, individuals rarely have enough clout or voice to shape public policy alone, but groups of like-minded individuals do. This chapter illustrates how American democracy encourages interest groups to form and explores the development of the American teachers' unions as education's dominant interest group. It explains how groups transform individual desires into group preferences by way of a bargain. In return for political clout, individuals surrender some individual identity and make the implicit promise to support or oppose a group's political agenda. Groups like teachers' unions lobby for equal treatment of their members by some public policy, but they strongly prefer that the public policy benefit *only* group members, a goal that places participation in direct conflict with the norms of equality and inclusion. For example, unions that represent government employees often favor provisions that give only members a limit on working hours, lower payments for health care premiums, or time off from work for professional development. Group-based politics may also trump self-rule and thwart attempts to inform citizens of "what works," especially if what works is not in the interest of the members of a powerful group.

Interest groups do not form automatically even when a large number of people share the same occupation or political desires. Individuals may not be aware of groups or not have time for them, but when people do join a group, it is because the benefit to themselves outweighs the cost of membership. Those selective incentives for membership may be *purposive*, *solidary*, or *material*. Teachers' unions built their membership on the third of these incentives through collective bargaining, and the two major U.S. teachers' unions claim as members 85 percent of all public school teachers: 2.7 million in the National Education Association (NEA) and 828,000 in the American Federation of Teachers (AFT).[1] (Thirteen states prohibit teachers' "unions," but they nevertheless have teachers' "associations" that perform many of the same functions. In this chapter, unless otherwise stated, "teachers' union" refers to both types of organization.) Despite these numbers, collective bargaining for public-sector workers has been strongly challenged by fiscally conservative governors and state legislatures beginning in 2011.

The power of teachers' unions comes from interest groups' unique ability to benefit both legislators and government bureaucracy in return for special access to policymaking, a condition known as an *iron triangle*. This arrangement works best when there are only a few interest groups that want influence in the same policy area, so that legislators cannot play one group off another. Until recently, American education fit nicely into this model, but other education groups have proliferated and challenged the dominance of teachers' unions at the state level, suggesting that American educational policymaking can be better explained by *issue networks* than iron triangles. For example, teachers' unions long fought policymakers who sought to evaluate teachers by their students' academic progress. But by 2010, policymakers including the U.S. secretary of education had successfully pushed merit pay contingent on student performance, as a handful of states adopted versions of this public policy. In July 2011 NEA adopted a resolution acknowledging that teachers could be evaluated by students' scores on standardized tests as long as they were "scientifically valid and reliable."[2] Lawmakers could challenge teachers' unions' dominance in part because other interest groups suggested that teachers could be feasibly evaluated by student performance.

This chapter begins with two stories that illustrate the power and prominence of the American teachers' unions. New Jersey Governor Chris Christie proposed sharp cuts in educational spending in that state, but did not propose changes in how schools were run. He did not attack teacher tenure or propose state standards, yet the New Jersey Education Association staged a full-scale assault on the proposal. Some forty years earlier, the New York City United Federation of Teachers maintained its group identity despite strongly conflicting liberal goals—it chose teacher solidarity over one vision of civil rights.

In 2010, New Jersey Governor Chris Christie engaged in a heated battle with the legislature and the New Jersey Education Association (NJEA) to close an $11 billion state budget gap. The NJEA was incensed about $820 million in school aid cuts (about 11 percent).[3] Joe Coppola, the president of the Bergen County (NJ) teachers' union, dispatched a memo to union locals:

> Dear Lord . . . this year you have taken away my favorite actor, Patrick Swayze, my favorite actress, Farrah Fawcett, my favorite singer, Michael Jackson, and my favorite salesman, Billy Mays. . . . I just wanted to let you know that Chris Christie is my favorite governor.[4]

The internal memo promised an "in his face and hard-hitting" political strategy to "follow . . . every word and when he lies, call him on it."[5] The governor was not amused and called the death wish "perverse." He stopped taking phone calls from NJEA lobbyists.

On May 9, 1968, the Ocean Hill–Brownsville school board in New York City sent nineteen teachers termination notices. The board president said, "Not one of these teachers will be allowed to teach anywhere in this city. The black community will see to that."[6]

Eighteen of the teachers were white, including the United Federation of Teachers (UFT) chapter president, Fred Nauman. The school board wanted more community control of education; the UFT wanted teachers protected from arbitrary school board decisions. The school board wanted all-black teachers; the UFT was 90 percent white and predominantly Jewish.

Amid simmering racial tensions, Albert Shanker, the head of the UFT, led three strikes that fall to defend the rights of the rejected teachers. The fight exposed a bitter divide between the black community and white liberals over the failure of school integration in New York City. In response, the city terminated the community school board experiment. Though the union won and a judge vindicated all of the teachers, the city's former political alliances were destroyed. Now New Yorkers took their political cues from race instead of class and religion. The transformation turned the city's politics to the right.[7]

Growth of Group Politics in Education

For most of the history of American education, schools have enjoyed an immense amount of freedom and at least the potential for strong, democratic participation by residents. Until the 1960s most adults had children and grandchildren, so education was a salient issue for almost every adult in a community. A local school board could set the curriculum, hire and fire teachers as warranted (or not), tax and spend at a locally acceptable rate, and decide whether twelfth graders (or eighth graders) should graduate. Many states outside the South had school districts a person could easily walk across, and the numbers of students in them were small. One-room schoolhouses were common in many states until after World War II. For example, Wisconsin's 4,622 one-room schools enrolled almost one-fifth of the state's school population in 1945.[8] The last one closed in 1970. Even today, 46 percent of school districts have fewer than 10,000 students, and 20 percent have fewer than 3,000.[9] Small, relevant, real power: ideal characteristics of a direct democracy. As discussed in Chapter 1, the prospects for individuals in modern democracies seemed dim, but in such school districts, why would anyone need to join a group to make a difference?

The problem for democracy in American education was not parental responsiveness. During the twentieth century teachers' and administrators' groups fought for recognition and power within education—sometimes using democratic ends, sometimes appealing to other levels of government, and sometimes using aggressive tactics to advance their aims. The democratic dilemma for these groups is that school districts were ideally democracies of *parents* and other residents. Teachers and administrators could always be easily outvoted because they were a perpetual minority.

In Federalist 10, James Madison argued that the "tyranny of the majority" could be countered by many interest groups battling each other for political power. If there were only two or three groups, politics could easily become dominated by one of them. He recognized that in small places, groups might have trouble forming because of local elites, so in Federalist 51 he argued that a large country would undercut the choke hold of local opinion. A dominant group in one part of the country would not be dominant in another. At the federal level, minority groups from one part of the country would be on a more-or-less equal footing because, in Madison's view, all groups would be minorities.

Early pro-education groups recognized this local dilemma. In 1829, for example, the Western Literary Institute and College of Professional Teachers (WLI), an early education interest group, aggressively lobbied for teaching standards to ensure that local districts actually provided education.[10] Most school districts had unreliable funding from grudging taxpayers, and many settlers refused to send children to school at all except in the winter. The teachers and others who joined the WLI group sought to thwart local preferences—Madison's dominant local groups—by appealing to state legislatures for funding and mandates for quality education. The WLI and others saw federalism as an ally in these battles.

The WLI was not the only such group, and in 1857 the National Teachers' Association (NTA) formed in Philadelphia. This organization became the National Education Association in 1870. From the start, this organization was meant to lobby for more state funding for education. Although state affiliates of the NTA were private, an outside observer could be forgiven for thinking they were an extension of state government. In many states the secretary of education, sometimes called a commissioner of education or a superintendent of public instruction, was also the president of the state teachers' organization, and state departments of education organized the group's state conventions. These state-level groups overcame some of the local resistance to tax-supported education, as Madison might have predicted.

These state-level groups did succeed in convincing legislators that education was appropriately a *public* policy. By the beginning of the twentieth century government had clear authority to provide and regulate education despite continued, but weakening, parental resistance.[11]

At the same time, the NEA favored Progressive Era ideals: bureaucratic control and "scientific management." Leading reformers argued that professionals could make nonpolitical decisions based only on an impartial body of knowledge. These included Ellwood P. Cubberley, an educational administrator and researcher, and John Dewey, a towering educational reformer of the time (and also the owner of AFT membership card no. 1). Favored Progressive policies included compulsory attendance laws; larger schools; fewer school districts; and nonpartisan, appointed state secretaries of education.[12] Progressive Era policies were openly hostile to some elements of democratic norms, especially self-rule. Parents and other voters would have understood that these reforms were based on the best available research and left administration of them to experts. But many of these reforms also favored group interests. Who would define educational "science?" What organizations could give teachers an imprimatur of professionalism? Who would set teacher pay? In most cases, the answer was the NEA and in some urban districts, the AFT.

However, for teachers, those who actually had contact with students, many of these Progressive Era policies were ambiguous at best and catastrophic at worst. Teachers were not considered professionals or experts by many within the NEA and only grudgingly in the AFT. In 1904 Margaret Haley, a teachers' organizer whom NEA leaders desperately wanted to silence, gave a slashing, critical speech at the organization's national convention. The NEA had a carefully prepared rebuttal, given by the Denver, Colorado, district superintendent. He dismissed her statements and argued that unionism was a "lower plane of social life" marked by "selfishness and acquisitiveness." Instead, the NEA should strive for the "truths of ideal manhood."[13] In 1920 the NEA reorganized its national structure to prevent local teachers' associations from participating (only representative members from *state* education associations could attend). The AFT was open to teachers, but its membership was less than one-tenth that of the NEA in 1925.[14]

Teachers were already subject to the whims of local boards, parents, and principals and could be paid what was "available." This was aided by the strong norm in many communities against women holding paying jobs. If Miss Smith did not want to do what the board or principal asked, she could leave. Teachers often did not get lunch breaks, were required to do school maintenance like shoveling snow, and could be arbitrarily reassigned to unruly students by an unfriendly principal.[15] The administrator-centric politics of the Progressive Era left teachers with little recourse.

Group Benefits and Contemporary Teachers' Unions

If teachers wanted to have a strong voice in the political process, it was clear that the pre-1960s NEA was not the right group, but their alternatives were limited by state law.[16] Two paradoxes of pluralism hampered these individuals' participation in democracy. First, groups, including unions, do not form unless the benefits of joining outweigh the costs of membership.[17] The second paradox is that many interest groups *do not* emerge until *after* a public policy is enacted on the group's behalf.

Unions are not all about money. They lobby legislatures for protective laws, set standards for members, and train members to be effective in their careers.[18] They can improve employee morale ("I'm a member of a group that's working for me, so my boss will respect me.") and help employers communicate with their employees (the boss only has to talk to local union leaders to gauge how employees might react to a new work schedule).[19] Unions historically have offered utopian ideals about a new, truly equitable society, yet for most teachers, what is most important is what appears in their contracts, in words like these:

> The teaching day shall not exceed 349 minutes of classroom teaching, thirty (30) minutes for lunch and thirty (30) minutes for recess. Outside of the forty-five (45) minutes guaranteed prep time and a thirty (30) continuous minute block for lunch daily, up to eighteen (18) hours per year of the standard work day . . . may be assigned each teacher for supervisory duties.[20]

Ideals may inspire union members, but pay and quality working conditions are at the heart of a union. In virtually all school districts, the employment contract is the basic job of local affiliates, and whatever the NEA or AFT says about federal education programs or honoring American diversity, the contract governs the daily life of a teacher in school. Most union locals reach an agreement with their district's school board through collective bargaining, in which the terms are binding on both union members and their employer. The terms of the contract are among the most compelling material incentives a group can offer. If a union cannot show that it can meet management and win, why should anyone join it?

Unions can, and do, offer other selective incentives, such as purposive incentives ("I'm joining the union because it is the right thing to do.") and solidary incentives ("I'll join because it gives me an opportunity to talk with like-minded teachers."). Yet unions, like all organizations, go through cycles in which members are more interested in one form of benefit over another. New unions are dominated by idealists who have not received any material benefits (yet, they hope), so their leadership appeals to other workers by holding out a promise of better working conditions *in the future*, which is a *purposive benefit*. Joiners may then decide that rubbing elbows with other, forward-looking teachers inspires confidence and camaraderie that they do not experience while isolated in a classroom. These people join for the *solidary benefits*. But that takes time, and promising the future only works for so long. Only when the union actually delivers material benefits—more wages, fewer hours, better retirement benefits, protection against arbitrary firing—do many people join. The cycle can continue, too. The idealists who start the union may remember, bitterly, that paycheck increases are not really that empowering. If they take over the union, it may shed members as material benefits decline in favor of purposive benefits.[21]

The AFT eschewed the formalism and self-proclaimed professionalism of the NEA and deliberately organized itself as a *union* in 1916. Its goal was not the advancement of education or Progressivism, but benefits: teachers in the union did not think they were paid what they were worth. Many of its founding members were Socialists who denounced American capitalism and its working conditions, but their focus on material benefits placed them squarely in the contemporary American unionist movement.[22] Samuel Gompers, president of the American Federation of Labor at that time, expressed this sentiment exactly when he told a congressional committee that unions wanted more and better, always. He said, "I have not stipulated $4 a day or $8 a day or any number of dollars a day or eight hours a day or seven hours a day or any number of hours a day, but the best possible conditions obtainable for the workers is the aim. . . . It will not stop. . . . It is the effort to obtain a better life every day."[23] Fifty years later, the AFT-affiliated UFT became the dominant union in New York City due to its success in forcing concessions from the school board and city hall. The result of these union activities was not more idealism, or more meetings, but material benefits like increases in pay and protection against arbitrary firing.

Most NEA and AFT affiliates do not strike, but they still deliver substantial material benefits.[24] Few school boards relish drawn-out confrontations with teachers, and the number of strikes has fallen to fewer than 25 per year since 2003 in 13,628 districts, from 241 in 1975.[25]

Collective bargaining has made bread-and-butter issues routine and specialized. Newer teachers are less interested in the fights of the 1960s and 1970s, so the NEA and AFT have adopted elements of "new unionism" that emphasize quality practice. Newer members are drawn to professional development opportunities such as classroom-management techniques, ways to introduce aviation into a physics course, or strategies for teaching elementary reading.[26] When the Wisconsin Department of Public Instruction

(DPI) asked the Wisconsin Education Association Council (WEAC) for help rolling out the new teacher licensure requirements, it did so because it knew that teachers would respect professional development sessions conducted by the union.[27] But unions do more than just provide administrative help. One district union president said, "We're the professional development organization. We know what's going on around the country, and the actual professional development that I've received from the district has been very poor. . . . [Ours from the AFT] has been fantastic."[28]

The most concrete measure of union effectiveness is pay. (Unlike health insurance or retirement benefits, pay is relatively easy to compare across districts and over time.) Public school teachers in a union make approximately 21 percent more than teachers in the private sector who are not unionized.[29] Within public school districts, however, the link between collective bargaining and pay is less definitive. Most evidence suggests that teachers in districts with collective bargaining are paid somewhat more than public school teachers in districts without it, but other evidence suggests that teachers are paid about what they would get without bargaining—but never less.[30]

The second paradox—that policy precedes group formation—illustrates the path-dependent nature of pluralism. The benefits of joining a group lobbying on behalf of, say, low-income African Americans with four-year-old children were tiny. Through Head Start, policymakers created this target population to receive a distinct government benefit. Now significant government money was available, so groups could trumpet a material benefit of supporting or joining their cause.[31] Although these groups existed as latent interests, individual members had no way of identifying themselves as potential beneficiaries.

For example, the Ocean Hill–Brownsville strikes brought New York Jews into political alliances with the city's white Roman Catholics. Until the late 1960s, Jews had straddled two potential target populations, "white" and "minority." Being white brought political power, especially in a city long dominated by white Catholics; being a "minority" meant Jews could forge alliances with other minority groups to protest against conservative white politicians. But the racially charged ouster of Jewish UFT members from majority African American Junior High School 271 forced Jews to choose their identity, and they chose to side with white Catholics. That identity was conservative middle- and working-class values of individual merit, competition, and a common American identity—which downplayed group differences and emphasized a common racial identity.[32] In the 1970s, as New York City went bankrupt, Catholics and Jews made common cause to cut back the city's social programs at the expense of the black community.[33] Their latent group interest became an activated interest through the strikes, and they saw themselves as beneficiaries of joint action.

Teachers' unions also organized after potential members' latent interests were activated by changes the unions did not cause. The NEA's long insistence on professionalism downplayed (or suppressed, depending on the point of view) divisions between teachers and administrators. The organization wanted a place at the table, and its directors thought that adopting a deliberately provocative image would threaten their influence, and NEA members could not be striking against each other. Don Cameron, the executive director of the NEA from 1983 to 2001, makes the case strongly in his memoirs of the organization:

> In 1957, NEA was the largest publisher of educational material in the United States. NEA's approach to higher salaries for teachers was predicated on the lunacy that improving education and printing comparative teacher salaries would somehow inspire school boards, legislatures and the tooth fairy to do right by America's teachers. . . . [W]hile the organization pontificated about low pay and bad working conditions for teachers, it rejected any practical way to do anything about them.[34]

Although a few militant teachers' delegations organized successfully before the 1960s (and associated with the AFT, not the NEA), the benefits of organization were hamstrung by state laws making unions and strikes illegal.

This changed in the mid-1960s as state legislators rushed to enact collective bargaining laws for government employees.[35] In 1959 Wisconsin enacted the first one, though it prohibited strikes. By 1969 thirty states had some form of collective bargaining or required arbitration; by 2006, forty-five states and DC did (North Carolina, Texas, and Virginia prohibit it, and Georgia and South Carolina have no law about it).[36] The NEA was forced to rethink its stand on collective bargaining, and after significant internal turmoil, administrators were expelled from the association, which became a teachers' union in all but name.[37] Though it continued to fund an impressive research division, its members demanded collective bargaining rather than salary rankings.[38] In the main, this transformation occurred *after* state laws changed. Teachers who associated radicalism with the big-city teachers' unions now found themselves grouped with teachers all around their state. (Albert Shanker had been a card-carrying Socialist—a radical—in his youth; see box 5.1.) Legislators created a target population, and unions activated the latent interests of that population. Joining a union was not a step of civil disobedience now or even "political." Legislators encouraged it, and in many states enrollment was almost automatic.

Certainly legislators were influenced by other unions' priorities, including President John Kennedy's Executive Order 10988, which authorized federal employees to bargain collectively. But public sector unions, like the NEA and AFT, were bit players in most of the country until collective bargaining gave teachers' unions genuine material benefits to offer. School boards and district administrators would be *required* to listen to complaints about working conditions. Teacher militancy spiked in the decade after collective bargaining laws passed (to the point where some observers thought that some laws might be repealed).[39]

How might the unions be different if collective bargaining *had not* appeared for public employees in the 1960s? Certainly the unions would not be the political power that they are today. It is easiest to see path dependency by thinking about what might have been different had states opted to introduce collective bargaining for government employees (like teachers) in 1935. (The federal Wagner Act of 1935 permitted only private employees to bargain collectively.)

The AFT would probably look something like it does today. It would be more militant, as it still had many locals that were dominated by communists in 1935. It was already successful in large cities, including New York, Chicago, St. Paul, and Atlanta, and may have quickly monopolized other city districts. The greatest difference, though, would have been the position of its main competitor, the NEA. In the 1930s the NEA was firmly controlled by school and district administrators, who were even more resistant to unionism than they would be in the 1960s.[40] Thus, the AFT might have been able to move into smaller American districts as well.

Where would the NEA be? Given the prevalence of AFT-affiliated unions in the cities already, the NEA would have had to look elsewhere for membership. After all, there were 119,001 school districts in the United States in 1938–1939, and 49 percent of public elementary and secondary schools had only *one* teacher![41] Assuming that the NEA's leadership would have pursued collective bargaining at all, the thousands of tiny school

BOX 5.1   Albert Shanker

Albert Shanker (1928–1997), the president of the American Federation of Teachers for twenty-three years, was either a "right-wing Socialist" or a "neanderthal liberal," depending whom one asked. In the midst of his career, some suggested he was a racist while others lauded his commitment to low-income, nonwhite teachers' aides. Though Shanker never entered electoral politics, his blessing was courted by both Democratic and Republican educational reformers.

After running out of money to finish graduate school at Columbia University in New York, Shanker became a substitute teacher in Harlem. He found the conditions appalling, and in 1959 he left his post as a math teacher to organize the Teachers' Guild, a New York City teachers' organization (now the United Federation of Teachers). Within three years he was the organization's secretary, and two years later he was president. The UFT blossomed under his leadership as the union grew from 5 percent of the city's teaching staff to 97 percent in 1968. He led a successful three-week strike in 1967, demanding smaller classes and higher school funding. He won the more divisive 1968 Ocean Hill–Brownsville strike. (He was jailed for his involvement in both strikes.) He struck again successfully in 1975.

In the 1980s Shanker became a strong proponent of innovation in schools and endorsed the findings of *A Nation at Risk*; with Ray Budde, he championed the creation of teacher-run charter schools. He supported testing and accountability for students—and for teachers. In 1989 he said, "business as usual in the public education system is going to put us out of business. . . . It's no surprise that our school system doesn't improve: It more resembles the communist economy than our own market economy." In his view, schools needed to encourage innovation through incentives while retaining teacher protections. One of those incentives was National Board for Professional Teaching certification, a national exam.

Shanker's pro-union, pro-incentive positions made him maddeningly difficult to categorize. He was pragmatic. Comic and filmmaker Woody Allen spoofed Shanker in a 1973 film, *Sleeper*, saying Shanker had destroyed civilization with a nuclear bomb. The charge stung, but Shanker felt that he soon redeemed himself. New York City came within days of filing for bankruptcy in 1975, and the city pressured unions to buy municipal bonds to stave off default. Every union agreed to do so, though the UFT was last. Shanker had strongly resisted helping the city because he worried that it would roll back teacher benefits won just months before. He relented after a meeting with the governor of New York, and UFT bought $150 million in city bonds. Shanker said, "Woody Allen said if I had a nuclear weapon in my hand I would use it. Here I had it and I didn't use it."

Source: American Federation of Teachers, President's Office (2005); Kahlenberg (2007); Roberts (2006); Shanker (1989).

districts would have posed a formidable organizational challenge. When democracies are small, organization is not that necessary for governance. When they are large, however, voters cannot directly oversee politics without organizations.

Prominent educational policymakers, and especially the NEA, claimed bigger districts could offer better education to students and produce education more efficiently for taxpayers.[42] They were wildly successful. By 1967–1968, the United States had only 22,010 districts (in 2008–2009, there were 13,628), and just 4 percent of schools had only one teacher. Larger school districts provide more complex organizations and more employees. Without consolidation, the NEA may well have become simply a think tank rather than a teachers' union. District consolidation made collective bargaining practical nationwide.

It is difficult to form a team when there are only one, two, or three teachers. Teachers are much easier to protect from the whims of local voters and principals if there are many of them in one district. For an analogy, think about a small grocery store. Mr. Smith makes his first dollar at a single storefront with four employees. Mr. Smith hired all of them personally, but he is also on the job every day evaluating their performance at stocking shelves and providing chipper customer service. The business is successful, and Mr. Smith opens more stores and expands into another town. Now Mr. Smith needs standard job descriptions and a standard contract so he can evaluate employees with whom he does not work. Employees have potential benefits, too. If they decide Mr. Smith is a poor boss and coordinate their efforts, Mr. Smith is more likely to listen to their complaints, because they can threaten to walk off the job. Four employees would be easy to replace, but four hundred would be difficult. This logic bolstered the UFT's power in 1962. It called a one-day strike in 1962. Only 10 percent of the city's teachers struck, but those five thousand teachers were just too many to fire, despite New York law empowering the school board to do just that.[43]

Contesting Union Strength

Group-based politics is not just good for the group, however. Strong interest groups can also benefit sitting legislators and government organizations. At the state and local levels, American educational politics resemble iron triangles. A dominant interest group influences both legislators and bureaucrats in return for support of the interest group's desires (which helps it keep its own members). In education, legislators need teachers' unions for votes, ideas, and campaign cash. State employees in the Department of Education need buy-in from teachers to implement new policies smoothly. They also need the union to lobby legislators to support state spending on education.

Politically, it is dangerous to ignore American teachers' unions. The NEA's and AFT's affiliates are the largest political donors in the United States. Combined, they contributed $68 million to state and federal candidates in 2008—more than any other organization except the Democratic and Republican Parties. Virtually all of that money went to Democratic candidates.[44] Teachers' unions are up front about their political activity and are aware that their work often pushes an agenda contrary to the ideal of democratic self-rule.

For example, both the NEA and AFT are strongly opposed to tax limitation measures, which require voters to approve raising taxes.[45] And both unions have strongly supported state constitutional amendments locking in education funding *statewide*. In 2000 the Colorado Education Association (CEA) strongly supported that state's Amendment 23. The amendment, which requires *state* funding to be increased by inflation plus 1 percent every year for ten years and then by inflation, passed. NEA affiliates tend to be suspicious of charter schools (much more so than AFT affiliates), partly because of the widespread democratic participation the charter schools may offer.[46] Using Colorado as an example again, the CEA opposes more charter schools, in part because "[m]ost charters are written and implemented by parents [who] typically waive state laws regarding teacher employment."[47]Although money does not necessarily swing elections, the unions have nearly four million members.[48] Many of these teachers are eager campaigners (in Chris Christie's New Jersey, the NJEA placed 105,000 phone calls to urge members to vote against him and for the incumbent governor, Jon Corzine).[49] During election season, the sheer numbers of teachers going door to door or calling on potential supporters can swing close elections. And there is strong evidence that union-backed candidates for local boards of education are more likely to win than those not supported. One study found that union-supported candidates won 76 percent of the time.[50]

But friendly politicians are not the only ones who benefit from strong teachers' unions. State bureaucracy, especially state departments of education, benefit as well. For example, in 1994 the Wisconsin DPI rolled out a new model for teacher certification. The DPI replaced the existing test-for-certification with a multi-stage process whereby teachers would be mentored at their first assignment and later evaluated by a peer-review board.

Setting standards for certification was a legal responsibility for DPI, so it would not have required any outside support to implement the new requirements. But officials knew that without the support of teachers (who were supposed to serve as mentors), the regulations could go badly wrong. Existing teachers could sabotage the program by refusing to serve as mentors. Because existing teachers already hold licenses and jobs, the state would have little leverage to compel volunteering. Perhaps worse, the most experienced teachers might view the program as an uncompensated add-on to already busy days, which would leave the less-experienced teachers to mentor others. Or teachers could shirk the requirements by writing positive, form-letter-like reports with little interaction with the license-seeker. Both shirking and sabotage would undermine the purpose of the program.[51] To avoid this problem, DPI enlisted the state NEA affiliate, WEAC, to help promote the new regulation to its members. This aided buy-in and gave the department needed political support.[52]

The successful roll-out also demonstrated that unions can have benefits for employers as well as employees.[53] In the Wisconsin case, DPI was able to increase the commitment of employees (teachers) to the new mentoring program, and it was able to incorporate feedback collected by WEAC from teachers. While unions may help teachers with district bargaining, the unions also help administrators respond to teachers' concerns *before* complaints lead to bitter, unhappy employees.

Yet critics of democratic pluralism worry that it thwarts self-rule by giving well-financed groups a free hand to press legislators in their favor.[54] Others suggest that groups thwart voter understanding through manipulation of class, race, or economic symbols.[55] The evidence that groups do either of these successfully is mixed. Despite the obvious strength of groups like teachers' unions, their influence is not absolute.[56]

Pluralism's effects are limited by other political processes. First, James Madison's large American republic does encompass diversity. Since the 1960s, interest groups in Washington, D.C., have multiplied. Though the teachers' unions are very well funded, they have no monopoly on educational policy—a distinct difference from school districts and even state capitals. Second, a significant part of selling a new public policy is the framing of the target population. If legislators want to attack a powerful interest group, they will probably try to portray ("construct") that group negatively. Third, political policy priorities shift with the national mood. The strong federal emphasis on reducing poverty in the 1960s gave way to choice, competition, and standards in the 2000s. Groups that do not adjust their public face find themselves outside political power.

Pluralism is also limited by federalism. In state capitals, teachers' unions are *the* dominant interest group, and they lobby on issues as diverse as property taxes, labor laws, hotel taxes, vehicle taxes, and state constitutional conventions.[57] But at the national level, the NEA and AFT have competition. The day-to-day work of teachers is not done nationally, so the benefits of the NEA for federal legislators or the U.S. Department of Education are much less. Instead, dozens of interest groups and think tanks fill the policy space with ideas to reform the system or keep it the same. The density of interest groups at the national level in educational policy means that no single interest group is as influential there as in the states.[58] Some are influential in narrow policy disputes—the National Association for the Education of Young Children (NAEYC) on preschool and kindergarten policy, or the National Alliance on Mental Illness (NAMI) on education for individuals with disabilities, for example. Others provide studies and policy suggestions on many facets of educational policy but do not have the same deep buy-in that NAMI or NAEYC might have—like the Economic Policy Institute, Brookings Institution, Heritage Foundation, or the Thomas B. Fordham Institute. Teachers' unions simply do not have the stage to themselves in Washington the way they (almost) do locally and in states.

Because of the proliferation of national groups, policy scholars suggest that "iron triangle" does not describe interest groups' influence as well as "issue network."[59] Issue networks are informal, temporary associations of specialists, interest groups, and officials that seek to influence government on a particular issue, but once the issue is addressed, the association disbands. In this situation, policymakers can shop for ideas and may be able to play one group off another. Politicians may not receive the same level of political support from such networks, but they are also less beholden to any single group. Most dramatic is when the unions' supposed allies turn against them—something very possible at the national level. For example, teachers' unions have been critical of the reform agenda of the Obama administration. Both President Obama and Secretary of Education Arne Duncan have strongly supported merit pay, charter schools, and even school "reconstitution" (wherein district

TABLE 5.1   Whom Does Public Policy Benefit? Constructing Target Populations

	POSITIVE POLITICAL IMAGE	NEGATIVE POLITICAL IMAGE
POLITICALLY POWERFUL	**Advantaged** Senior citizens Taxpayers Suburban schools Parents	**Contenders** Teachers' unions School bureaucracy For-profit charter school operators Educational reformers
POLITICALLY WEAK	**Dependents** Elementary-age children Special-needs children Teachers Parochial schools	**Outsiders** High school dropouts Children schooled at home

Note: These groupings are *political constructions*, not moral evaluations. These same groups might be constructed differently in different policy contexts.

Source: Adapted from Schneider and Ingram (1993).

or state officials fire *everyone* in a school because of students' low academic performance). AFT president Randi Weingarten said, "Deliberately or not, President Obama, whom I supported, has shifted the focus from resources and innovation and collaboration to blaming it all on dedicated teachers."[60] Although the Obama administration's Race to the Top emphasized state and local union buy-in, it claimed to privilege understanding over pluralism (as in Obama's "Invest in What Works Initiative").[61] Obama can do this because major interest groups are still major, but not dominant, in Washington, D.C.; issue networks are.

Because all public policy eventually gets a public airing—where ordinary voters can pressure legislators—*how* policymakers talk about the targets, costs, and benefits of a proposed policy can boost its chances. Defining a target population is not necessarily a fair, even-handed process (see table 5.1). Policymakers can construct the target population positively ("This policy will help children in poverty.") or negatively ("We need to fire incompetent teachers."). These constructions are just that—constructions. "Children in poverty" could be framed by some legislators as children of illegal aliens who burden an underfunded education system. The same population is now given a negative construction. "Incompetent teachers" can also be cast as teachers who would improve with additional professional development and classroom support.

Positively constructed populations are hard to attack in the policy process. Few politicians want to go on record as barring parent involvement in schools or closing high-performing schools. Negatively constructed populations find it difficult to win. Later, this chapter shows how the fights over merit pay and collective bargaining are not so much over whether unions should protect incompetent teachers as over how to define an incompetent teacher.

For example, unions were able to capitalize on collective bargaining laws to build membership and advance teachers' pay and benefits, but they feared being perceived as harmful to education. Even during the membership drives of the 1960s, the unions were boldly proclaiming "Teachers Want What Children Need."[62] This bolstered a positive construction of collective bargaining. In this construction, the targets of the policy were not teachers; they were kids. By the 1990s this construction was severely strained, and politicians, including 1996 presidential hopeful Bob Dole and governors in California, Pennsylvania, Michigan, Wisconsin, and other states successfully constructed union-friendly legislation as benefiting *unions*, not kids. In the 1990s Michigan Governor John Engler successfully gutted many of the Michigan Education Association's (MEA) legislative victories by framing it as a brass-knuckles union rather than a kid-friendly professional association. Engler routed the MEA on school choice, property taxes, and academic testing, in large part because he was able to construct the union as a "diehard defender of the bankrupt status quo."[63] Similarly, New Jersey Governor Christie has tried to undermine public confidence in NJEA:

> I believe the teachers in New Jersey deserve a union as good as they are, and they don't have one. And they should start demanding to get a union as good as they are, because I believe the teachers in New Jersey in the main are wonderful public servants and care deeply. But their union—their union is a group of political thugs.[64]

Christie's pronouncements aside, unions faced a different challenge in 2011 as governors and legislators questioned whether their group benefits violated the democratic norm of equality. State legislatures around the country debated the value of collective bargaining by public sector unions, of which the largest are teachers' unions. New Jersey, Ohio, and Wisconsin all enacted bills to exclude benefits from collective bargaining; Massachusetts's lower legislative chamber passed a bill to similarly limit public sector union power; Illinois reduced bargainable items; and legislators in New York, Michigan, and California sought to limit bargaining in other ways. The immediate cause of this wave of legislation was serious fiscal imbalances in state and local government budgets. School districts spent approximately 22 percent, or $73 billion, of their instructional budgets on benefits in 2008–2009.[65] Many state legislators and governors saw reducing the power of unions to bargain for benefits as a way to give local governments more flexibility in balancing their own budgets, especially as legislators cut state aid to those local governments. Others thought that governors and legislators were using the fiscal situation to launch a thinly veiled attack on public sector unions. Republican candidates made historic gains in the November 2010 elections and won more seats in state legislatures than at any time since 1928, and many (but not all) of the original bills were pushed by Republican governors and strongly supported by Republican legislators. Leaders of public sector unions denounced the bills as attempts to weaken a longtime political foe. Although most legislators denied the charge, public sector union members are more heavily Democratic than private sector union members, and their organizations rarely support Republican candidates.[66] For Republicans, reducing the power of unions would weaken future Democratic opponents, because they would no longer have access to union campaign help.[67]

The most prominent supporters of these limits, especially Wisconsin Governor Scott Walker, argued that the issue was less about finance or politics than about the democratic norm of equality. Wisconsin is significant because it was the first state to propose and pass the limits. Newly elected Governor Walker called a special session of the legislature in February to address a $137 million budget shortfall by requesting a handful of changes—including restricting collective bargaining to matters of pay and requiring public sector unions to be recertified every year. (A "certified" union is one that employees have authorized by vote to represent them in collective bargaining.) Like other governors, Walker argued that limiting collective bargaining would allow school districts and other local governments to recoup a 10 percent cut in state aid, depending on the district, without eliminating programs.[68] But Walker also cast public sector union benefits as unfair and unequal by arguing that union members should share the same economic sacrifices as private sector workers. "I hope that our state employees feel as if they've been treated fairly over the years," Walker said, "But—like all of us—they should recognize that we are in

FIGURE 5.1   Joe Heller, "I Thought We Voted for Fiscal Sanity Last November"
Source: Courtesy Joe Heller. © 2011 *Green Bay Press-Gazette.*

difficult economic and fiscal times. . . . We must right size our government. That means reforming public employee benefits"[69] (see figure 5.1).

Initially, state-level public sector union leaders complained about the bill, arguing that the state was saving very little money for the controversy it was generating, but when the president of WEAC realized that the changes would undermine the union's power in every school district as well, she called for teachers to flood the Capitol as protesters.[70] Some ten thousand teachers and other union activists did so, and several hundred teachers called in "sick" to attend the protests, causing almost twenty school districts to close due to lack of staff, including the state's two largest.[71] Opponents of the measure charged that the changes were an attack on working Wisconsin families, because 18 percent of families in Wisconsin have at least one member on the government payroll.[72] This brought about a four-week sit-in that filled the building with deafening chants and drumbeats in an attempt to derail the bill. In the midst of the din, the state assembly held a continuous sixty-one-hour debate that ended with the bill passing the house, but not before tempers flared: one Democratic legislator threatened a Republican legislator with death and another threw bottles at fellow legislators. In the confusion after the bill's passage in the assembly, all fourteen of the Democratic state senators fled into hiding in Illinois. (Although the Republicans held a majority, the state constitution requires 60 percent of the state senate to be present for certain legislation.) After three weeks, Republicans modified the bill to pass it without the Democrats.[73]

Walker signed the bill. It was immediately challenged in state court; Democrats tried to recall Republican senators who had supported it, and Republicans tried to recall Democrats who had fled the state. Despite the uproar, Walker did not budge from his position that changes in collective bargaining made sense for protecting public education and that the changes were fair. Indeed, he argued that even some public sector workers had begun to think the law made sense.[74]

Whether Walker's framing of the issue marks the beginning of a decline in union strength in Wisconsin is an open question. The state supreme court upheld the law, and Republicans retained their state senate majority after recall elections were held. But Walker's actions have deeply polarized Wisconsin's electorate. Walker has both kept strong Republican support and energized Democrats. By August 2011, 87 percent of Republicans in Wisconsin approved of the governor's work, but 93 percent of Democrats disapproved of his performance in office. Similarly, 53 percent of residents supported limiting collective bargaining, yet 52 percent opposed the law as passed.[75]

The Wisconsin case illustrates the role of constructed target populations used by legislators and policymakers. Whether collective bargaining is about protecting "working families" or about "fairness" between public and private sector workers may have very little bearing on *any* of the policy questions. The policy might be the same. To take another example, say lawmakers are proposing rules to support school systems attended by recent immigrants' children. Politicians using the term "illegal aliens" may sound more punitive than those talking about "children of undocumented migrant workers," but they may actually be talking about the same bill. The terms can build or break *political* support for policies, as low-information voters use these shortcuts to evaluate lawmakers' stands on the issues.[76]

Interest groups may lose influence if the public loses faith in their goals. Here, democratic majoritarianism trumps pluralism, especially for big groups. Small groups may be able to keep a low profile when their positions are controversial, but groups the size of the NEA and AFT cannot duck their positions. Their members are direct beneficiaries of the $308 billion spent annually on teachers and teaching (spending in 2007–2008).[77] Both the NEA and AFT tend to adopt federal policy goals as their own so as to shape them. As with organizing, interest groups tend to follow (not lead) the federal government.

The federal government's goals for education have drifted considerably since the 1960s.[78] In the 1960s federal policymakers argued that education could overcome decades of discrimination against African Americans and propel Americans out of poverty. In their view, educational policy would promote democratic inclusiveness and self-rule. By the 1980s critics such as Diane Ravitch, E. D. Hirsch, and Secretary of Education William Bennett argued that the federal policy of the 1960s and 1970s had done much to advance inclusiveness—but had undercut *academic* achievement.[79] They argued that depriving students of academic knowledge shortchanged their future participation in the democratic process as knowledgeable voters and undercut their career readiness. In 1994 federal policy identified academic achievement as a pressing policy goal on a par with improving the conditions of poverty. By 2002 the transition was complete. Although the policymakers who drafted No Child Left Behind (NCLB) argued that its antipoverty elements continued to have value, they also argued that the pressing goal was to overcome a stubborn academic "achievement gap" between different races and ethnicities of students (see Chapter 3).[80]

The onslaught of academic, standards-based education in the 2000s proved challenging to the teachers' unions. What teachers' unions wanted—carefully limited working hours, assigning teachers based on seniority rather than need, and blocking teacher assessments by principals and peers—might not be what students needed. The unions continue to press for these, but only after changing their visible, public, national goals.

In 1968 Albert Shanker, the president of the New York UFT, said that he did not represent children—he represented teachers.[81] That hard-hitting, confrontational, unionist line still exists in teachers' unions around the country, but many of the teachers who think this way were hired in the 1960s and 1970s. They are now retiring, and new teachers tend to be less interested in unionism than in professional development.[82] Later, as AFT president, Shanker retreated from this position somewhat in the 1980s. He came to advocate educational reforms from curriculum standards to charter schools. In 2006 the AFT strongly supported some merit pay programs.[83] (The NEA, on the other hand, is deeply suspicious of school choice and an opponent of merit pay.)[84] Indeed, union supporters are again arguing that "the common good of educators that teachers' unions pursue is largely congruent . . . with the education interests of the students they teach."[85]

A final weakness of group-based politics is that groups are not monolithic. One union organizer in Ohio lamented that, "We have [some noncentral city parts of the state] where teachers do not see that their representative doesn't vote for public education. They just don't think about that."[86] Others have noted a shift in new teacher priorities, as they are less likely to support the "old unionism"—aggressive, confrontational, and radical—and even less likely to be Democrats. The president of the Los Angeles teachers' union told researchers that 30 to 35 percent of new California teachers were Republicans.[87] As Madison hoped, the conflict among multiple groups (especially at the federal level) ensures that other democratic norms do not disappear in the shadow of pluralism.

Unions and Merit Pay: Teaching for Results

Union negotiators usually walk away from the bargaining table with a good deal—not always with their preferred outcome, but rarely with the worst case. Even New Jersey Governor Chris Christie was only partly successful in restricting educational spending in New Jersey. But outside the bargaining room, the overwhelming emphasis of federal and state policy on academic proficiency and career readiness threatens unions' central claim. Unions—indeed, all interest groups—are based on the assumption that members share *common* interests. They would not be a group otherwise. Certainly this makes bargaining easier and preserves an important political message for the teachers' unions (such as, "Teachers are all quality professionals, and you can trust your children to any of them.").

Since the 1960s policy research has shown that, of the policy inputs that government can control, teachers are by far the most important factor in students' learning. (Democratic governments cannot directly control the most important influences on education: family situation, race, neighborhood, and income.)[88] Critics argue that treating all teachers uniformly may not produce better outputs. Thus there is a policy problem: variable inputs (teachers) being expected to produce the same outputs (student performance).

One possible solution to this problem is ending teacher tenure. Tenure specifies a careful, deliberative process for firing teachers. It also protects teachers from being fired for their students' academic performance. This has frustrated reformers, but Washington, D.C., school chancellor Michelle Rhee successfully forced its AFT-affiliated union to weaken tenure protection in 2010 (see box 5.2). Unions argue that the problem of poor teachers is not a problem of firing, but of hiring. If schools and districts took more care, they argue, many bad apples would never face a classroom to begin with.[89] But even ending tenure opens the question of how to evaluate teachers.

A less contentious public policy that faces the same dilemma of evaluation is merit pay, sometimes called pay-for-performance. The AFT has supported versions of merit pay, but the NEA remains skeptical. Proponents of merit pay note that existing pay policies reward loyalty to a school district and additional education, neither of which has much effect on student learning.[90] Virtually every public school district in the United States uses a "single pay schedule."[91] Teachers are paid based on years of experience and accumulated graduate credits and degrees. That means that most teachers can look forward to a pay raise every year they work. (Technically, teachers would advance another step on the pay schedule. The actual raise, if any, would be set through collective bargaining.) The single pay schedule means that high school physics teachers are on the same scale as kindergarten teachers. This emphasizes the unions' argument that all teachers are professionals, whether they teach five- or fifteen-year-olds. But teachers are not all the same. Younger teachers are less committed to their district than older teachers—but they are also much less likely to *stay* teaching, especially if they have a good-looking college transcript.[92] And urban school districts lose high-quality teachers at a much higher rate than do suburban schools.

For example, in Denver, Colorado, teachers with fewer than twelve years in the district are twenty times as likely to leave the school district as those with more than twelve years.[93] In New York City, 25 percent of teachers receive their bachelor's degree from the least competitive colleges (per Barron's). Some 16 percent of teachers in the suburbs do. Overall, 60 percent of teachers leave their first teaching assignment.[94] Many districts, both urban and rural, struggle to fill high school science and math posts.

Beyond their college qualifications and teaching specialties, not all teachers can teach well. Any student knows this, and so do teachers and principals. A 2003 survey of K–12 public school teachers found that 78 percent said they knew of at least "a few" teachers who "fail[ed] to do a good

BOX 5.2   Michelle Rhee

Michelle Rhee left her post as chancellor of the Washington, D.C., school district after Mayor Adrian Fenty lost his reelection bid in 2010. When Fenty first approached her about the job, she said, "I warned him he wouldn't want to hire me, . . . [but] he said he would back me—and my changes—100 percent." He was true to his word, and Rhee credits his loss to her controversial tenure, which lasted from 2007 to 2010.

Rhee's tenure in the District of Columbia drew national attention. Both *Time* and *Newsweek* ran cover stories on her work in the District, and Davis Guggenheim gave her a lead role in the film *Waiting for Superman* (2010). All this despite running the 108th largest school district in the country and having no school or district administrative experience before Fenty's offer. But Rhee did come highly recommended—by the chancellor of New York City schools, the largest school district in the country. Why?

Rhee is a firm believer in the effect of teachers on student learning. She signed up with Teach for America, a nontraditional teacher education program, in the early 1990s and flailed badly in her first year. But over the next two years she and another teacher were able to move a cohort of students from the bottom test percentile to grade level. Fifteen years later she applied that experience to D.C. by purging what she called "incompetent teachers." She fired more than 270 teachers and closed more than twenty schools. D.C.'s test scores rose. Although those test scores are the subject of a continuing controversy after some schools' tests had an unusual number of answers erased and corrected, the District has found no evidence of widespread wrongdoing as of this writing. (Rhee's focus on teaching is still felt in the District. Using the system Rhee designed, her successor fired 206 teachers for poor performance in 2011.)

In that process, Rhee bolstered her reputation as "dramatic, often authoritarian," as one of her critics has characterized her. She is aware of her reputation and has said, "[D]uring the civil-rights movement they didn't work everything out by sitting down collaboratively and compromising . . . this is the time to stand up and say what you believe, not . . . feel good about getting along." She is unapologetic. After she resigned, she was not worried about fighting, firing, or being forthright. Instead, she said her failure was to "connect the dots." She had not sold parents on the connection between firing teachers and D.C. improving its schools.

After leaving D.C., Rhee started Students First, a group to promote similar reforms nationwide.

Source: Gillum and Bello (2011); Kahlenberg (2011); Rhee (2010); Ripley (2008); Turque (2011).

job." Only 28 percent said that tenure meant that a teacher worked hard and did well in the classroom.[95] Principals can also tell the award winners and those who should have left last year. Students who score highly on achievement tests are more likely to come from classrooms with teachers whom principals identify as good teachers. They are not as able to distinguish among teachers who are near to average performance.[96]

The disconnect between official teacher equality (as implied by the single pay scale) and the actual diversity in their ranks raises dilemmas about equity and understanding. First, for equity, teachers are legally treated equally in their districts regardless of their particular merits. From one perspective, this is *exactly* the democratic project: all comers may participate—at least within the bargaining unit. But parents, students, and taxpayers have an argument, too. Should students expect equally effective teachers? Or at least an equal minimum standard? Critics of the pay scale argue that urban students learn less and less well in part because fewer top-notch teachers are willing to work with them.[97] If more high-talent teachers are concentrated in the suburbs, does that violate democratic equality?

Second, understanding suggests that citizens can only self-govern if they are knowledgeable about the choices they make. Teachers' unions have long argued that teachers know best, so unions fulfill this norm if their claim is true. In 1985 AFT's Albert Shanker said that teachers "ought to have the power to make the decisions because we know more—more about what is right and wrong to do in the education of children."[98] But if teachers are not all equal, principals and district superintendents may be better judges of what effective teaching looks like.

How does merit pay address these dilemmas? The first policy question asks, *Is there a problem?* Critics of the single salary schedule are certain that there is. For them, schools should produce gains in learning achievement, and both unions and their critics agree that teachers are at the center of student learning. Unions acknowledge that the "best and brightest" do not choose, and do not stay in, teaching as a career. And both unions and critics agree that some schools are not desirable for teachers.[99] Even the storied UFT in New York agreed to a concession that teachers in some more challenging schools would receive extra pay to help fill the slots.[100] The answer, then, is yes, there is a public policy problem.

The answers to the other three policy questions—when, for whom, and what—are contentious. When: Should only needy districts be given extra cash for teachers? For whom: Should all teachers receive a pay boost? What:

Should pay be linked to performance, credentials, or experience? Or a combination? About 20 percent of American students are in school districts with some form of merit pay, but the *what* of the policy is drastically different between states.

Here, American federalism demonstrates both the best and worst aspects of democracy. Best, in that policymakers have dozens of already-enacted models to analyze. Does Denver's ProComp ("Comp" for compensation) policy, which rewards individual teachers, work better than Alaska's School Performance Initiative, which gives bonuses to *everyone* in a school at once for the school's overall performance? Why do only some districts choose to participate in Florida's Merit Award Program (only twenty-three of sixty-seven in 2008–2009)?[101] Worst, in that most of the programs called "merit pay" programs do not reward the same things; merit pay for schoolwide performance is much different than merit pay for individual student learning growth. When policymakers propose a "merit pay" program, they are confronted with research about "merit pay" that may analyze a program totally unlike the one under consideration. Further, state legislatures enacted all of the existing merit pay programs *before* policymakers had evidence that they would work. It was not voters who made decisions on uncertain evidence in democratic discourse; it was state legislators.

For some people (and these are the most prominent), performance pay could encourage teachers to boost individual student achievement. Others say that merit pay could keep younger high-quality teachers from leaving the profession. A third group argues that merit pay probably will not do anything for existing teachers. Instead, bright college graduates who would not otherwise think twice about teaching might enter the profession. First-year teachers might make more than the advertised salary because they do their job *well*.

A thorough policymaker will insist on program evaluation after lawmakers enact a change. Merit pay has been evaluated in a handful of studies and experiments. Unfortunately for both proponents and detractors, the evidence is mixed.

Two major evaluations illustrate the difficulties. The first, an evaluation of the Denver ProComp program, found suggestive but very positive results. Teachers hired after the program was enacted were required to participate, and their students' test scores were consistently better than those for Denver teachers overall. Also, high-poverty schools were able to retain more of their teachers, although there is still more turnover at these schools than at those in the suburbs.[102] On the other hand, a study of Nashville, Tennessee, mathematics teachers found no effect at all despite bonuses of up to $15,000 for improved student performance.[103]

The first evaluation encouraged the local AFT affiliate. The positive findings, especially regarding teacher retention, showed that some of the gambles made were beneficial. Indeed, one reading of the study appears to show that the system attracted higher-performing new teachers, so the school district might see long-term gains in excellent teaching. But the ProComp study also found very small effects for existing teachers—that means that a bonus, even a big one, was not likely to inspire significant difference from existing teachers. That is the same conclusion that a policymaker could draw from the Nashville experiment. There, only existing teachers had an opportunity for a bonus, and there was no discernible effect. The NEA argues that the Nashville study shows "merit pay doesn't work," but suggests that attracting higher-talent teachers requires higher pay for all.[104]

How has pluralism affected merit pay? The Denver AFT affiliate can point to a relatively good working relationship with the school district administration. One of the goals of "new unionism" was more collaboration with districts on common interests, and the Denver Public Schools and the union seem to have accomplished some of that goal. For the union, though, it can make sure that whatever becomes of ProComp, it can maintain some measure of job protection. The NEA's opposition to merit pay places it at risk of being on the wrong side of voter mood—it fought the Colorado plan but lost. It risks losing political clout, as the MEA did in Michigan when it opposed Governor John Engler's school reform plans. Indeed, in 2011, only 27 percent of American adults said they oppose merit pay, but 72 percent of public school teachers oppose it. Some 20 percent of American adults support teacher tenure, whereas 53 percent of teachers do.[105]

Conclusion

Merit pay may or may not "solve" teacher quality problems, and the pervasiveness of teachers' unions in the policy debate hampers a full test. That is a good thing for pluralism—the unions are trying to block a policy opposed by many teachers who might not otherwise have any voice in the process. It may be good for children to escape the strong testing regimen required by

NCLB and opposed by the unions. And it may improve the overall quality of teachers that collective bargaining helps protect teachers from arbitrary firing and ensures that the district carefully specifies working conditions. Although teachers' unions have come under attack in 2011 for collective bargaining and benefits that governors framed as too generous compared to the private sector, they continue to offer material incentives to members. Even if state policymakers successfully limit the scope of collective bargaining to issues of pay only, unions could still provide professional development for members and policy expertise to state departments of education.

But the fact that interest groups are not fully accountable to the local voting public poses a democratic dilemma between self-rule and well-informed decision making. The NJEA was able to swing its members against Governor Christie in New Jersey's 2009 gubernatorial election (though not enough to defeat him), but he branded their efforts as antidemocratic. In 1968 the UFT successfully thwarted local control in the Ocean Hill–Brownsville neighborhood. Many Republican and a handful of Democratic governors in 2011 curtailed collective bargaining to help state and local officials balance their budgets in response to voter concerns. Is Christie on track? Was the UFT justified? Should unions be able to bargain on benefits? Democratic norms do not provide the answer.

Suggested Readings

Allegretto, Sylvia A., Sean P. Corcoran, and Lawrence R. Mishel. 2008. *The Teaching Penalty*. Washington, DC: Economic Policy Institute.

American Federation of Teachers. http://www.aft.org/.

Coleman, John. 2010. "*Citizens United* and Political Outcomes." http://users.polisci.wisc.edu/coleman/Citizens%20United%20and%20 Political%20Outcomes.pdf. Accessed January 20, 2011.

Economic Policy Institute. http://www.epi.org/.

Moe, Terry. 2005. "Teacher Unions and School Board Elections." In *Besieged: School Boards and the Future of Education Politics*, edited by William G. Howell, 254–287. Washington, DC: Brookings Institution Press.

Murphy, Marjorie. 1990. *Blackboard Unions: The AFT and the NEA, 1900–1980*. Ithaca, NY: Cornell University Press.

National Education Association. http://www.nea.org/.

Podair, Jerald E. 2002. *The Strike That Changed New York: Blacks, Whites, and the Ocean Hill–Brownsville Crisis.* New Haven, CT: Yale University Press.

Schneider, Anne, and Helen Ingram. 1993. "The Social Construction of Target Populations." *American Political Science Review* 82 (2, June): 334–346.

Timar, Thomas B. 1997. "The Institutional Role of State Education Departments: A Historical Perspective." *American Journal of Education* 105 (May): 231–260.

6

....

Understanding History, Understanding Students

"WE WANT IT ALL," summarized John Goodlad in his book, *A Place Called School*.[1] He identified four groups of goals that American policymakers and citizens expect from schools. Academic goals are for children to read, write, think, and argue clearly. Vocational goals prepare students for work in the armed forces, technical careers, or college education. Social and civic goals teach them about a common American culture, assimilate new immigrants, provide public health services, and ensure nutritional diets. Finally, schools serve individual goals. Through all of these, schools are meant to bring children to faith in democratic government. In this view, American students should be rational, understanding participants in democratic discourse.

The norm of democratic *understanding* strikes at the heart of American educational policy and the policy question, *What should government do?* Other norms help direct policymakers toward who should make decisions about public policy, how those decisions should be made, and who will be affected by public policy, but policymakers promoting understanding in policy must tackle two major dilemmas. The first is untangling a contested definition of what democratic understanding means. Does it mean that citizens can *comprehend* political discussion, or does it mean that citizens *share the same interpretation* of political issues? For educational policy, the range of answers to this question drives the debate over school curriculum and academic tracking. This chapter summarizes the debate over the Progressive Era educational reforms that dominated the twentieth century and continue to shape policy debates. The second dilemma is *who* should decide what students should learn. This dilemma pits parents against schools, and state governments against local and federal solutions. States have strongly resisted "national standards" in the name of local control, but the waves of reform over the last forty years increasingly have forced districts to adopt *state* standards instead, and perhaps soon national standards from the Common Core State Standards Initiative. The controversy that democratic understanding stirs up has led policymakers to abandon most of the goals Goodlad identified for schools; instead they have opted for academic standards aimed at economic competitiveness.

Policymakers trying to prepare students to be knowledgeable political consumers face *loose coupling* as an additional roadblock to policy implementation. This chapter introduces how ideal bureaucracies would work and shows the limitations of treating schools like bureaucracies. A *tightly coupled* bureaucracy is one in which front-line workers readily comply with decisions made by their overseers, but schools have no clear hierarchy because teachers do not work for their principal, and district superintendents do not work for the state superintendent. Thus, when the state superintendent launches an initiative, both teachers and principals have tremendous discretion in how to respond. The incredible diversity of schools and districts discussed in Chapter 2 allows them to be models of experimentation and self-rule, but this diversity often thwarts policymakers' attempts at meaningful educational reform.

"Thousands of Southern blacks fought in the Confederate ranks, including two black battalions under the command of Stonewall Jackson," according to *Our Virginia*, a fourth-grade history textbook by Joy Masoff. It was approved by Virginia's textbook review committee and adopted throughout the state for the fall of 2010. Unfortunately for Masoff, no major historian agreed with her statements. As a last gambit, Confederate President Jefferson Davis had pondered forcing slaves to fight for Dixie, but his advisors warned him that fighting slaves would be freed slaves.[2] Davis abandoned this last effort to stay fate. There were no black battalions; there were no thousands.

Masoff stood by her statement, although she admitted that she had obtained the information through a Web search. She settled on Web pages posted by the Sons of Confederate Veterans, a Civil War group, as the source for her claims.[3] A handful of blacks did fight for the Confederacy, according to historians, but only a handful. African Americans did work as cooks and servants, but that is much different than front-line fighting.[4]

The state's textbook committee recommended the book as "accurate and unbiased." The disputed sentence touched a nerve—only a few years before, Georgia had had a tense showdown over redesigning its state flag to eliminate the Confederate saltire cross because of the legacy of slavery. How did such a statement make it through the committee? Although it was only one sentence in the book, it questioned "the legitimacy of emancipation itself," according to Yale University historian David Blight.[5] It repeated a stock claim made by pro-Confederate groups downplaying the role of slavery in the Civil War.

Governor Bob O'Donnell was "deeply disappointed" by the review committee's recommendation, especially after he learned that the committee comprised three elementary schoolteachers who were paid $200 each. None was an American history specialist; and neither was Masoff, the author of the text! O'Donnell ordered that the Virginia Department of Education overhaul its book approval system.[6]

Should Governor O'Donnell have been involved at all? Twenty states have state textbook lists like Virginia's, which local districts use when stocking classrooms in the fall. Who should judge whether students are learning the right information to become informed, understanding democratic citizens? Or, in terms of public policy, *When should the government intervene?*

Governor O'Donnell and countless school boards have discovered that meddling with school curriculum raises the ire of parents and interest groups alike. Americans fight over interpreting American history (How should the interaction between Native Americans and early settlers be taught?), discussing religion (Should the Pledge of Allegiance be unconstitutional because of the phrase "under God"?), and pedagogical techniques (Should children read with phonics or whole language?).

What makes democratic understanding so volatile? There are two major hazards that threaten policymakers when they venture into these waters. Defining what *democratic understanding* means can infringe on self-rule and participation. There is no commonly accepted version of what a student should "be like." What should a student learn in school? Just academics? Life skills? Tolerance? Ethics and morals?

Defining Understanding

What does understanding mean for practical policymaking? Does it suggest that citizens *comprehend* political discussion, or does it mean that citizens *share the same interpretation* of political issues?

The first interpretation suggests that well-educated citizens are able to comprehend the policy consequences of government action. This ideal only requires citizens—and legislators—to share a common language. For example, New Hampshire Senator Daniel Webster made references to classical antiquity with impunity. And Martin Luther King Jr.'s political speeches were filled with biblical and political allusions. In his "I Have a Dream" speech, King mentioned the "promissory note" of the Declaration of Independence, alluding to Lincoln's second inaugural address, which used the identical imagery of debt. Both Webster and King knew there was strong political opposition to their proposals, but they could expect that their audiences would be able to follow their logic and allusions. There was a widely shared language and body of knowledge. This interpretation of the norm fits well with modern calls for common, basic national standards. Policy scholars across the political spectrum now argue that *all* students would do better in more rigorous, more academic courses. This consensus has reframed the standards debate—even the National Education Association has adopted this language.[7] As discussed later in this chapter, politicians now talk the language of standards rather than the language of individualism.

As the first interpretation of democratic understanding was gaining wide political acceptance and empirical support in the 1980s, some policymakers and legislators used the norm's positive framing to attach policy using the second, volatile definition. Should students *share the same interpretation* of democratic policy, or at least share some core values? This interpretation of democratic understanding created a dilemma for policymakers between self-rule and pluralism.

Exhibit A in this firefight was the controversy over a teaching method called Outcomes-Based Education (OBE).[8] This method tried to combine the best aspects of the Progressives' individual-focused model (described later), with the recognition that high standards for all students helped all students learn more. Proponents argued that "95 percent of students . . . can learn a subject up to high levels of mastery."[9] In OBE, the state would establish certain competencies ("rubrics") that all students would have to meet before moving on to the next topic or grade level. Teachers would not be tied to this or that type of teaching, so long as students could demonstrate "mastery" of the particular outcome. Many schools adopted a three-letter grading scheme: "A" for advanced mastery, "B" for mastery, and "I" for work in progress. If students failed, they could re-read a section of the textbook, try an experiment again, or consult with the teacher. Eventually, every student could master every outcome at his or her own pace. The logic was that *instruction* should vary rather than the results. ("Everybody can get an A—if they have the appropriate opportunity to learn.") *Opportunity to learn* meant that students would be expected to know academic material only after they had been taught the material with appropriate methods. This approach became controversial because policymakers could not agree on what those methods might be. OBE answered that question by encouraging students to try to pass a rubric's standards without a penalty for failure. OBE's lead proponent, William Spady, suggested that the method would help "undermine the potential use of evaluation (testing and grades) as a mechanism for the control of student behavior."[10] Thus, there were uniform standards but students could learn in a way best suited for them.

Some argued that this was not fair to academically gifted students (because the standards could not be *that* high), and others worried that the repetition of course material for less-gifted students would set them up for failure in real-world settings. But these charges were not any different than those made against Progressive reforms.[11] If these had been the only critiques of OBE, it would have entered teaching pedagogy as yet another method to help struggling students in a demanding environment. But these were not the only criticisms.

OBE proponents encouraged educators to look far beyond content outcomes to "transformational" outcomes. Schools should "equip all students with the knowledge, competence, and orientations needed for success."[12] OBE proponents urged school districts to decide what skills and values a competent citizen in the future would need to be successful. In other words, what did a successful democratic citizen do and value?

It was that last question that challenged the democratic norm of self-rule. Forty-two states worked on some form of outcomes-based education, and the most controversial standards were almost uniformly related to the "orientations" or "values" that students would have to demonstrate to graduate. For example, Pennsylvania's draft standards included requirements that "all students exhibit self-esteem" and that "all students would advocate the preservation and promotion of cultural heritage."[13] Other states included citizenship and "appreciation" of history. The apparent attacks on self-rule values were explosive. Although many critics of OBE were religious conservatives, teachers' unions were also hesitant about the method's potential to require teacher evaluation and cross-district comparisons. Criticism revolved around funding, values, and local control of the curriculum.[14]

For example, Ohio adopted new state rubrics that defined "what children should know, be able to do, and be like." Ohio State Superintendent Ted Sanders's intent was for schools to address democratic citizenship, so he was encouraging schools to talk about respect, participation, and understanding different points of view. But vocal parents did not see it that way. They fumed that the "state was telling our kids what to believe."[15] John Goff, who was an assistant superintendent in the early 1990s, remembered being on the road with Sanders to promote the program:

> Ted and I were in a church in western Ohio talking about the new standards. They were *mad*. I wasn't sure we were going to make it out alive—and not metaphorically. The standards said they would set what students would know, be able to do, and 'be like.' Including that phrase was the worst thing we ever did.[16]

Ohio Governor George Voinovich sent an uncharacteristically shrill note to the state superintendent. "I was not tipped off that all of this Outcome Based Education has been controversial in other states. . . . I feel like I've been blind sighted [sic]," he wrote. "I think it is imperative that you put together a very understandable document on what this is all about, so I understand it."[17] Private schools thought that OBE was a National Education Association (NEA) takeover plot, and public school advocates railed against the cost.[18] Sanders had to pull the plug on the standards.

The Ohio parents were not angry that the state was setting standards per se, but because the standards were conflicting with their own *individual* philosophy of education. How could students show they were respectful, tolerant, or open to other points of view? To these voters, OBE sounded as if the *state* was going to define respect, tolerance, and acceptable points of view. Sanders abandoned this vision of democratic understanding; Ohio adopted academic achievement standards instead. Many other states were backed into the same corner: trying to define the norm of democratic understanding was thwarted by the norm of self-rule.

Exhibit B was the inflammatory rhetoric of academics, politicians, and bureaucrats that surrounded the release of the *National Standards for United States History* in late 1994. The U.S. Department of Education supported and published many voluntary curriculum guidelines in the 1990s (usually called "standards," although the federal government did not hold states to them), and all attracted critics (e.g., Did the science standards expect students to learn too much too soon? Should calculators be encouraged in mathematics courses?). But none drew as much vitriol as the history standards.

In 1992 the U.S. Department of Education and the National Endowment for the Humanities (NEH, also a federal agency) gave $1.4 million to the National Center for History in the Schools (NCHS) at the University of California, Los Angeles, to draft a set of history standards. Lynne Cheney, the chairwoman of NEH, was originally enthusiastic about and highly invested in the standards. She and other supporters of strong, content-based, traditional curriculum urged that the standards should reintroduce American history into elementary and secondary schools. (Many school districts had replaced history with social studies, an amalgam of economics, sociology, and civics.)[19] NCHS had already produced the highly regarded history guidebook for teachers called *Lessons from History*.[20]

So far, so good. Gary B. Nash, a professor of history at UCLA, headed the effort, working with twenty-nine other organizations and prominent historians. They produced a 600-page document covering ten "eras" and thirty-one standards, beginning with pre-Columbian America. As an aid to teachers, the document also contained some 2,500 classroom activities and teaching examples. A teacher perusing the guidelines would have no trouble building a history class for any grade level. Nash and his colleagues aimed to produce a document that would help children be democratic citizens who understood how contemporary politics are shaped by conflict in the past. "We want students really to interrogate the data. We want them to exercise their own judgment in reading conflicting views of any piece of history and understand that there are multiple perspectives on any particular historical era," Nash told Charles Gibson, an anchor on ABC's *Good Morning America*, in 1994.[21] An excellent definition of democratic understanding.

But in October 1994, five days before NCHS was to release the standards to the public, Lynne Cheney launched the first salvo in a two-year fight over the document. Cheney blasted the standards she had sponsored, chastising Nash and others for producing a document that included no mention of Daniel Webster, Robert E. Lee, or Thomas Edison, but one mention of Mansa Musa, six of Harriet Tubman, and nineteen of Joseph McCarthy and McCarthyism. She charged that "various political groups, such as African-American groups and Native American groups . . . complained about omissions and distortions." She wrote that the standards were a product of "an academic establishment that revels in . . . politicized history."[22] To Cheney and her supporters, it seemed that the standards praised pluralism at the expense of democratic understanding.

Cheney's attack was notable, as it came from the (now former) NEH chairwoman who had approved the project. But the increasingly conservative national mood of the mid-1990s proved fertile ground for her criticisms to multiply. Radio host Rush Limbaugh devoted a show to tearing pages out of a history book, saying, "Here's Paul Revere. He's gone. Here's George Washington as president. Look at all these pages in this book. He's gone."[23] The Family Research Council produced its own set of history standards, which were much shorter and much more traditional.[24] Nash and his colleagues responded in kind, calling Cheney and her supporters "shock troops" engaged in a "blitzkrieg" against professional historians.[25] Nash also denigrated the "mossback historians" who dissented from the NCHS standards.[26]

But Limbaugh, the Family Research Council, and other nonhistorians on the right of the political spectrum were not the only critics. In 1995 the U.S. Senate condemned the standards 99 to 1 and insisted that future work have a "decent respect for . . . United States history."[27] Some prominent professional historians panned them as well. Most notably, Diane Ravitch and Arthur Schlesinger Jr. together offered tempered, but still severe, criticism of the standards. Both Ravitch and Schlesinger were lifelong Democrats and professional historians, and both later blogged for the unabashedly liberal *Huffington Post*. Like Cheney, however, Ravitch was at the U.S. Department of Education from 1991 to 1993 and had signed off on the initial history project (see box 6.1).

Yet Ravitch and Schlesinger called the standards "an embarrassment." They noted that the standards implied that the United States was responsible for the Cold War and that westward expansion was due only to the "greed and rapacity of 'restless white Americans.'" They said that many

BOX 6.1 Diane Ravitch

"We are disrupting communities, dumbing down our schools, giving students false reports of their progress, and creating a private sector that will undermine public education without improving it," Diane Ravitch wrote in early 2010 in the *Wall Street Journal*. "That is why I changed my mind about the current direction of school reform." Her statements—and the release of her 2010 book *The Death and Life of the Great American School System*—prompted one former ally to accuse her of a "philosophy of resentment and futility" and "bizarre hypothetical nostalgia."

Ravitch received a Ph.D. in history in 1975 for her work on the growth of urban public schooling in New York City. That work, and her mentor, Lawrence A. Cremin, made her skeptical of using schools as tools to remake society. She frequently argued that schools were fundamentally undemocratic and harsh when they did not give *all* children a solid, academic foundation. Her commitment to academic learning was so strong that, as a Democrat, she took a post in a Republican administration in 1991, chiefly to promote it. After her time in the Department of Education, Ravitch served on the boards of pro-school-choice organizations and helped oversee the National Assessment of Educational Progress for the Clinton and second Bush administrations. Ravitch now blogs for the *Huffington Post* and *Education Week*, and she is a professor of education at New York University.

Thus, her seeming change of heart in 2010 puzzled her former allies. Ravitch appeared to disown school choice, student assessment, and even her own previous statements, such as, "We must give poor kids a chance to escape schools that are cruelly not educating them." Yet Ravitch's statements were not so far out of character. During her academic career she has railed consistently against what she sees as fads in school reform. She challenged twentieth-century educational reforms, especially the push to replace academic subjects with "practical" learning, in her books *The Revisionists Revised* (1978), *The Troubled Crusade* (1983), and *Left Back* (2000). She advocated national standards as an assistant secretary of education, yet when the national history standards were released in 1994, she called them an "embarrassment."

That she has weighed contemporary school choice policy in the balance and found it wanting would only be her most recent judgment. To her, assessment testing seemed to be watering down the curriculum, not expanding it. Neither seemed to be promoting the academic curriculum she has spent thirty years promoting.

Source: Ravitch (2001, 2010a, 2010b); Carey (2010).

of the teaching examples were absolutely "politically biased, moralistic, and judgmental."[28] Schlesinger later wrote that adamant defenders of the standards—and their adamant critics—were guilty of using the standards as "social and political therapy."[29]

After the U.S. Senate condemned the guidelines, a widely regarded pro-standards educational policy group convened a panel of historians to suggest revisions; the changes were provided to Nash's group, NCHS. NCHS eliminated 400(!) pages, dropping all of the teaching examples and fundamentally reorienting many of the standards. Although Nash continued to defend his first offering (reminding readers in 2004 that NEH had called the original document "remarkable in its ambition [and] its clarity"), he boasted that the revised standards had "fulfilled their assigned role: to raise the standards for teaching history and provide guidance . . . for bringing history alive."[30]

How did Nash, who so clearly articulated the tie between American history and democratic understanding, fall into a national fight over political correctness and the American past? The policy window opened because politicians across the political spectrum at that time believed that standards improved education and, like the Puritans, were concerned that history might be "buried in the grave of our forefathers." In the late 1980s and early 1990s, states had been moving to adopt standards in other academic areas as well. A policy window is an opportunity for policymaking when opposition to some change is weak and the public is dissatisfied with the status quo and seems willing to change. But open policy windows *do not* mean that public policy is enacted—only that it is openly debated for viability. According to historian Sean Wilentz, the standards' authors "seem to have been mighty naive" about what the political response would be, and the lead authors later recognized that they were playing with fire.[31]

Like Virginia Governor O'Donnell, Nash and his colleagues discovered that, "history, like politics, is about . . . identity."[32] Was slavery a major cause of the Civil War? Or was it simply about Northern aggression? Some Southerners' identity was linked to the answer, and the textbook *Our Virginia* provided fodder for the debate. Similarly, the history standards unsettled individuals' values about America. Was Joseph McCarthy *the* defining figure of the twentieth century (as the numerous references to him might suggest)? Was the Cold War the product of a militaristic America (as depicted in the original history standards) or a realistic response to a shaky totalitarian superpower with nuclear weapons (as depicted in the revised standards)?

The teaching examples in the original history standards strongly implied that democratic understanding meant students *shared* a particular set of interpretations about the American past: America was a collection of competing groups seeking their own interests, and political elites of the past were craven. They failed "to balance *pluribus* and *unum* and to place the nation's democratic ideals at the center of its history."[33]

Parents, Puritans, and Progressives

The balance between *pluribus* and *unum* remains extremely difficult to strike. While Goodlad identified the many goals students may have in school, the contentious fights over the National History Standards and *Our Virginia* illustrate that Americans do not have a clear preference about *who* should set academic, vocational, and social goals. In the early colonies, families made the primary decisions about their children's education, but three centuries of demands by elite policymakers and interest groups for social order and a *common* culture have successfully wrested most educational control away from individuals.[34]

Massachusetts enacted America's first school laws to preserve social order in the interest of the majority. Although most Americans think of "back to basics" as meaning the three Rs of reading, 'riting, and 'rithmetic, schools did not start with *those* basics. For the Puritans, schools in America were meant to produce moral citizens who would make virtuous decisions. Recall from Chapter 1 that when Massachusetts' legislators nixed reformer Horace Mann's pleas for state oversight of schools, they argued that schools were well-endowed to preserve "the morals, the religion, [and] the politics of the state."[35] Neither academic performance nor personal aspiration was a purpose of schooling for the Massachusetts legislature, but it argued that children could not be virtuous without careful, deliberate instruction.

In the 1640s the Congregationalists of the Massachusetts Bay Colony saw the passing of traditional society. In the New World, the social bonds of church, family, and community were stretched to the breaking point. Frequent famines undercut community bonds, and the vast, sparsely inhabited frontier provided a means of escaping from community mores. The colony enacted a series of laws in the 1640s to counter the degradation of society. In the 1647 law, the Old Deluder Satan Act, the Massachusetts divines warned that without instruction in religion and industry, history might be lost.

The Puritan divines argued that individualism could be bridled by teaching girls and boys to read; the Bible would help them ward off the temptations of the devil. The laws required teaching literacy and some "honest, lawful calling" at public expense. Thus, schools were meant to reproduce social order first and learning second.[36] By all accounts, they were tremendously successful at promoting learning. Although there are no definitive numbers, some historians estimate that 90 percent of men and 80 percent of women could read in New England. Back in England, only 60 percent of men in towns, and much less than half of those in the countryside, could read. By 1800 literacy was almost universal for whites in the United States, and among African American slaves it was 15 to 20 percent.[37]

New England schools, however, could not maintain civilization in the 1600s. As in Reformation Era Europe, the Bible was a two-edged sword. Giving the Bible to individuals to read provided a common language and cultural framework that could support social order, but it also meant people did not have to rely on their social betters for understanding.[38] Puritan education sought to quell individualism, but animated it instead. Rhode Island filled with dissidents from the Massachusetts Congregationalist order after the 1640s, and the Great Awakening of the 1720s threatened the power of the rationalist clergy, who were politically dominant. In the West religious sects rebelling against authority of all kinds multiplied—so many in upstate New York that it was known as the "burned-over district" because of the fires of religious revival.[39] Though many of those westward settlers brought a semblance of education with them, schools tended to be minimal and sporadic well into the nineteenth century. Schools could not maintain social order.

Could they maintain democracy? This too, was an open question. In the nineteenth century many Americans thought schooling was tinged with antidemocratic elitism. In the 1850s Georgia legislators rejected state oversight of education twice. One historian's gloss held that Georgia had rejected the "conservative idea that education should descend gradually from the higher institutions to the masses of the people."[40] Some twenty years later, that state banned public monies for funding any education past eighth grade.[41] Economics also competed with education. Ohio legislators, for example, were more interested in direct economic development than in state funding for education. In 1828 they sold all of the land given to the state by the federal government for education and used the money for funding railways, canals, and roads.[42] They did allow school districts to raise money if local voters approved (few did). Other states had similar experiences. These Americans believed that using education as a means to perpetuate order was *un*democratic. For them, the democratic norm of understanding did not come from socialization in school but through individual experience. Individualism, then, carried the day. The answer to *when government should intervene* was "as little as possible."

Throughout the nineteenth century, self-styled progressive reformers like the Western Literary Institute and National Education Association labored to overcome these strong antischooling impulses, with little success. But Europe's late-nineteenth-century troubles gave American reformers an opening. Immigrants poured into America's cities from Europe, bolstering urban political machines. Reformers, who became known as Progressives in the first third of the twentieth century, charged that such machines were warrens of graft and corruption. In their view, politicians used the machines to enrich themselves and thwart "true" American values, even though they did provide jobs and income to immigrants, who frequently arrived with little formal education and few skills suited for work in an industrializing society. Many also brought radical political ideas that seemed to threaten American democracy.

Ellwood P. Cubberley was one of the leading Progressive reformers in education. (His book, *Public School Administration* [1916], was the gold standard textbook in colleges of education into the 1940s.) He argued that these new immigrants were

> illiterate, docile, lacking in self-reliance and initiative, and not possessing the Anglo-Teutonic conceptions of law, order, and government, their coming has served to dilute tremendously our national stock and to corrupt our civic life. . . . Our task is to . . . implant in their children, so far as can be done, the Anglo-Saxon conception of . . . popular government, and to awaken in them a reverence for our democratic institutions.[43]

In other words, Cubberley argued that schools should—must—imprint the democratic norm of understanding on students.

The NEA and other Progressive groups capitalized on the influx of immigrants to force many cities to centralize their school systems, handing administration to experts.[44] Progressive policymakers succeeded in transferring educational oversight from partisan, elected officials to appointed superintendents or nonpartisan boards in many states to break urban machines and "politics." In line with Cubberley's prescriptions, Progressives wanted to maintain social order through the schools. Schools would impress upon children that this was a "republic, . . . one nation, indivisible"(from 1893). Students would learn English and indispensable industrial habits of promptness, obedience, and personal cleanliness. Although Progressives were a diverse group of reformers, many agreed that the government should intervene to make immigrants safe and useful in modern America.

Progressives dramatically changed contemporary policymakers' answers to *what government should do*. Before the late nineteenth century, school curriculum emphasized academic subjects like grammar, Latin, and mathematics. Virtually all American schools included religious study of a Protestant character. Children learned by memorization. Schooling transmitted cultural values, but very little in the way of career readiness. In Goodlad's terminology, schools focused on academic and social goals while virtually ignoring vocational and personal goals.

Led by John Dewey and Cubberley, the Progressives would have none of this. Packing children off to school to memorize Alfred, Lord Tennyson's "The Charge of the Light Brigade" might have been a useful diversion when home and work were scarcely separate—when a child was either in the kitchen or in the field. Families that had provided training for their children (and resistance to formal schooling) were no longer suited for the new age. Cubberley attacked parents' individualism directly, claiming that "each year the child is coming to belong more and more to the state, and less and less to the parent."[45] Dewey, one of the most prolific writers on American education in the country's history, took a much kinder view of immigrants but still attacked the traditional curriculum and argued that children, not parents, should drive it. He argued that the curriculum should be tailored to children rather than children to the curriculum.

Dewey and others introduced vocational and personal goals into the core curriculum of school. Above all, schooling would be practical, and students would be sorted into classes that would fit their perceived abilities and likely future career, a process later called *tracking* or *ability grouping*. Then, subject matter was to be presented in such a way as to match children's own activities, in what was called the *project method*. John Dewey argued that if children were not at school, they would be playing, reading, coloring, or doing some other such activity: "What, then, could be more natural than making the school's curriculum of such material?"[46] Thus, schools were to simultaneously "serve the individual" and the "welfare of the entire community."[47]

From the Progressive point of view, this child-centered, vocation-driven education would enhance the democratic project. Schools encouraged students to cooperate with other students in learning, and teachers would help direct students to learn the consequences of their activities. Sorting students would promote the best kind of learning for any kind of student. Reformers argued that these were democratic values: individualism, understanding, and inclusion.

Although the Progressive Era petered out in the 1930s, its educational norms, ideals, and policy proposals persisted and presaged seventy years of conflict about how education could bolster democracy. It was a conflict, yes, but Progressives and their heirs argued from the winning side. For example, the nation's first direct federal educational spending, the Smith-Hughes Act of 1917, was to support schools' vocational education programs to prepare students for specific careers, rather than a general education. Some desegregation lawsuits in the 1950s were built around the claim that black students did not have access to the same school materials used for vocational education as white students had. James B. Conant, president of Harvard, persuasively argued that only the large high school could offer students appropriate vocational educational experiences; his opinion precipitated wholesale school district consolidation in the 1960s (see box 6.2). Smaller schools harmed students, Conant wrote, because "although the [non-academically talented student] constitutes a majority of the student body, he is obliged to study courses which at best only the top quarter of his class can pursue with profit."[48] Small schools merged to become bigger ones, just as school enrollments were booming after World War II. In 1965 James Coleman and his colleagues used dramatic disparities in the availability of materials between schools as evidence of unequal educational opportunity.[49] This Progressive view suggested that children could not understand modern democratic life if they did not have access to a wide range of specialized learning opportunities.

Until the 1970s, opponents of child-centered, practical education had been successfully framed as out-of-date elitists. An NEA field secretary called critics of this curriculum "unintelligent" and "unethical" and called

BOX 6.2   James B. Conant

James B. Conant (1893–1978) would frequently introduce himself as having "worked at Harvard." It was true, but only in the most technical sense. Conant had been an organic chemist at the university in the 1920s and may have been in the running for a Nobel prize for his work in chlorophyll. He never got the award, because Harvard took him away from that work when it elected him president in 1933. He held that post until 1953.

During that time, he revolutionized how Harvard—and much of American higher education—recruited students and faculty. Conant stayed out of college and political controversies while in the Chemistry Department, but once he became president, he moved quickly to demolish Harvard's tight-fisted admissions policy. When Conant arrived at Harvard, the best way for a student to be admitted was to be related to Harvard alumni. Conant found this repugnant and created a merit-based scholarship system to open the school to middle- and low-income students from around the country—the "meatballs," he called them. He also allowed women to attend classes at Harvard through an agreement with nearby Radcliffe College. Faculty, too, felt Conant's meritocratic glare. In a sharp departure from his predecessors, he would not offer employment to faculty unless they were engaged in excellent, original scholarly research. "You will become a member of the aristocracy in the American sense only if your accomplishments and integrity earn this appellation," he told one graduating class.

Conant made Harvard into an internationally renowned research university. His success there propelled him into national and international politics. During World War II, President Franklin Roosevelt recruited him to attract top talent to work on the secret atomic bomb and other foreign policy projects. Later he was the U.S. ambassador to West Germany and an advisor to President Eisenhower.

This perch gave Conant a national audience for his views on education. Although he was a critic of his contemporary, John Dewey, he shared Dewey's belief that education could overcome barriers of income and class. He suggested that high schools be large because small schools could not offer enough courses to meet all students' needs, especially academically talented students. Larger schools could group students by ability and hire better-trained teachers.

If Harvard could be meritocratic, Conant thought, high school should be also.

Source: O'Connell and O'Connell (1997); "The Inspector General" (1959); Halberstam (1952).

their criticism an "attack on the community."[50] Another observer claimed that many educators believed the critics were doing "the work of the devil."[51] They could demean their critics this way because those critics were at the margins of the debate.

Critics did not see it quite that way. What had they done to be in league with the Old Deluder himself? While the NEA, Conant, and others advocated student-centered tracking to bolster democracy, critics on the left and the right argued that sorting students, whether by ability or interest, actually undercut self-rule, weakened inclusion, and destroyed democratic understanding.

Democratic self-rule means that individuals are able to make consequential decisions about what to do, where to live, and how to judge political actions. Although individuals can and do make poor choices, democracy assumes that *collective* choice outweighs individual mistakes. As Madison argued in Federalist 51, as long as no single faction becomes too powerful, democracy can preserve individual liberty, including the liberty to make bad decisions. The framers of the U.S. Constitution attempted to preserve this liberty by splitting Congress into a directly elected House with short terms and an indirectly elected Senate with longer terms. The House was supposed to be responsive, even to wild popular passion. The Senate's insulation was supposed to stop the worst excesses of democracy. Congress does not always work that way, but the design shows the weight that the framers placed on liberty.

Critics conceded that schools providing vocational training to most and academic training to a few may have been efficient and practical, at least in the short term. But who would do the choosing? A few experimental schools could help students make intelligent choices about learning activities, because these schools had a very low student-teacher ratio, which guaranteed that students received substantial individual attention. (Notably, these included Dewey's own Lincoln School in Chicago, where the ratio was six to one.) Virtually no other schools had the resources to evaluate every child. Instead, they relied on community employment needs, standardized testing, assumptions, or stereotypes. Despite the promise of being child-centered, tracking removed individual choice. Progressive education consigned students to vocations based on the judgments of teachers, administrators, or other professionals.

Some critics alleged that Progressive educational reforms undercut democratic inclusion. These were foes of school sorting, who made virtually the same argument that proponents of racial inclusion have made: less-industrious, less-talented, and less academically inclined students would obviously benefit if they were in the same classrooms as top-tier performers. Concentrating less-motivated students in less-demanding classes, ironically, would make success in life even more difficult.[52] They argued that social divisions of income, race, and geography were strong in American democracy, and schools that did not share curriculum standards would perpetuate those divisions.

The effect of tracking on inclusion appeared to be most invidious for African Americans. As discussed in Chapter 3, many Southern states had sharply increased spending on African American schools in the 1930s and 1940s to fend off desegregation. Much of that spending was split between improving the facilities of black schools and bolstering vocational training. A mass migration of blacks from the South to the North in the 1920s and 1930s meant that the South was hemorrhaging workers. To provide for the states' economic viability, Southern policymakers turned to tracked education to train a new generation of skilled laborers—as long as they were black. That likelihood continues. Blacks nationwide were and are disproportionately assigned to vocational tracks. Whites, especially upper-middle-class whites, have been much more likely to receive traditional, college-bound training in junior high and high school.[53]

Finally, critics argued that by banishing the traditional curriculum and catering to children's own (tracked) interests, schools actually weakened democratic understanding.[54] Flannery O'Connor wrote sarcastically in 1963:

> The devil of educationalism that possesses us is the kind that can be cast out only by prayer and fasting. No one has yet come along strong enough to do it. In other ages the attention of our children was held by Homer and Virgil, among others, but by the reverse evolutionary process, that is no longer possible; our children are too stupid now to enter the past imaginatively. No one asks the student if algebra pleases him or if he finds it satisfactory that some French verbs are irregular, but if he prefers [John] Hershey [a contemporary journalistic author] to Hawthorne, his taste must prevail.[55]

Though Progressive reformers were adamant that "all" children should have their "rightful heritage to a satisfactory education," they meant that students should have courses that were interesting or useful to them.[56] In fairness, the Progressives were reacting against a dry academic tradition that was heavily dependent on rote learning, a pedagogy that left many to wonder what the contemporary usefulness of Latin grammar was. John Dewey and other Progressives successfully undercut this traditional schooling.

By one measure, Progressives did succeed in educating all children. In 1900 some 75 percent of elementary-aged children and only 11 percent of fourteen- to eighteen-year olds were in school. As a result of compulsory-attendance laws passed at the urging of Progressives, virtually all elementary-aged children and 90 percent of fourteen-to eighteen-year-olds were in school by the 1960s.[57] Under Progressive curricula, most children would now share the schooling *experience*, but they would no longer share a common *curriculum*. The Puritans gave colonists a common language; the Progressives spurned it.

Both the reformers and their critics were making empirical, testable claims, but they rarely provided evidence to let legislators or voters make a democratic decision. Tracking could aid achievement in and after school, or it could strengthen within-school segregation. As happened with the Elementary and Secondary Education Act (ESEA) and James Coleman's 1966 study (see Chapter 3), legislators moved faster than policy analysts—first to introduce tracking on a wide scale, and then to boost the academic goals of school at the expense of other curricula. Had legislators waited, though, they might not have had any clear direction about what they should have done. Although policy scholars have shown that tracking does not always do what proponents promised it would, it has not resulted in worse segregation than was already present in schools. But critics were dead on when they decried the "dumbing-down" of the "nonacademic" track.

Proponents' first claim was that tracking would improve *all* students' school outcomes, thus boosting their potential to evaluate claims made by a democratic government. Conant hoped that nonacademic tracks would make education relevant for "the majority of the student body." Conant's theory of action was that children's learning and participation in school would improve if teachers gave them relevant, practical, educational opportunities. What *outputs* might a researcher look for? One would be academic performance. Proponents of vocational education thought math and reading could be learned better in a realistic setting than by rote or other traditional methods.[58] Another output would be graduation. If students saw how learning would be useful in future careers, they might stay in school longer and be likely to become more productive democratic citizens.

Academically, tracking does benefit students—but only those students in academic tracks.[59] Some educational reformers argue that this benefit comes from pulling the least-talented and least-motivated students out of the classroom.[60] In their view, tracking discriminates against those in nonacademic tracks by segregating schools. Principals do appear to group elementary students in classrooms based on their likelihood of academic success, so this criticism is serious.[61] And policy research has convincingly shown that schools place students in tracks for reasons unrelated to their academic abilities, especially school staffing needs and parental involvement.[62]

Other reformers suggest that nonacademic tracks are not necessarily a problem, but low-quality curriculum is. Some scholars estimated that if all high school students were assigned to an academic track, overall mathematics achievement would rise. Gains for nonwhite students would actually be greater than those of their white counterparts.[63] Similarly, in schools with multiple tracks, placing students in classes one or two levels above their assigned level actually increases their academic achievement in both English and mathematics. Assigning them to lower groups reduces their scores.[64] It appears that tracks *do* segregate students by ability and *do* increase inequality between groups, but the results suggest that schools expect too little from any of their students.

The second claim made by Progressive reformers was that real-world education would help students see the importance of learning and therefore stay in school.[65] They were right to argue that staying in school was much better for learning than dropping out of school—even students in the least academic, most vocational tracks learn more in school than their peers who do not finish.[66] But does targeting education to students' interests actually *keep* them in school?

Maybe, if the curriculum is challenging enough. The same researchers who estimated mathematics gains argued that placing all students in an academic track would raise the overall graduation rate 10 percent, even after accounting for other factors that contribute to dropping out of school.[67] But the actual practice of tracking appears to lower the aspirations, academic and otherwise, of students in nonacademic tracks. Vocational students leave high school with lower self-esteem than they start it with.[68] Little wonder, if, as researchers have found, teachers in academic classes have more teaching experience and teachers in general have higher expectations for academic-track students.[69]

The history of American Progressive educational reform illustrates the paradoxical nature of democratic debate over public policy. Progressives like Cubberley and Dewey lauded the unifying aspects of school: let us make the new immigrants in our own image, the majority, "The Quality" and not "the equality," as Owen Wister wrote in the Progressive Era novel, *The Virginian* (1902). But to do so, Cubberley proposed strong central control, and Dewey proposed radically individual education, because in their view children could not effectively participate in democracy unless they understood their individual social station in life. Critics responded that such self-rule undercut norms of inclusion and understanding. Instead, they claimed that a common, majoritarian curriculum would give *individuals* a common language to understand choices made in democratic government.[70]

National or Federal Understanding?
The Growth of Curriculum Standards

At the beginning of the twentieth century, leading educational reformers called for practical, child-focused education models. Students would do individual "projects" to show they had learned a useful set of skills. By the end of the century, leading educational reformers were championing uniform academic standards that would be assessed by standardized tests. Both sets of reformers believed they were advancing democratic understanding. Progressives sorted students into socially useful occupations; standards boosters tried to define a common language for democratic discourse. Both had strong ideas about what a citizen in a democracy should know.

This section of this chapter considers an additional dilemma that *both* groups of reformers faced: despite increasing involvement by the federal government in American educational policy, American schools were and are fragmented.[71] Both groups sought to bolster state (and federal) control of education—the only way to ensure that all students were appropriately prepared for democratic citizenship. Initially many state lawmakers were reluctant to take power from local school districts, but as schools took larger portions of state budgets, they, too, saw reasons for demanding results. It was *Time for Results*, as the National Governors' Association titled a 1986 report.

Why are schools so fragmented? The root problem is that they are not an ideal bureaucracy. Ideal bureaucracies have *unitary command, no resistance to policy changes, perfect communications,* and *ample time to enact decisions.*[72] Few bureaucracies actually match this ideal, but schools fall far short of it. The core of their failure stems from the lack of unitary command. *Unitary command* means that there are clear lines of authority, or, what the boss says, goes. Schools in many states report to multiple overseers who may or may not report to each other. An elected school board, for example, may be able to hire and fire a superintendent but not principals. Only in rare schools can principals hire teachers, and in even fewer can they fire them. Although a school board has to follow state education regulations, school boards are not controlled by state departments of education—but in some states, the Department of Education may take over school districts if the school board does not meet certain standards.[73] *Schools* are not necessarily subject to the Department of Education, either. For example, Wisconsin State Superintendent Herbert Grover told local television reporters that he would not send any of his six children to the DeSoto public schools because the district had substandard curriculum according to state standards. "I had teachers crying on the phone to me," he said.[74] What was notable was that the *state superintendent* had to resort to the local media to get the district's attention!

Schools are instead a model of loose coupling.[75] Many significant policy decisions are made in the classroom by teachers. But loose coupling opens up a host of problems. Front-line workers like teachers have a great deal of discretion in how they carry out the wishes of their superiors. School-teachers design their own lesson plans, evaluate their students' work, decide how strict their discipline will be, and otherwise set the tone for their classrooms. Once teachers close their doors, their classrooms are essentially theirs alone. If teachers dislike a new reform, they may find it tempting to resist it behind the closed door in the hope that it is only a passing fad. Compounding loose coupling is the vast uncertainty surrounding the technology of schools. (In this context, "technology" means how schools transmit information and values rather than laptop computers and HDTV.) This is not an unreasonable approach, because children's learning styles are not well understood, and they vary significantly. ("Why can Isaiah just make 50 flashcards and ace the exam, but it seems like I have to read the textbook 50 times?") The Coleman Report, discussed in Chapter 3, foreshadowed the problem: schools themselves seemed to have remarkably little effect on children's learning and social outcomes. Although that finding has been shown to be less dire than it was originally thought, even Coleman's critics had to concede that schools were not the panacea Progressive reformers and U.S. judges had thought they were.[76] Uncertain technology easily leads to poor communication, because different actors in educational policy may have different theories of action, different hypotheses, and different jargon.

Neither loose coupling nor uncertain technology was seen as problematic for most of American history. Because many states simply required that there *be* schools, local school districts and schools made educational policy for themselves; there was no "coupling" necessary between state reform efforts and teachers' actions. Leaving teachers to respond to children's needs bolstered the image of a teacher as a professional, as the NEA claimed (see Chapter 5). If teachers were professionals like doctors or lawyers, they could be trusted to solve the problems posed by uncertain technology individually. Even when the policy debate over education shifted from provision to production in the 1930s and 1940s, politically ascendant Progressives and their heirs demanded changes to educational inputs, including more centralization and overhauls of the curriculum. Later, when the courts found persistent inequality between schools in the 1960s, judges, and newly empowered teachers' unions argued that greater financial resources were an appropriate remedy. Proponents of desegregation and integration argued that schooling children in the same facilities had a salutary effect on their education; again, this is an educational input. When educators and the courts called for more inputs—more funds, more teachers, better facilities—state policymakers complied. Focusing on inputs allowed politicians to claim that they were improving American education and allowed policy analysts to collect easily measurable statistics, but that focus also meant that policymakers could not diagnose the problems of loose coupling or uncertain technology. If all policy analysts had were input measures, there was no way to know how well a policy translated inputs into educational outputs and outcome (see Chapter 4).

Yet by 2010, the Obama administration was calling for "rigorous interventions in the lowest performing schools" and "performance targets" for schools, districts, and states.[77] The administration also sought to make all students "college and career" ready. These were calls for output measures. Not only were education professionals no longer trusted, but *state* policymakers had to prove their worth, too. What happened? It is not as if advocates of Progressive education or local control have disappeared. Some educational policymakers still advocate "authentic assessment" (essentially the Progressives Era project method), vocational education, and social skills.[78] Many teachers and professors in colleges of education still denounce testing and even standard-setting.[79]

Instead, the policy problem has shifted. At the start of the twentieth century, reformers complained about educational *access*. Toward the end, the policy issues of equal educational *opportunity* and economic competitiveness moved to the fore. When lawmakers saw the problem of American education as access, Progressive reforms seemed to fit the bill. Building more schools would serve more students, but these reforms alone seemed ill-suited to addressing equal opportunity or competitiveness.

The first policy issue was equality of opportunity for democratic understanding. Progressive education advocates, such as James B. Conant, tried to frame their reforms as equalizing. Conant had helped write the NEA's 1944 report *Education for All American Youth*, which advocated career tracking. The issue became a policy problem when James Coleman and others found glaring disparities in schools and in academic achievement in the 1960s. But Coleman's report and subsequent research (discussed previously) shows clearly that many Progressive reforms made academic education *less* equal.

Academics replaced access in public conversation as American competitiveness declined in the 1970s. In that decade, the United States lost its world economic dominance as America's dependence on foreign oil was revealed in embarrassing detail when Middle Eastern states cut off oil. At the same time, American schools seemed to be producing worse results. Many achievement test scores had been falling for more than fifteen years, especially in high school grades. Average scores for the mathematics portion of the SAT college entrance test, for example, fell more than 22 points between 1966 and 1976.[80] Between 1969 and 1982, high school science scores on the National Assessment of Educational Progress fell half a standard deviation—a significant drop.[81] One policy organization claimed that in 1985, 44 percent of seventeen-year-olds were only marginally literate.[82] The cover story of the June 16, 1980, issue of *Time* magazine claimed that half of the nation's parents complained their students did less homework, and the parents blamed lazy teachers. American high schoolers performed poorly in international comparisons exams, and Americans were worried about the comparisons with up-and-coming economic competitors like Singapore and Japan.[83] In 1983 the U.S. Department of Education released *A Nation at Risk*, which combined all of these challenges into one document:

To keep and improve on the slim competitive edge we still retain in world markets, we must dedicate ourselves to the reform of our educational system. . . . A high level of shared education is essential to a free, democratic society and to the fostering of a common culture, especially in a country that prides itself on pluralism and individual freedom.[84]

It is worth noting that some claimed that the educational "crisis" was overblown. *A Nation at Risk* did overplay some of the declines in achievement data.[85] Many of the low aggregate test scores of the late 1970s returned to late 1960s levels by the end of the 1990s, suggesting that students were performing about the same as their parents had thirty years before, and that the reforms of the 1980s and 1990s had had little effect on students' average knowledge.[86] Others claimed that conservative politicians were maliciously defining a public policy problem in order to undercut American public education.[87] Whatever the merits of these claims, it was not just the apparent declines in test scores, an output measure, that empowered educational reformers.

The public production of education also faced a trust deficit. The oversold social programs of the 1960s—the national War on Poverty that did not eradicate poverty, and national civil rights victories that did not prevent racial violence—and the stagnating economy of the 1970s gave life to new conservative political movements. Political trust in government buckled after President Richard Nixon's Watergate cover-up and the weak presidencies of Gerald Ford and Jimmy Carter. The decline in confidence was palpable. Until 1974, a majority of Americans expressed general confidence in government, but in no year since Watergate have more than half of Americans trusted government most of the time. (This malaise was interrupted only once, and that was when a majority of Americans trusted their government in the month after the terrorist attacks of September 2001. In 2010, only 22 percent of Americans said they trusted government most of the time, near the record low of 17 percent in 1994 and 2008.)[88] When President Ronald Reagan told Americans in 1981 that "government is the problem," he was only stating what many Americans "knew" by experience.

Thus the policy problem was poor academic performance, but it was compounded by Americans' severe lack of trust in *public* policy. In 1978 an article in the respected education journal *Phi Delta Kappan* noted that even the leadership of the NEA and American Federation of Teachers (AFT) seemed genuinely worried that tuition tax credits would lead to a mass exodus from the public schools.[89] A June 16, 1980, *Time* article quoted Professor J. Myron Atkin from Stanford University: "For the first time, it is conceivable to envision the dismantling of universal, public, compulsory education as it has been pioneered in America."[90]

Of course, that is not what happened. State policymakers and legislators felt the pulse of the decline and linked the policy problems to solutions that think tanks, teachers' unions, and others had been advocating. Legislators' and governors' strong belief that education could be linked to economic growth prevented them from abandoning compulsory public education.[91] When this critical juncture appeared, state policymakers preserved public, tax-supported schools by introducing major reforms to the structure of public education. Proponents hoped these reforms could turn the traditional bureaucratic model of education on its head.

Traditional bureaucracies rely on internal regulation ("red tape") to ensure fairness to their employees and citizens.[92] In line with demands from the NEA and AFT, lawmakers had imposed many regulations on schools to ensure equal treatment of teachers and to guarantee an element of freedom in teaching. This equality resulted in lengthy contracts and significant red tape (see Chapter 5). Even today, it can take years to remove a teacher due to these protections.[93] But this red tape can stifle the democratic norms of majority rule and self-rule. When bureaucracies are too far out of line with public desires, they lose their reputation for competence.[94] And schools did.

State lawmakers offered a "horse trade," as Tennessee governor and future U.S. secretary of education Lamar Alexander said in 1986.[95] Instead of relying on internal regulation, Alexander argued that schools should respond to external accountability. Alexander had no problem extending more money to schools or dropping some regulations—but only if those actions produced results in line with state standards. (Alexander has called for other "horse trades," too, on merit pay and school vouchers.) Alexander's proposal had the benefit of maintaining public, tax-supported education while forcing schools to respond to majority wishes. School personnel would not set the standards; the state would. Standards could apply to anything, but legislatures and governors could ensure that academic goals would be foremost.

A combination of low trust in government, high anxiety over economic competitiveness, and a growing conservative political mood combined to open the policy window for external, state accountability standards. As a result, states made Alexander's trade, first in the South and later in every state. There have been five major waves of reform since the 1950s (see table 6.1).[96] Although the metaphor of a "wave" suggests that one reform comes in as another goes out, in practice the reforms layer one on another. This creates conflicts and confusion in schools and districts and illustrates why schools, unlike ideal bureaucracies, rarely have sufficient time to enact changes before they are asked to change again.

The first wave was expanding access to schooling along the lines of Conant's vocational high schools and the U.S. Supreme Court's desegregation efforts (discussed above and in Chapter 3). The second wave washed over public education in the 1970s and 1980s, but accelerated after the release of *A Nation at Risk*. States focused on forcing schools to offer, and require, academic classes. Four years of high school English and three of math became a common requirement. States bolstered their school building requirements. None of these standards were too far afield of what schools were already doing, and state legislators were not specifying *what* should be taught in four years of English. Educators still had the prerogative; they just had to be more academic.

A third wave also began with *A Nation at Risk* but did not crest until the mid-1990s. The National Governors' Association took up education as one of its core priorities in 1986, under the direction of Lamar Alexander and bolstered by fellow Southern governors, including future president Bill Clinton. The organization urged schools and districts to restructure themselves to improve education. Both Republican and Democratic governors endorsed the National Governors' Association report *Time for Results* (1986), which called for academic standards and some form of accountability. President George H. W. Bush styled himself the "education president," and he pushed legislation to boost national involvement in education.

This third wave also increased teacher training requirements. State departments of education boosted course requirements for *teachers*. Policymakers were now tampering with the gains teachers' unions had made in the 1960s and 1970s and challenging the dominance of experts in education. For example, the University of Wisconsin initially refused to change its course requirements to conform to new teacher certification standards required by the state's Department of Public Instruction. Professors argued that the state was trespassing on academic freedom and teacher professionalism. Well and good, State Superintendent Herbert

TABLE 6.1   Waves of Reform in American Education

Universal Education *(1950s to 1970s)*	The combination of rural school consolidation and court-ordered desegregation efforts created what most Americans think of as a "public school" for the first time. Reformers like James Conant argued that schools should serve students of all ability levels, and courts required schools to include all students regardless of race or learning ability.
Competency *(1970s to mid-1980s)*	State legislatures, especially in the South, dramatically increased *state-mandated* course-taking requirements for graduation, especially for less academically gifted students. In 1973 two states had such standards; in 1983, thirty-four did. Many states further increased these requirements in the mid-1980s again. (For example, from one English course in high school to four.)
Excellence *(1983 to mid-1990s)*	An originally low-profile committee issued *A Nation at Risk* in 1983, thereby igniting a decade of reform boosting "excellent" education. The U.S. secretary of education frequently highlighted how unfavorably U.S. students compared with students in other countries in some evaluations. Gifted-and-talented education programs received substantial attention in many states.
Content Standards *(1994 to present)*	American governors and President Clinton pressed for schools to require meaningful, academic content in classes. OBE was one version of this reform, in which students had to master rubrics before moving to the next outcome. Controversies erupted over model math standards and model history standards, severely weakening their political appeal. The Common Core Standards revived this reform.
High-Stakes Accountability *(1999 to present)*	Some states had been using standardized tests for several years before 2002 to track students' and schools' performance, but the No Child Left Behind Act brought schools nationwide into a testing regimen that threatened major school changes unless student scores progressed toward proficiency. President Obama's Race to the Top continues high-stakes assessment by offering rewards for schools and districts that meet goals.

Source: Linn (1998); Smith and O'Day (1991).

Grover said, but he threatened to ban new UW graduates from teaching until the state university relented. Grover won.[97]

The fourth wave, beginning in the early 1990s, furthered the revolution with school choice and accountability testing. A key complaint from think tanks and policy activists was that public schools undercut self-rule and trapped students in unequal school systems.[98] Reformers argued that school districts had monopoly power over where children went to school. Although the public, external accountability reforms could help parents know if a local school was up to snuff, short of moving or opting for private schooling, they could not influence the school system. In 1991 Minnesota lawmakers adopted this critique and passed legislation that would allow parents or others to create public "charter schools," mostly free of school regulations but still subject to public accountability.[99] In theory, these schools would fail if they failed to educate children. The state also permitted students to transfer between public school districts. Now not even the state was monitoring success, but educational consumers (and their parents) were. School choice is discussed in Chapter 7.

School choice did not take off until the late 1990s and even then never had the depth of impact accountability testing has had. Although school choice has grown substantially since the 1980s, it only directly affects students and teachers who learn and work in those schools. Testing has contributed to substantial changes in school curriculum, school activities, and policymakers' language about schools (for example, schools "in need of improvement" were schools that did not make sufficient gains in standardized test scores rather than schools with a high drop-out rate, incidents of violence, or even concentrations of students in poverty). Testing had become pervasive by mid-decade. Ohio, for example, had a ninth-grade proficiency exam in place from the late 1980s. In response to business concerns, Governor George Voinovich targeted it for overhaul. He and the Ohio Department of Education revamped the test and later linked it to state educational funding.[100] Vermont created state standards for the first time.[101] Wisconsin Governor Tommy Thompson became so frustrated with the pace of standard-setting by the Department of Public Instruction that he gave the task to the lieutenant governor instead.[102]

The No Child Left Behind Act (NCLB) heralded the fifth wave, high-stakes accountability. Although states had experimented with rewarding or punishing students and schools based on test results in the 1990s, this wave became federal policy with NCLB. Unlike the previous three waves but like the first wave, the federal government motivated states to change and then try to seize the initiative before the federal government required more changes.

It is important to note that *state* governments were the key players in educational reform. State policymakers watched the growth of standards with a mixture of satisfaction and trepidation, and they have consistently tried to thwart federal efforts at defining curriculum. Defining what a student should know takes government power into the heart of what was a family decision in the colonial period, then a district decision in the nineteenth century, and then a state decision in the twentieth. At each step, the norm of democratic understanding stepped away from the norm of self-rule. Once state legislators and state bureaucrats drew up state standards, there was little reason to think that national standards were far behind. Why should mathematics in Texas be different than mathematics in Vermont? But it is also important to note that the standards movement, which once tried to include instruction in democratic values through OBE, now focuses narrowly on Goodlad's academic goals. The controversy is still there, but schools' success is measured in academic terms.

In the bipartisan environment of the standards movement, core curriculum advocates saw an opportunity to push national guidelines to give meaning to "excellence." In 1987 some 84 percent of Americans told the Gallup Poll that they supported national standards.[103] President George H. W. Bush called a governors' summit on education in 1989 that explicitly called for national goals and noted that governors knew of education's labyrinthine bureaucratic structure. In a report from the summit, the governors noted that, "National goals will allow us to plan effectively, to set priorities, and to establish clear lines of authority."[104]

They partly succeeded—at least until the controversy over the national history standards gave ammunition to foes. One policy response to *A Nation at Risk* would have been to create national academic standards and measure them with an exam like the National Assessment of Educational Progress (NAEP). In 1994 President Bill Clinton had lawmakers introduce a bill to create national voluntary standards and suggest national testing. Originally the bill provided money to states to develop their own standards as long as a panel called the National Education Standards and Improvement Council (NESIC) approved them. Both proposals took heavy fire from conservative

Republicans, liberal Democrats, and the NEA. Republicans disliked the federal intrusion into state educational policy, and they continued to call for the abolition of the U.S. Department of Education. Democrats and the NEA vehemently opposed the focus on student performance and accountability.[105] Congress buckled and made standards voluntary.

As discussed previously, the history standards were released and dressed down by Lynne Cheney within six months. Two prominent historians noted that the furor "seemed proof to many that the whole effort to formulate national standards was a terrible mistake."[106] In November 1994 Democrats suffered historic losses in Congress, and the new Republican Congress was far more hostile to federal activity than even many of its more conservative members had been the year before. Although the new Congress failed to abolish the U.S. Department of Education, it did scuttle NESIC. States would have the lead on standards.

The policy window closed as conservative Republicans and liberal Democrats headed for the exits, though only temporarily. In 2000 a conservative Southern governor became president. George W. Bush took the position of core curriculum supporters, that the norm of understanding meant that students should have shared knowledge. But standards and accountability would be tempered by a strong commitment to the norm of self-rule.

Bush urged Congress to write these commitments into the No Child Left Behind Act, which he signed within a year of taking office. The 1994 version of ESEA had required state standards and some form of accountability. Although that was a revolutionary change to ESEA's original commitment to funding the inputs of education, it left the teeth of the requirements up to the states. Bush and many policymakers argued that leaving accountability up to the states had only empowered interest groups to water down accountability to prevent fundamental and, in their view, necessary changes. Indeed, the test-score gap stagnated in the 1990s (see figure 3.1).

On one hand, NCLB forced states to enact tough accountability requirements. The law requires annual testing of students to meet academic standards and public comparison of the results. Republicans who had fought this federal mandate in the mid-1990s came to Bush's aid. Representative John Boehner (R-Ohio), who had publicly urged fellow members of Congress to kill Clinton's Goals 2000, now argued that Bush's proposal was a golden opportunity to shape ESEA on conservative lines by emphasizing accountability and self-rule. Liberal Democrats, especially Senator Ted Kennedy (D-Mass.), saw that nonwhite parents and their interest group supporters (normally rock-solid Democratic voters) were increasingly angry about the dismal conditions of urban public schools. They were beginning to turn away from *public* production in favor of a core conservative policy proposal, publicly funded vouchers to pay for *private* schools.[107] Democrats ultimately went along because, as the chief lobbyist for the Council of Chief State School Officers recalled, "If pressure wasn't put on the schools to change, the public system would produce too much evidence that we needed a voucher system, and that would ultimately destroy the public school system."[108]

Although Bush attempted to include vouchers in the proposal (as his father, George H. W. Bush, had done in a bill in 1991), the opposition from Democrats proved too intense. Instead, NCLB included two weaker provisions that emphasized the norm of self-rule when a student's assigned public school did not meet state standards as measured by state-designed tests for more than one year. States would have to provide *individuals* with remedies. One was a requirement that students be allowed to transfer to a school in the district or another district that did meet standards. Districts would have to notify parents of other school choices, including charter schools, if a school did not meet standards. This preserved public oversight but allowed parents to opt-out of schools that *they* deemed unacceptable. A second remedy was a mandate that districts provide individual tutoring.

As conservative Republicans would not stand for either national standards or a national test, NCLB only required public accountability for *state* standards. As discussed in Chapter 3, state policymakers were left with the ultimate power to create both *what* students should learn (content standards) and *how well* students learned them (performance standards). Although this produced wildly differing levels of educational assessment, it preserved a semblance of a federal separation of power.

As Congress worked on the successor to NCLB in 2010 and 2011, states moved preemptively to avoid federal standards. In the summer of 2009 the National Governors' Association and the Council of Chief State School Officers had begun work on a new round of national standards in English and mathematics, called the Common Core State Standards Initiative. In June 2010 they were released, and forty-three states adopted them within a year. Like *A Nation at Risk*, they tied academic performance to economic competitiveness: "With American students fully prepared for the future, our communities will be best positioned to compete successfully in the global economy."[109] Although this effort gained early traction, it is not clear how states will actually implement the Common Core Standards, nor is it clear how they will mesh with NCLB once it is reauthorized by Congress. Further, such standards will still face the challenge of loose coupling.

This effort drew strong support from the Obama administration, which repeatedly praised *state*-driven reforms as models. In its proposal for the new ESEA, the administration explicitly called for "states to adopt state-developed standards"—but highly recommended the "lead of the nation's governors and state education leaders," that is, the Common Core State Standards Initiative.[110] At an address to a national governors' group, Secretary of Education Arne Duncan sought to short-circuit conservative Republican concerns: "Some people will raise concerns that common standards across states will lead to federal over-reaching . . . [but] education is a state and local issue. You pay 90 percent of the tab, and our job is to support leaders like you."[111] Yet despite the softer rhetoric, the administration's $4.35 billion Race to the Top program still encouraged states to present systematic reform plans that required strong, public accountability, and state standards.[112] That focus caused some to wonder whether the Obama administration was listening to the chorus of NCLB critics, including the NEA and state governors (see box 6.3).[113] At the same time, Duncan reiterated support for individual choice through charter schools.

Although states appeared to have dodged federal control of the curriculum, since democratic understanding would be defined by fifty different states, those standards would be narrowly tailored to literacy and mathematics. Despite this success, and despite Secretary Duncan's tribute to state and local policymakers, NCLB had narrowed state and local options considerably. States *had to* adopt statewide, test-based academic standards; states and teachers *had to* use data to evaluate educational progress of students; and states *had to* provide educational options for students in schools that did not meet standards, even if state law did not already provide for it.[114] And states still face challenges from the bureaucratic nature of schools. Schools are difficult to reform because school boards, principals, and teachers actually implement educational policy, and they may still be implementing the last wave of reform when another wave begins. Teachers and principals may become cynical and try to undercut new reforms or

---

BOX 6.3   Race to the Top and No Child Left Behind: Two Sides of
the Same Coin?

State political capacity: Can the state show that teachers' unions and local school districts will support state reform efforts? Does the state department of education have the autonomy and scope to implement genuine reforms? Have previous reforms produced substantive results?

Curriculum standards: Is the state participating in a multistate curriculum standards effort (e.g., the Common Core Standards Initiative)? Are the standards meaningfully assessed?

Accountability systems: Does the state maintain data for all assessments over time? Does it encourage schools to use the data to improve teaching and learning?

Teacher and principal effectiveness: Are teachers and principals evaluated annually? Do evaluations include an assessment of student learning growth? Are teachers and principals encouraged to work in high-poverty areas and in high-need fields (like math and science)?

Focus on low-performing schools: Does the state identify its lowest performing schools? Does the state have policies to "turn around" these schools?

General education funding; enabling charter schools: Does the state have stable *state* revenues devoted to education? Does the state permit public charter schools and provide them access to public facilities? Are charter schools evaluated for outcomes?

Source: U.S. Department of Education (2011b).

---

complain that they are not being treated professionally. States face challenges both from the federal governments above and districts and schools below.

Conclusion

The 1990s were tumultuous years for American educational policy. Before 1989 most policymakers accepted that the greatest flaw in promoting high-quality education was lack of equitable learning opportunities, poor facilities, low funding, and underpaid teaching staff and believed that education should be tailored to a student's needs and interests. Not only would child-centered education keep them in school longer, but it would spark greater interest in learning.

That consensus showed serious signs of strain as Americans turned on government-led reforms in the late 1970s. Policymakers tried incremental changes in the 1980s—boosting funding, limiting class sizes, tightening teacher requirements—but this effort failed to stop the collapse. By the time President Bill Clinton took office, policymakers on both the left and right saw that American public education could not sustain majority support without significant concessions to the norm of self-rule and a new definition of democratic understanding.

The 1990s began with an attempt to downplay individualism and emphasize commonality. Outcomes-Based Education preserved the individual attention of Progressive reforms, but its advocates encouraged schools to present a common interpretation of democratic values. The original draft of the national history standards reinforced this interpretation of democratic understanding. But as the Puritans had discovered in the seventeenth century, the norm of self-rule runs very strong in the American democratic experiment; in this case, so strong that the standards withered under congressional reproach. The states went their own way as policymakers replaced the Progressive vision of education with a relentless focus on a common set of academic "basics." By 2009 President Obama's secretary of education agreed, "[It was] the only way to achieve the vision of equality spelled out by our founders."[115]

Suggested Readings

Abernathy, Scott Franklin. 2007. *No Child Left Behind and the Public Schools.* Ann Arbor: University of Michigan Press.

Bailyn, Bernard. 1960. *Education in the Forming of American Society.* New York: W. W. Norton.

Common Core State Standards Initiative. http://www.corestandards.org/.

Dewey, John, and Evelyn Dewey. 1915. *Schools of To-morrow.* New York: E. P. Dutton.

Goodlad, John I. 1984. *A Place Called School.* New York: McGraw-Hill.

Hirsch, E. D., Jr. 1987. *Cultural Literacy.* New York: Vintage Books.

Nash, Gary B. 2004. "Lynne Cheney's Attack on the History Standards, 10 Years Later." *History News Network* (November 8). http://hnn.us/articles/8418.html.

National Council for Accreditation of Teacher Education. http://www.ncate.org/.

Ravitch, Diane. 2000. *Left Back: A Century of Battles Over School Reform.* New York: Simon & Schuster.

U.S. Department of Education. "Race to the Top." http://www2.ed.gov/programs/racetothetop/.

Vinovskis, Maris A. 1999. *The Road to Charlottesville: The 1989 Education Summit.* Washington, DC: National Education Goals Panel. http://govinfo.library.unt.edu/negp/reports/negp30.pdf.

Weick, Karl E. 1976. "Educational Organizations as Loosely Coupled Systems." *Administrative Science Quarterly* 21 (1, March): 1–19.

Wilentz, Sean. 1997. "Don't Know Much About History." *New York Times Book Review* (November 30): 28–29.

7

··

Self-Rule and
Structuring Success

ALTHOUGH THE ABILITY OF CITIZENS to rule themselves is central to democracy, previous chapters have shown how frequently the norm of *self-rule* conflicts with the other norms of democracy. After *Milliken v. Bradley* (1974), self-rule made inclusion through desegregation efforts difficult. Self-rule permits some voters to fund local education dramatically more than others. The norm of participation can boost self-rule if many citizens participate, but the group-based politics in the United States can suppress weaker groups or even prevent them from forming at all. The norm of understanding may not conflict with self-rule, but citizens making their own decisions are under no compulsion to make informed decisions.

This chapter extends the discussion of self-rule in another direction: Should individuals be able to trump decisions made by members of Congress, state legislators, and school boards and make decisions about public policy for themselves? Policymakers who argue that American educational policy is unresponsive to individual needs—because of bureaucratic limitations and teachers' union strength—have advocated *school choice*. School choice enables some parents to opt out of traditional public school arrangements to pursue *individual* self-rule. This chapter builds on the discussion in Chapter 4 about the nature of education as a *public* policy. Chapter 4 discussed whether government should provide or produce education, and it noted that policymakers had largely settled the debate in favor of production, with the U.S. Supreme Court's blessing. This chapter considers whether government production of education can coexist with individual choice about what that production should look like. If education is a *public good*, it is unlikely to be offered except if the government produces it, and decisions about education should be made jointly because it is for the public, common good. If education is a *toll good*, individual choice seems appropriate, but only within limits. Different parents will have different preferences about what an appropriate education is, but government may need to enforce certain rules and subsidize the effort.

Both policymakers and parents seeking school choice face the troublesome dilemmas of self-rule. When should the norms of equality or inclusion trump local wishes? When should public policy limit choice because some choices might undermine academic quality or the norm of understanding? The political decision to balance self-rule with other democratic norms rests in policymakers' consideration of the *nature* of educational policy. After addressing this question, the chapter considers four forms of school choice: Tiebout choice, open enrollment, vouchers, and charter schools. Tiebout is driven by individual choice and occurs when residents can choose where to live based in part on the level of services, including public education, that governments provide. The other three forms are deliberate public policy choices through which governments can encourage individual self-rule.

Annette Polly Williams was Wisconsin's longest-serving woman in the state legislature when she retired in 2010. She lost her first two elections before she went on to win in 1980 and then the next thirteen elections as a Milwaukee Democrat. A native of Mississippi, she moved to Milwaukee in 1948 as a girl. She entered politics in 1972 as a campaign assistant for her cousin, who became Wisconsin's first African American state senator, and in 1982 she filed a lawsuit against the state's redistricting plan because she thought it violated African Americans' access to equal representation in the state legislature.

But her most enduring, and most controversial, political accomplishment is the Milwaukee Parental Choice Program, the first large-scale voucher program in the United States, which was enacted in 1990. She argued that low-income, African American children were systematically excluded from better schools despite busing and magnet schools. "That was the hypocrisy of desegregation," she said. "It was supposed to be for the interest of *our* children. . . . Yes, they put good schools in the inner city, but the inner-city children couldn't go to them."

Williams championed the program despite staunch opposition from the Milwaukee Federation of Teachers and the Democratic Party. She said her constituents were frustrated and angry at the public school district, but she never had any intention to take on the school district. Indeed, the program was originally limited to 1,500 students (out of about 100,000). But Williams argued that the only way to remedy this situation was to give low-income parents a choice of any public or private school, religious or not. "These are not exclusive private schools; they are community schools," she said.

Williams never wavered in her commitment to maximum school choice for low-income students—as long as it was for low-income students. When the mayor proposed raising the income cap to keep middle-class families in Milwaukee, Williams vigorously protested, and she won. She was no supporter of forms of school choice that did not specifically help low-income students.

The voucher program never won over the Democratic caucus or the teachers' unions in Wisconsin, and they continue to attack it. Even as Democrats tried to kill the program in 2010, Williams's foes called her a tenacious defender of Milwaukee's poor. Williams held off her party one last time before retiring, and the voucher program continues.[1]

Education's Toll Road

Direct participation by ordinary voters is not very effective for making public policy for all citizens or even providing individuals with their own desires. Voter education, attention, and diversity all work against the norm of self-rule. For most public policies, low voter control is alarming but probably not that troublesome to overall democratic control, depending on the *nature* of the public policy. Policymakers regularly grapple with the question, *When should the government intervene?* Their answer depends on what kind of "good" (product or service) the policy problem suggests (see table 7.1). For goods that anyone can get without a direct cost (like air), it makes sense to restrict how much say any one person or any one private group has over,

TABLE 7.1   Nature of Public Policy Goods

	RIVALROUS	NONRIVALROUS
EXCLUDABLE	**Private**: markets can provide efficiently: *class enrollment, school supplies*	**Toll**: markets underproduce without subsidies or other incentives: *information, teaching credentials, college degrees*
NONEXCLUDABLE	**Common pool**: individuals overuse without regulation: *public parks, fishing grounds*	**Public**: markets will not produce: *national defense, mandatory vaccination programs, concerts in public parks*

for example, clean air policy. It is a public good. But the government also provides or regulates some toll goods, for which there is some incentive for private organizations or individuals to provide them, especially with government help. Goods may also be private goods or common pool goods. When the government *does* provide these goods, low voter participation may dangerously undermine the norm of self-rule.

Public goods are those for which there is no incentive for a private group to provide them for others. Providing national defense does not make sense for a private company, because the company could not limit safety to just those people who paid for the security. Because everyone gets the benefit of protection regardless of whether they pay (they are nonexcludable), too few people pay for the service. Further, "safety" is not used up as it is provided, so the effects of national defense persist even when F-16s are not patrolling New York City (it is nonrivalrous). Everyone can enjoy the benefits of national defense, but no one has an incentive to pay for it because there is no way to deny the service to nonpayers, called *free riders*. Government has to *compel* people to pay for defense if it is to be provided at all.

Toll goods are similar in that there is only a limited incentive for private organizations to provide a good or service. Private groups *might* provide these goods because they are excludable, so a group can charge for the goods. (A person has to pay for the right to drive on a toll road.) Some people will pay for the benefits. But toll goods are not used up (they are nonrivalrous), so when they are provided, the consumers could share the good with others without paying extra. Private organizations may produce toll goods, but they will not produce enough for everyone who wants them, because the organizations may not be able to charge every user of the good equally. Because toll goods are underproduced, governments often provide legal protection or payment to encourage private groups to produce them. For example, the Indiana Toll Road is part of U.S. Interstate 80/90. The state of Indiana operated the road until June 2006, when the state leased the road to a private company for seventy-five years. The road might not have been *built* at private expense, but once it was constructed, there was sufficient incentive for a private group to *operate* it. Similarly, knowledge is nonrivalrous and will likely be underproduced without some government assistance. Copyright law, for example, encourages authors to write because they can receive compensation from selling copies, even though once one person has read the book, he can tell his friends the plot. Education is nonrivalrous for the same reason.

Because public goods benefit society as a whole, it makes sense for individuals to have limited say in their provision. (Should one person have monopoly power over providing national defense or public health?) Self-rule for public goods is satisfied even if state or national legislators make policy decisions because the benefits are widely shared. But toll goods provide *individual* benefit because they are excludable, and individuals must decide to receive the good. If the U.S. Congress mandates that drivers must drive on toll roads, drivers are likely to be angered by its intrusion on their driving plans, because that action intrudes upon self-rule. Similarly, if Congress passes laws to require school choice by individuals, but few people choose a school other than where they would have been assigned anyway, then self-rule will probably trample on other norms of democracy, as only a well-connected minority will take advantage of the option.

Private goods are both rivalrous and excludable, meaning that the private market has strong incentives to produce enough goods and to respond quickly to consumer preferences. School supplies are an example of private goods: pencil manufacturers will produce enough pencils for back-to-school sales because children will use them up and their parents are willing to buy more of them. Common pool goods are rivalrous but nonexcludable. Individuals over-consume such goods because it is difficult to prevent people from using them or even to make them pay for them. A school offering free Internet access to students is likely to face an overconsumption problem, because the cost to a student for using a little more bandwidth is small, but if all students use a little more bandwidth, Internet service will become sluggish for everyone. (Thus many open-access Internet services impose limits on how much a user can download at one time, in order to prevent this problem.)[2]

So, is K–12 education a public good or a toll good? American educational policymakers have given both answers at different times. K–12 education has characteristics of both public and toll goods.

For education to be a public good, it has to be equally available without incurring an identifiable individual cost. Until the mid-twentieth century, this assertion was false in the United States (and it continues to be false in much of the world). Although most states required education to be *available* by the late nineteenth century, the states did not require the same spending or the same kind of education, even internally (see Chapter 4). Some states did not even go this far. For example, until the Civil War, Georgia's school system consisted of state-recognized private academies. The bulk of these schools' expenses were paid by the parents of students; others simply hired tutors.[3] Obviously Georgia policymakers saw education as nearly a private good. (It was not quite a private good, because the state still officially recognized the academies, and the state did provide minimal school funding for "poor schools.") Education did not meet either the availability or the cost requirements.

That did not stop Progressive Era educational reformers early in the twentieth century from vigorously fighting to *make* education a public good. They convinced legislators to pass mandatory attendance laws and fundamentally overhaul school finance laws to reduce spending inequality between districts. These changes made public education a quasi-public good by removing the individual cost and mandating that all children participate. Public education moved closer to the nonexcludable ideal, but it still excluded some children. African Americans, recent immigrants, and rural students had far fewer school resources available to them. Teachers taught different curriculum to different students, so there *was* an individual cost, because students' life choices were narrowed by the choices of school officials (see Chapters 3 and 6). Despite these shortcomings, Progressives tried to minimize the dilemmas posed by self-rule by maximizing a form of democratic equality. Among other changes, they successfully shut down small school districts, eliminated many school board elections, and centralized school district administration.[4]

Seen as a toll good, education would have to be produced in some sort of market. Schools (or tutors) would have to receive a benefit for their services, and parents would need to have a choice about their children's schooling. The market would not have to be efficient or robust—remember that toll goods tend to be underproduced unless there is government assistance—but there has to be a real choice. These conditions are rarely met in pure form. Parents have long had the option of private schooling, but both the cost and the geography of the schools limit their contribution to a market.[5] (Does Ethan live close enough to St. Thomas Aquinas Catholic School to attend?) If a student lives in rural America, there is often no choice, because there are not enough students to support both private schools and public schools.[6] Nevertheless, most urban and suburban Americans have multiple education choices. Both public and private schools *are* rewarded for their services. A large portion of public school funding is based on student enrollment, and private schools receive tuition from each enrolling family.

Policymakers who treat education as a toll good assume that parents will also treat education as a toll good. That is, policymakers assume that parents will participate without coercion. For example, the No Child Left Behind Act (NCLB) requires states to post schools' aggregate test scores. The theory behind this policy was that parents can pressure the school board to improve education. If the school does not improve to parents' satisfaction, they can pull their children out of the school. (Some states have even stronger legislation, as in California, where parents can, and have, forced a public school to shut down.)[7] But if *most* parents do not use the information, policymakers exacerbate the dilemma between self-rule and the norms of equality and inclusiveness.

Why? The minority of parents who *do* use NCLB's information are likely to be highly motivated and involved in their children's education. They are also more likely to be married, highly educated, and own their homes—in other words, these parents are not like the average parent.[8] Students with parents like these are also likely to do much better in school (see Chapter 3). If a school posts poor results and these parents act on the information, critics argue that the remaining schools will only become worse. The students left behind will not have the academic benefit of high-performing peers, weakening democratic inclusion. As active parents select better schools, the new schools' advantages increase, undermining democratic equality.

The Progressives were so successful because they understood how *institutions* would lock in their vision of education even if they lost political power.[9] The apparent success of government planning during World War II bolstered many Americans' acceptance of the expert-led government Progressives advocated, and they accepted the institutions of large high schools and centralized administration. When the turmoil of the 1960s and 1970s destroyed that faith, path dependency made those institutions difficult to change, further weakening public confidence in the system. Counterreformers said public education could be saved if policymakers reenergized the norm of self-rule. Legislators would have to abandon Progressive assumptions about government expertise and give *parents* a choice of schools, either within the public system or between the public and private systems. Proponents said improving self-rule could be done without abandoning the achievements of desegregation and financial equity—or the public school system. Policymakers must consider whether that choice is appropriate for the nature of the good.

School Choice as Self-Rule

As a public policy, school choice is a deliberate compromise between self-rule and other democratic norms. The local school board is supposed to represent community preferences about what children should learn and how they should learn it, and parents who pull their children out of their assigned school effectively overrule the school board. Should parents be able to opt out of local democracy this way? Parents might be poorly informed and their decisions might be harmful to their children or to the inclusive aims of education. This argument is made most sharply by critics of parents who educate their children at home, but it is also made by those who argue that public schools are the only institution that deliberately teaches democratic values.[10] The NEA's former executive director, in an attack on school choice, argued that

> America's public schools reflect the broad values of American society . . . They are society mixing bowls that place students in daily contact with other kids, other beliefs, other races, other cultures, and other values. Their exposure to this wide range of American society enhances their life experiences, abets their socialization, and strengthens their character.[11]

But if there is no "best" way to educate diverse children, then relying on experts is not necessarily superior to relying on parents. If there are strong minority viewpoints about the balance among the norms of democracy, the public good view of education may create the majority tyrannies that James Madison warned of in Federalist No. 10.[12] If policymakers believe there is a need to guarantee education, but there is reason to believe that there is no "one best way" to produce education, the policy should be treated as a toll good. John Stuart Mill, the English political theorist, made precisely this argument. He was strongly in favor of compulsory education, but did not believe that the government could adequately account for individual needs and preferences. He argued that, "[The] importance of individuality . . . involves, as of the same unspeakable importance, the diversity of education."[13] He proposed a voucher-like choice system, but his observation undergirds all school choice policy proposals. School choice, especially among publicly funded schools, is one way to allow parents to participate in the public policy process—by choosing a school acceptable to them—while ensuring that schools are available and meet minimum standards.

Private Schools and Tiebout Choice

Open enrollment, vouchers, and charters are relatively new, but Americans have been able to choose private schools longer than there have been tax-supported public schools. Private schools have the advantage of being able to offer specialized curriculum, unique philosophies, or religious instruction that is not available in government-produced education. Private schools have steady appeal—in one representative survey of urban and suburban *public* school parents in Massachusetts, 39 percent said they would send their children to private schools if cost were no object.[14] Teachers in private schools tend to have a strong, shared sense of mission that translates into positive effects on learning and behavior for many children.[15] Yet private schools also have direct costs. Parents must pay tuition to the school on top of public school taxes. They may have transportation time and fuel costs if they do not live close to the school. In some places, there might not *be* an available private school. These barriers have kept private enrollments low. In 2007–2008, 10.7 percent of U.S. students attended private schools; in 1970–1971, 10.5 percent did.[16]

Even without private schools, American federalism has always guaranteed some choice. Federalism allows different units of government to respond to different voters. For example, one city might spend a lot of its taxes on the upkeep of city parks but not very much on road repair. A neighboring town might advertise its low taxes to attract home buyers—but will not install sidewalks. When there are many units of government with different levels of services, residents can choose which government to live under. This is called *Tiebout choice*.[17] Over time people will sort themselves into cities and towns that provide the services they want; residents of these small governments can decide how much they value certain services and tax themselves appropriately (see Chapter 4).[18] Various cities, states, and school districts will always be unequal in some way, but that is because people have different expectations of government. Despite the glaring conflict with the norm of equality, proponents of Tiebout choice argue that this diversity allows citizens to have meaningful choices.[19]

American school districts are almost as abundant as counties, cities, and towns. The 13,628 U.S. school districts serve anywhere from fewer than ten to more than one million students (see table 2.2). Most major metropolitan areas in the United States have clusters of many small school districts. Detroit, Michigan, for example, has more than fifty school districts within easy driving distance of the city. Sometimes these districts simply overlap suburbs, but in some states, cities have multiple school districts within them. Many states still have school districts reminiscent of one-room schoolhouse days. Vermont has 291 regular school districts for 89,999 students; if students were evenly distributed across the state, there would be 309 students in each district. The sheer number of school districts guarantees a choice of curriculum, demographics, and tax rates. Districts are small enough in many places that families can easily move between them should schools be "bad." Tiebout choice can exist within school districts as well, as families buy homes in more attractive school attendance zones. That increases parental satisfaction and implies that parents can exercise real self-rule within the existing tax-supported, public school system.

But Tiebout choice has drawn strenuous criticism. First, it can reinforce economic segregation. A top selling point for residential property is its school district.[20] ("Sure, the house needs a kitchen make-over and you'll have to rip out the shag carpeting, but it is worth $10K extra because it is in District 20!") "Good" districts—generally those with higher test scores—tend to have highly educated parents and relatively more affluent residents. These residents value education highly and are likely to be very involved in their children's schools, and even residents without children may be willing to pay a premium to live there. In one version of the argument, homeowners know that they may someday sell their homes, so they want them to be worth as much as possible. Therefore they support schools and school taxes simply to keep property values high.[21] This cycle is self-reinforcing. Good districts win tax increases to support property values; they spend more on schools; residential property becomes more expensive; more affluent families "buy their way in" to the district; and new families support tax increases. It is difficult for poor residents to afford to live in these school districts, because both the property values and the taxes are high.

Second, Tiebout choice can aggravate racial segregation if homeowners use race as a proxy for governmental quality. In 1971 federal judge Steven Roth held that the Detroit, Michigan, public school district had deliberately segregated its schools by race (see Chapter 3). In other cities, judges had ordered busing within a school district to create equal percentages of whites and blacks in each school. But Roth was a careful researcher; he saw that the number of whites in the school district was sinking fast. Surely some movement was racially motivated, but the city's schools were becoming less desirable due to increasing violence and reports of decreasing academic test scores. Many whites "voted with their feet" and left for the more expensive suburbs. To counter the trend, Roth ordered Detroit *and* fifty-three surrounding districts to bus children to create a racial balance. Detroit's plethora of small, close school districts was a textbook model for Tiebout choice, but Roth believed inclusion was more important than white parents' exercise of self-rule.[22] Although the U.S. Supreme Court overturned Roth and sealed off the suburbs in *Milliken v. Bradley* (1974), inclusion continues to conflict with expressions of self-rule.

Third, Tiebout choice assumes that people can move. Could a low-income African American actually pick up and move his family to Grosse Pointe, Michigan—a district eight miles from downtown Detroit, where 86 percent of students meet or exceed state math standards versus just 39 percent in the city? De facto residential segregation might be a roadblock (Grosse Pointe is 97 percent white), but the spiraling costs of living in a good school district would likely make the move out of the question. The price of "good schools" tends to put them out of reach for the poor, even though low-income families are *most* likely to move for schools—but only within districts.[23]

School Choice as Public Policy

Public schools do not have much incentive to offer parents choice within districts. The combination of efforts by educational reformers like John Dewey and James B. Conant and the school civil rights cases of the 1950s and 1960s persuaded lawmakers that self-rule could be pernicious, so democratic education should emphasize equality and inclusion. Lawmakers responded with extensive regulation of public schools. Conant and his supporters wanted big districts to encourage financial efficiency and vocational education. Unions wanted teachers treated equally wherever they taught. Civil rights groups worried that different schools would be racially tinged. Advocates for those with special needs said such students would be marginalized without deliberate regulatory intervention.[24] Their successes left parents with little direct control over what went on in local schools. American educational policy emphasized uniformity and expert control. Until that public policy regime reached a critical juncture, proponents of choice would not be able to overcome the inertia of path dependency.

The rising level of discontent with public schools, especially those in large, urban districts, pushed policymakers to reframe the rationale for American education.[25] Americans' unhappiness with the status quo suggested that school choices were underproduced, just as an economist might predict for toll goods. School choice advocates seized the opportunity.

Choice advocates suggested government support for private producers of education, ranging from private tuition tax credits to full vouchers. Proponents argued that choice addressed two *policy problems* better than the existing public policy did. First, they argued that the "public school monopoly" made public education inefficient and unresponsive. Inefficiency can apply either to money or results. Some argue that schools are financially inefficient because teachers' unions have been successful in securing high pay and expensive benefits regardless of teacher quality (see Chapter 5). Others suggest that schools have little incentive to improve teaching or choose academically demanding curricula because there is virtually no way to lose students. Schooling is then inefficient because the money spent has little relation to the academic outcomes. (Education is not the only public policy that has been criticized for this problem. The Congressional Budget Office found that many medical practices bill federal health programs based on the number of staff rather than on the treatment of patients.)[26]

Second, advocates argued that government-supported choice would bring the benefits of Tiebout choice to low-income students.[27] In a national survey, 45 percent of all whites and 60 percent of upper-income whites moved into a neighborhood after considering its schools, but only about 25 percent of African Americans at any income level did so.[28] Due to residential segregation, two-thirds of African Americans live in central cities. Making use of Tiebout choice to move to the suburbs may not be available for them. Indeed, even formerly staunch foes like the National Education Association begrudgingly accepted limited school choice to clamp down on low-income, nonwhite parents' preferences for a pure voucher program.[29] School choice would allow these parents to exercise democratic self-rule and improve their *efficacy*, that is, their belief that the government works *for* them.

Many school choice proponents (and especially voucher proponents) argued that schools had become focused on teachers and buildings rather than teaching and learning. Empowering parents to choose *any* option would force schools to compete for students. Good schools would be rewarded by having large enrollments (meaning more money), and undesirable schools would lose students and funding unless they quickly fixed their staffing and curriculum to meet the wishes of local parents, just as in an ideal, free market. Such competitiveness would bolster school accountability and academic performance.[30] Used in this way, school choice could maximize self-rule while improving democratic understanding. If urban schools could attract white, suburban students back into the city, choice might improve democratic inclusion as well. Indeed, this is what magnet schools were meant to do in districts that were attempting desegregation.[31]

Although American schooling can resemble a free market, the resemblances are those of distant cousins.[32] Competitive markets are characterized by low barriers to entry (it should be easy to start a school), actual competition (there must be more than one viable school choice), and full information (parents have to be able to compare schools).

First, opening a school requires heavy capital investment. A school has to have a building. Heating and cooling costs are virtually the same whether the school has 250 or 500 students. Teachers need training. Schools need teaching materials before any students show up. Although educational-materials companies exist to help start new schools, there is a strong disincentive to open enough schools.[33] In some districts, robust choice exists—but private and charter schools fill up.[34] Just as any other toll good, schools are underproduced.

Second, viable competition does not exist in most American school districts. Choice can work well if there are multiple public schools at every level and a network of private schools (often Catholic). It is no accident that the most prominent voucher programs in the United States are in the large cities of Cleveland, Ohio; Milwaukee, Wisconsin; and Washington, D.C. (Privately funded voucher programs also exist in New York City; Dayton, Ohio; and [again] Washington, D.C.) Charter schools, too, are also more likely in urban areas, although almost 25 percent of rural districts in some states have at least one charter school.[35] Rural students often have no choice except the public school.[36]

Third, parents must have sufficient information about schools to make a choice. School choice critics have charged that most parents making school choices rely on gut feelings rather than careful research.[37] Parents say they want high-quality teaching, challenging and appropriate academic curriculum, high levels of discipline and order, and small class sizes (usually in that order).[38] Parents could research most of these before sending their children to a school, and some do. But those who know this information are the *same parents who could use Tiebout choice*—they are more likely to be highly educated, upper-income, and white, and their children are *already* in high-performing schools.[39] Those without these advantages are less likely to know their school's qualities directly. Thus, unless lawmakers vastly increase the information that low-income parents receive, a "market" for education continues to favor those who might benefit from it least. Self-rule would benefit the most able, but weaken democratic inclusion for the rest.

As a public policy, school choice was not initially successful. A federal tax credit for private tuition nearly passed in 1978, and Ronald Reagan came into office in 1981 promising less government regulation and the abolition of the newly created U.S. Department of Education. But strong Democratic resistance and the publication of *A Nation At Risk* in 1983 undercut Reagan's efforts to weaken public educational regulations.[40] Instead, state governors like Lamar Alexander (Tennessee), Joe Frank Harris (Georgia), and Jim Hunt (North Carolina) became "education governors" and promised to shake up *public* schools through an intense *state* focus on results. These moves toward educational accountability had a distinct Southern accent, which also dampened choice proposals. Not only did most Southern states have large school districts (making even Tiebout choice difficult), but school choice had a strong, recent association with segregationist efforts of the 1950s. Self-rule could be more effectively expressed through at-large governors, who could take on state bureaucracy and local interest groups.

Governors around the country quickly adopted the language of accountability and results, but schools could not process the changes quickly enough, especially in urban districts. Former Milwaukee superintendent Howard Fuller spent more than a decade forcing the district to boost efforts for fellow African Americans. Extremely frustrated, he became a staunch supporter of vouchers. In 1995 he explained, "Choice is like a bomb that needs to be thrown into a system that is so bad, so rotten, that nothing else will work."[41]

That crisis reverberated in other states, and school choice reached a critical juncture about 1990. As policymakers began to emphasize the outputs and outcomes of learning (e.g., test scores, graduation rates) rather than the inputs (e.g., hours in class), the method of learning became less important. In *which* school a student learned to read and write was not as crucial as *that* the students learned to read and write. If parents were happier with their school as a result of choice, so much the better.[42] The Minnesota legislature created statewide, cross-district open enrollment in 1987.[43] Some states experimented with school-based management, in which teachers made all decisions.[44] In 1990 the Wisconsin legislature created the nation's first operational voucher program in Milwaukee.[45] Charter schools appeared in Minnesota in 1991, in California in 1992, and in seventeen other states by 1995; and in forty states and D.C. by 2011.[46] Each of these school choice policies made a different compromise between self-rule and other democratic norms. The most contentious policy options are open enrollment, vouchers, and charter schools.

Open Enrollment

Of the three public policy options that offer an element of self-rule in education to parents, open enrollment is the least controversial and requires little change to existing traditional public schools. Depending on the state, open enrollment may mean that parents can apply for their children to attend a different school than the one to which they would normally be assigned *within* their home school district, a different school in *another* school

district, or both. In most states, the receiving school can turn down appli-
cations due to lack of space; in some, the child's home district can deny
transfers for reasons specified in law, such as making the racial balance in
the district worse. (Recall that the Supreme Court ruled that cross-district
busing could not be imposed by federal legislation; this provision in open
enrollment legislation allows districts to prevent whites from sending their
children out of the district without actually moving.) Usually, school funding follows the child. Most states with open enrollment programs enacted
them in the late 1980s and early 1990s.

The original logic behind open enrollment was as a half-step toward
vouchers. If the government could provide vouchers to increase housing
options for low-income citizens and public financing to electoral candidates
to boost choice on election day, why could the government *not* provide
students with options for schools? Many proponents of open enrollment
saw it as a way to *prevent* private school vouchers, because parents who were
unhappy with their assigned public school had an easy and legal way to find
a *public* school that suited them better, reducing political pressure for private
tuition tax credits or vouchers. Open enrollment could preserve the
inclusion and equity that traditional public school supporters argue it
provides, and it would not undercut the influence of local teachers' unions.
Business groups have tended to support open enrollment because it
provides some element of a market to education; public schools would have
to respond to parents' desires or risk losing students. In Minnesota, the first
state with cross-district open enrollment, a business group's report said
open enrollment in Minnesota would force "profound structural change"
on school districts, for the better. The Minnesota Education Association
and Minnesota Federation of Teachers initially opposed open enrollment
because it could weaken some school districts' finances, which in turn would
hurt the pay and benefits of some members. The unions' policy directors
changed their minds when they became convinced that open enrollment
might force smaller districts to consolidate—a benefit for union members.
Larger, more financially secure school districts could give the union
members better and more stable pay and benefits.[47]

Open enrollment's potential for substantial educational reform was realized only when combined with charter schools, however. Because money
follows the child with open enrollment, some school districts discovered
they could use charter schools to set up programs to attract students from
neighboring districts or students who would otherwise be schooled at

home. In Wisconsin, for example, policy researchers found evidence that enterprising district superintendents were advertising "theme schools" to students in surrounding districts—and the surrounding district super-intendents were quite aware of the competition. In this case, public school districts *were* acting as if they were in a marketplace, although the academic changes were limited to charter schools.[48] In 2005–2006, Detroit lost some 27,000 students to charter schools outside the district, forcing the district to consider substantial staffing cuts and building closures, a trend that will continue because the state of Michigan took over the district's finances in 2009 and gave a state university direct control of the district's worst-performing schools in 2011.[49] Minneapolis and St. Paul also have lost a substantial number of students to open enrollment and charter schools, but as with Detroit, policy analysts have argued that some higher-income residents have stayed in the cities *because* they could send their children to other public schools.[50]

Open enrollment has had none of the dramatic impacts its supporters and detractors predicted, primarily because, with some exceptions, the number of students using open enrollment from any one district is too small to force a district to make curricular or policy changes. That said, most districts experience at least one transfer through open enrollment in states with the option. Open enrollment has enabled parents to select schools that are closer to their work and perceived as a better fit for their children.[51] Most transfers seem to occur between districts of similar affluence, but the primary factor parents consider appears to be academic quality rather than race or income. Indeed, for a program meant to head off vouchers, some have argued that open enrollment serves *as* a voucher program for good-performing, middle- to upper-class students who can afford to travel every school day.[52] For *individuals* open enrollment appears to fulfill the norm of self-rule.

Vouchers

Vouchers are the boldest of the school choice proposals. A school voucher is money given to parents to be spent at the school of their choice, public or private. Although some vouchers are provided by private foundations, these do not generate nearly the controversy that publicly funded vouchers do. Public vouchers have generated fiery debates about the place of "free" public schools and, especially, religion. Unlike charter schools or open enrollment, policymakers who support vouchers claim that publicly produced schools *cannot* satisfy all parents (see box 7.1).[53] For proponents, the satisfaction that parents draw from self-rule is more important to the democratic project than the inclusiveness that public schools may provide. Low-income parents who use vouchers are unabashedly positive about the private schools their children attend.[54] And supporters argue that public schools are already highly segregated by race and income, so vouchers could not substantively worsen segregation. Vouchers, they argue, may be the only way that some students can receive an education approaching that of suburban public schools.

Voucher programs have a long history, but very few have been enacted because of the controversy that surrounds them. They are on the political radar again, however, after strong conservative gains in state legislatures in 2010.

Some critics of vouchers argue that they undermine the quality of public education by allowing public funds to be spent on private schools that are not accountable to the public. Although vouchers *could* be used at public schools, virtually none of them are.[55] Private schools in most states are not required to hire licensed teachers, use approved curriculum, or even measure student achievement, much less report it. Teachers' unions, in particular, oppose vouchers on this point. They argue that collective bargaining requires districts and schools to carefully specify all of their teaching practices and make them transparent to the public (see Chapter 5).

For example, after Florida Governor Rick Scott proposed a statewide voucher program in 2011, the former state education commissioner worried that vouchers were "a system designed to fail" and would undercut public accountability. Public schools "work in an open, transparent arena— accepting all students—and must answer to parents and the public at large. . . . [Vouchers put] our fundamental system at risk."[56] An income-limited voucher program in Indiana drew a similar response. The chief of Indiana's district superintendents' interest group explicitly compared vouchers to school segregation. Vouchers are "divisive and treat other students like second-class citizens while failing to provide a superior education," he wrote.[57] In effect, these critics argue that vouchers turn "public" education into a public subsidy for a private decision. If so, vouchers risk undoing the improvement in democratic equity and inclusion that courts and civil rights reformers fought for in the twentieth century.

BOX 7.1   Milton Friedman

In 1985 the economist Milton Friedman (1912–2006) said that he had escaped Washington, D.C., in 1943 "before I caught Potomac Fever, a deadly disease for someone whose primary interest is scientific." Oddly for one who had escaped the fever, Friedman's economic theories and advice swirled around politicians from Franklin Roosevelt to Ronald Reagan and around the world from Vietnam to Eastern Europe. He may have had a scientific "interest" in monetary policy and free markets, but his passion for the subject led him to barnstorming political campaigns.

Friedman's abiding faith in individual freedom undergirded his economic theories. "The free market is the only mechanism that has ever been discovered for achieving participatory democracy," he wrote. He was a foe of government regulation of business, professional licensing, and the military draft. (Indeed, Friedman said he personally lobbied members of Congress against the draft in the 1960s.) He consistently held his position, even when it led to unpopular stands. For example, in *Capitalism and Freedom* (1956), Friedman argued that government-mandated desegregation efforts would be counterproductive because they would force some individuals to act contrary to their own wishes, undercutting the basic policy goal of improving race relations.

He was also a staunch critic of government control of education. Although he accepted that governments might require education, he thought that uniform public schools compromised individual freedom. To accommodate both the requirement for education and individual freedom, Friedman suggested publicly funded vouchers that could be redeemed at either public or private schools. Vouchers would permit students and their parents to choose what *they thought* was the most appropriate education, not government policymakers. The government could still operate schools, but individuals would not be compelled to attend them.

Unlike many academics, Friedman was an ardent public exponent of his ideas. He actively campaigned for an amendment to the Michigan constitution to limit government spending. He starred in a ten-part television series in 1980 espousing his ideas. In 1996 he and his wife, Rose, created a foundation to support school choice in all fifty states. The Foundation for Educational Choice continues to advocate school choice generally and especially vouchers.

Source: Friedman (1985/2004); Noble (2006); The Foundation for Educational Choice (2011).

In response, many voucher supporters argue that they are not advocating privatizing education. Indeed, some have argued that vouchers are the only way to generate true educational *equality*. Why should a student be penalized by a local school district's tax base? The state could calculate a family's ability to pay, a district's expenses, and an "ideal" individual school financing level. Each family would then receive an "equal" amount, based on their own particular circumstances, to be used for educational purposes.[58] Governments can still control who receives vouchers and can specify which schools can accept them. Giving vouchers to all parents would almost certainly prompt many middle-income parents to move their children to private schools, but both the Cleveland and Milwaukee programs—and the sixteen other voucher programs that exist as of this writing—target vouchers to low-income students.[59] This limit helps keep the policy focused on the original policy problem: low-income parents cannot exercise Tiebout choice. Schools accepting vouchers do have to conform to state law, and if private schools have to abide by fewer regulations, that is the fault of the legislature and not voucher programs. In Wisconsin, for example, vouchers must go to a *school*. It may be public (highly regulated) or private (less regulated, but still subject to laws). In most programs, vouchers cannot be used by a parent to fund schooling at home or to send a student to a school in another state.

The second incendiary debate surrounding vouchers is whether allowing tax funds to go to religious institutions is an unconstitutional "establishment of religion." Legislators amended the Milwaukee, Wisconsin, voucher program to allow students to choose religious schools in 1996. The Cleveland, Ohio, voucher program allowed that choice from its inception. Critics argue that self-rule can harm the norm of inclusion. In their view, a voucher program could result in "taxpayers being forced to fund private and religious schools teaching things that would make many of us deeply uncomfortable . . . ideas that are repugnant or even hateful," according to a board member of the interest group Americans United for Separation of Church and State.[60] In their view, religious education promotes divisiveness. Although opposition from such a group is not surprising, some religious private schools are also opposed because they fear government intrusion. But for many others, especially urban Catholic schools, vouchers have proven a lifeline to keep their doors open even as shifting city demographics weaken their traditional student populations.[61] Although teachers' unions, school administrators' associations, and most Democrats opposed vouchers for multiple reasons, critics sued both cities' programs on religious grounds. The court record on such church-state issues was not consistent, and the courts ultimately let both programs stand.

The courts did have a consistent question, though. Who got the money? Both New York and Pennsylvania had passed statutes in the 1960s to keep religious schools open. Their legislators argued that stable schools, public or private, ensure quality, safe neighborhoods. Legislators also argued that subsidies for parochial education were less expensive than educating the same children in public schools. But because the money was directed to religious *schools*, the court found the programs unconstitutional (*Committee for Public Education and Religious Liberty v. Nyquist* [1973] and *Sloan v. Lemon* [1973]). Even though some 96 percent of Cleveland's vouchers went to religious schools, the court said no, vouchers were not direct aid to religious institutions. In *Zelman v. Simmons-Harris* (2002), the U.S. Supreme Court held that the Ohio voucher program did not create an "excessive entanglement" with religion because the vouchers were sent to *parents*, who then chose a religious school. Direct aid is unconstitutional, but so long as parents choose, the U.S. Constitution does not prohibit the practice.

The victory for vouchers was not final. In American federalism, the U.S. Supreme Court cannot rule on the meaning of state constitutions. Many states have "Blaine amendments" in their *state* constitutions to prevent funding of religious schools. Most were added in the late nineteenth century to discriminate against Catholic schools, but during the twentieth century state courts interpreted them to prevent funding of any religious education. In 2004 a Florida appeals court, for example, found that Governor Jeb Bush's statewide voucher program fell afoul of religious separation.[62] Likewise, the Douglas County, Colorado, school board unanimously voted to create a voucher program in 2011 to bolster "choice and accountability" in the district—and to help it balance its budget. Parents receiving vouchers would get only 75 percent of the money the district would have spent on the student; the district would keep the remaining 25 percent. Despite the existence of other school choice programs in Colorado, and despite the link to shoring up the district's budget, a state judge in Denver still found the program unconstitutional, because the money might go to religious schools.[63] And the Washington State Supreme Court ruled that even tax-funded scholarships for *college* cannot be used for religious instruction (upheld by the U.S. Supreme Court in *Locke v. Davey* [2004]). Knowing this challenge, Nevada Governor Brian Sandoval has suggested amending his state's constitution to explicitly allow such vouchers. Such an amendment would thwart an unfriendly state court.[64] More than any other challenge, religious controversy has made vouchers difficult public policy to enact and sustain.

Charter Schools

The charter school concept was policymakers' middle-of-the-road response to the perceived academic perils of traditional public schools and the constitutional threats of a free-range voucher system. Charter schools must accept the public accountability of the public school system because they *are* public schools. In many states, local school boards authorize them to operate, and the schools often reside in public school buildings. Their students are subject to the same state tests, and teachers are often subject to the same licensure requirements as in the public system. Charters must accept any student that a traditional public school must. Thus charter schools preserve decisions made by majority rule. Charter schools also incorporate some features of private schools that many parents say are attractive. The foremost feature is that charter schools do *not* have to use the same curriculum that other district schools use. Charter schools may cater to students with interests in engineering and aerospace, performing arts, and E. D. Hirsch's "traditional" academic curriculum.[65] They can emphasize boot-camp-like discipline or free-flowing Montessori instruction. In many states charter schools are free to experiment with different class times, require uniforms, or meet in unusual locations (like a national park or industrial setting).[66] Charter schools also require parents to choose to enroll their children.

Charters combine the accountability of traditional public schools and the choice of private schools. For some educational reformers, charters were framed as a back door to introduce market-like pressure on traditional public schools through competition.[67] For teachers, charters offered an opportunity to be treated like professionals and make substantive decisions about how schools were run.[68] For school districts, charters could compete with private schools (or other districts) to bring in additional revenue— really the reverse of vouchers.[69] Charter schools also have attracted both conservative and liberal supporters in high places, unlike vouchers. President Barack Obama's Department of Education's Race-to-the-Top competition pressured states to enact charter school legislation, and if they

TABLE 7.2   Growth of Charter Schools, 1991–1992 to 2009–2010

Year	States Permitting	Schools Open	Students Enrolled
2009	40	4,919	1,620,316
2008	40	4,638	1,441,214
2007	40	4,299	1,291,404
2006	40	3,999	1,163,222
2005	40	3,689	1,017,519
2004	40	3,383	897,643
2003	40	2,959	789,479
2002	40	2,559	666,038
2001	38	2,313	580,029
2000	37	1,941	458,664
1999	37	1,542	349,642
1998	35	1,122	
1997	30	721	
1996	26	432	
1995	19	254	
1994	11	100	
1993	8	36	
1992	2	2	
1991	1	0	

Source: Various state departments of education; National Alliance for Public Charter Schools (2011). Enrollment data before the 1999–2000 school year are not reliable.

already had such laws, to make charter schools easier to open. U.S. Secretary of Education Arne Duncan applauded charters because they bring "new options to under-served communities" and introduce "competition and innovation" to public schools.[70] The charter compromise would seem to satisfy the democratic norms of pluralism, inclusion, *and* self-rule, and charter schools have increased rapidly in the United States (see table 7.2). But the compromise did not satisfy either choice critics or voucher supporters.

Opponents of charters believe that they "cream" the motivated and talented students out of traditional public schools, leaving them to struggle with the less-engaged students who are left behind. Similarly, critics say that charter schools increase school racial segregation by giving active parents, who are more likely to be white and middle- or upper-income, a tax-supported "escape" from overwhelmingly black or Hispanic schools. As evidence, critics point out that white students make up 29 percent of California's student population but fully 38 percent of that state's charter school enrollment.[71] They also point to what appear to be almost single-race charter schools, especially for African Americans. For example, in the Oklahoma City metropolitan area, 40 percent of charter schools but only 5 percent of traditional public schools are 90 percent or more nonwhite. In the Dayton, Ohio, metropolitan area, 74 percent of charter students but only 17 percent of traditional public students are black.[72] Using these data, charter schools appear to be agents of resegregation by attracting nonwhite students out of apparently less-segregated traditional schools.

Because charter schools have the freedom to offer specialty curriculum, some charters *do* cater to racial or ethnic heritage. For example, one Harambee charter school in Philadelphia, Pennsylvania, describes its philosophy this way:

> The foundation of our instruction is a value system known as the NGUZO SABA. . . . [The] Nguzo Saba was developed and proposed during the Black Cultural Revolution in the Sixties as a necessary minimum set of principles by which Black people must live in order to begin to rescue and reconstruct our history and lives.[73]

Clearly, the school is catering to African American students even though its specialty focus is not particularly racial or ethnic (it is science and technology). This school's founders, and those of others like it, placed the norm of self-rule above an unfulfilled promise of inclusion.

Critics also take aim at the assumption that the competition that charter schools provide will improve traditional public schools (note the quote above about vouchers failing to provide "superior schools"). Early choice proponents frequently made grand claims about the salutary effects of competition. For example, two prominent charter proponents argued that "[choice] has the capacity all by itself to bring about the kind of transformation that, for years, reformers have been seeking."[74] Others have argued that parental self-rule would result in students being placed in appropriate, academically challenging environments. Choice would be much more efficient than relying on existing public school bureaucracies.

But dozens of studies show that charter schools do not necessarily result in better academic performance. Both national and city-specific studies of charter school students have found that most charter students perform at about the same level as their peers in traditional public schools.[75] If research findings such as these continue to hold, pro-school-choice policymakers may regret framing school choice as a means to academic improvement. According to critics, given these mediocre results, the potential harm to inclusion and weakened majority rule are not worth the steep increase in satisfaction that self-rule gives parents.

Charter proponents dismiss the allegation that charters are agents of resegregation. They admit that charters in general are not challenging the status quo, but they are not worsening it, either.[76] Research showing charters as sharply out of line with local demographics tends to compare charters to district, city, or metropolitan averages. Thus, when critics say that the Milwaukee *metropolitan* area charter schools are 50 percent black but only 23 percent of its traditional school population is black, they overlook the extreme segregation between Milwaukee and even its within-county suburbs (the city is 31 percent white, but the county, excluding the city, is 89 percent white).[77] In large districts, even using district averages is difficult to defend, because charters tend to draw from the surrounding neighborhoods, which may also be highly segregated.[78] In some states, charter schools can draw students from other districts, but there is no strong evidence that race is a major pull for out-of-district transfers. It is certainly not the case for Milwaukee. In 2008–2009, 327 students transferred into the Milwaukee Public School District, but 4,235 transferred out.[79] Apparently charter schools *in* the city are not drawing students *into* the district, so it is unlikely that they would be any more integrated than schools in the district. Charters may not improve democratic inclusion, but they are unlikely to undermine it any more than Americans' existing housing patterns do.

As for test results, all but the most fervent defenders of school choice admit that the promise of large performance gains was oversold.[80] As a rule, neither charters nor vouchers dramatically increase test scores. But lumping "charters" together is problematic; more so than lumping together, say, all traditional public elementary schools when talking about fourth-grade reading achievement. Traditional elementary schools tend to have approximately the same curriculum with approximately equally experienced teachers. Charter schools do not. One of the advertised benefits of charters is their diverse programs, and *some* charter school models *do* show strong academic improvement. Many charters are tailored for low-performing and otherwise at-risk students. It is unlikely that schools with an at-risk focus will be turning out ninety-ninth-percentile test scores, but they might turn low-performing students into average-performing students.[81] Charter programs with intense discipline, extra time on academic tasks, and core academics can be extremely successful in besting comparable traditional public school students. One such model is the "Knowledge Is Power Program" (KIPP). KIPP charters appear to boost students' achievement by more than a full year of schooling in math and almost a year in reading.[82] In short, some charter programs are successful—just as some teachers are unusually effective.

The dramatic variation in charter schools and charter performance only sharpens the dilemma of self-rule for policymakers. As public policy, if only a minority of charters are more educationally efficient than traditional schools, is greater individual self-rule worth the risks that charter critics fear? Does government have a responsibility to protect parents from making poor educational decisions for their children? If a particular charter is effective, should districts be *required* to copy its program? If not, are traditional schools undermining democratic understanding by ignoring success?

Conclusion

There is no norm more associated with democracy than self-rule. Elections encourage choice among candidates, federalism provides choice among governments, and school choice caters to diverse preferences in education. School choice reformers argued that individual self-rule could overcome the problems of unresponsive school bureaucracies. Open enrollment gave some parents an option to exercise choice by moving their children to different public schools, but reformers still sought more thoroughgoing choice. By defining education as a toll good, these reformers argued that schools could cater to individuals preferences with government support, whether through a government-funded voucher or public charter schools.

School choice reformers could not demonstrate whether self-rule benefited more than just its target population. That is, did school choice offer real benefits beyond making parents who choose very pleased with their children's schools? Can lawmakers expand self-rule without compromising democratic inclusion, majority rule, and understanding? Is self-rule compatible with stringent accountability?

School choice seems here to stay as both liberal and conservative organizations support school choice through charter schools. As the U.S. Department of Education pushes for more charter schools and states push for more accountability, policymakers will continue to face difficult decisions as they balance self-rule with the rest of democracy.

Suggested Readings

Chubb, John, and Terry M. Moe. 1990. *Politics, Markets, and America's Schools.* Washington, DC: Brookings Institution Press.

Fischel, William A. 2001. *The Homevoter Hypothesis: How Home Values Influence Local Government Taxation, School Finance, and Land-Use Policies.* Cambridge, MA: Harvard University Press.

Fuller, Bruce, and Richard F. Elmore. 1996. *Who Chooses? Who Loses? Culture, Institutions and the Unequal Effects of School Choice.* New York: Teachers College Press.

Henig, Jeffrey. 1994. *Rethinking School Choice: Limits of the Market Metaphor.* Princeton, NJ: Princeton University Press.

Hess, Frederick M. 2010. "Does School Choice 'Work'?" *National Affairs* (Fall): 35–53.

Howell, William G., and Paul E. Peterson. 2006. *The Education Gap: Vouchers and Urban Schools.* Rev. ed. Washington, DC: Brookings Institution Press.

Smith, Kevin B., and Kenneth Meier. 1995. *The Case Against School Choice: Politics, Markets, and Fools.* Armonk, NY: M.E. Sharpe.

Tiebout, Charles M. 1956. "A Pure Theory of Local Expenditures." *Journal of Political Economy* 64 (5, April): 416–424.

Zimmer, Ron W., Brian P. Gill, Kevin Booker, Stephane Lavertu, Tim Sass, and John Witte. 2009. *Charter Schools in Eight States: Effects on Achievement, Attainment, Integration, and Competition.* Santa Monica, CA: RAND Corporation.

8

···

Devolving the Dilemma?

CAN AMERICAN EDUCATIONAL POLICY be democratic if it is created democratically? American policymakers expect schools to produce kids who can read, debate, and find quotients proficiently. Americans want their children to be ready for a meaningful career. And small-d democrats want schools to help students believe in democracy—in majority rule, in participating, in including everyone's view, in equality, and that these norms culminate in good, responsive government action. They want children to believe that democratic government is believable.[1]

This dream seems universal. Educational reformers from the Puritans to Obama's secretary of education have argued that education serves as a national glue that promotes democracy. With that, Thomas Jefferson, Horace Mann, Ellwood Cubberley, John Dewey, James Conant, James Coleman, Gary Nash, and Diane Ravitch could agree. But the terms of the debate have changed. Horace Mann's vision of education in the 1840s, designed to encourage a common, mainline Protestant culture, was far removed from Gary Nash's and Gary Orfield's calls for integrated, multicultural schools in the 1990s and 2000s. Yet all thought their proposals would make Americans a better-governed, more equal people.

This chapter recapitulates the five norms of democracy that organize this book, but though democracy is self-rule, participation, understanding, inclusion, and equity, it is, above all, conflict. As one democratic theorist noted long ago, it is impossible to design an election system that is both logical and fair.[2] There are simply too many policy options for any *one* option to garner majority support. Yet a system cannot be democratic if one person, or one group, can dictate what public policy should be. This is the great paradox of American educational policy. To produce anything like what Americans want from schools, educational policy *cannot* simultaneously satisfy each democratic norm. Policymakers draft educational policy in this arena of conflict. *They* rank the norms of democracy; *they* try to forge compromise between democratic ideals and democratic practice.

Mann and Nash were no different. Mann preferred equality; Nash favored inclusion. And both confronted skeptical legislators and disbelieving citizens. In Mann's America, most people, including his own state legislature, did not think education was a public responsibility. The answer to the policy question, *Is there a problem?* was a firm "no." That most Americans did not go to school regularly did not trouble legislators or the public. In the seventeenth century, the Puritan leadership of the Massachusetts Bay Colony had to force towns to hire schoolmasters, because many town governments (which were famously participatory) did not want to spend the money. As it was, many Americans thought schools were for moral instruction, and there was not much schools could provide that a supportive home could not.

From his post as commissioner of education, Mann's position on government involvement in education was obvious. He tried to boost support for tax-supported education by offering attractive answers to *When should government intervene?* In his view, Massachusetts in the 1840s was becoming dangerously overcrowded, and overcrowding inevitably led to social chaos. Legislators needed to act to stop the poor from revolting against the government. (Massachusetts legislators scarcely needed to be reminded of farmer Daniel Shays's nearly successful rebellion in 1786. He and eighteen hundred impoverished farmers marched on the state's courts and eventually captured the Supreme Judicial Court with muskets and pitchforks.) Education could do more than encourage public morals. Mann argued that, "Education, then, beyond all other devices of human origin, is a great equalizer of the conditions of men—the balance wheel of the social machinery. . . . It does better than to disarm the poor of their hostility toward the rich: it prevents being poor."[3] Education would be determined by prevailing majority views. A common, uniform education for all children would secure Massachusetts's economic future.

Mann's Massachusetts argument has been echoed and amplified by educational interest groups from the frontier Western Literary Institute to today's National Education Association. Immigrants would gain access to power. Crime in cities would fall. Employment would rise. A college education would open new horizons for all. The likes of Cubberley, Dewey, and Conant would echo Mann as they promised that "more and better education can solve whatever problems exist."[4] This, as two critics call it, was the "education gospel."

Mann won the argument. Some 150 years later, Nash and his colleagues were not debating *if there was a problem* but *what the government should do.* Their debate was not whether education could prevent poverty or increase democratic participation—they "knew" that it could. Instead, Nash and others struggled to use public schools to correct what they saw as vast inequities in representative government. Were higher-income, more-suburban, and white citizens more likely to believe in self-rule? To form interest groups? To use government to their own ends? Yes, yes, and yes. Government has a distinct upper-class bias, and self-rule, participation, and majoritarianism seemed destined to trump inclusion and equity.[5] But judges and activists seized the centralized, Progressive school machinery to elevate the contributions of low-income, more-urban, and nonwhite citizens to American society (as in New Jersey's *Abbott* lawsuits; see Chapter 4). Nash and his team were only writing history standards that brought this perspective to the curriculum. Surely, they thought, Americans who *were not* part of Mann's common, mainline Protestant culture should have their story told, too. In Nash's view, inclusion could bring equity to American democracy.

The conflict Mann and Nash encountered was not unique to them. As policymakers incorporated other norms into educational policy, they faced stiff opposition from others who valued different norms more highly.

Inclusion

Riots, firebombs, and deliberate sabotage accompanied integration—but not as many as segregationists promised. In the early 1950s the NAACP's Thurgood Marshall noted with satisfaction that despite warnings from state officials about violence, "nothing happened except that Negroes were admitted [to state law schools] just as if they had been attending school for years back."[6] Marshall was optimistic that when white Americans saw that "nothing happened" when blacks attended school, self-rule would peacefully yield to the norm of democratic inclusion.

But Marshall and fellow civil rights activists understood the attraction of self-rule over education, and they knew that using the courts threatened the norm. The future Supreme Court justice did not think that challenge insurmountable, though. Instead, he charged that Southern governors were actually perverting self-rule to maintain segregated schools. He was convinced that the Southerners' efforts to privatize education would backfire. "The white citizens [of segregated states] are not insane enough on segregation to be willing to turn over millions of dollars of their tax money invested in schools to private institutions where they will have little, if any, control over the education of their children," he said.[7] Marshall argued that whites would accept inclusion if only to preserve self-rule.

Since the civil rights reforms of the 1960s, though, policymakers and the public have become skeptical of the promise of integration. Despite major reforms in civil rights, a series of riots in the late 1960s undercut many white Americans' acceptance of inclusion. A Gallup Poll in 1967 found that only a minority of Americans thought government should do more to improve education or job training for blacks. Instead, most Americans wanted the government to stop rioting by force.[8] The promised academic gains did not materialize from desegregation, either. When the Supreme Court ended stronger, mandatory desegregation policy with *Milliken* in 1974, the court invoked self-rule. While noting that "few judges" were "qualified" to oversee school districts, Chief Justice Warren Burger wrote, "Substantial local control of public education in this country is a deeply rooted tradition."[9] The ruling was a crushing blow to advocates of integration: the courts had just opened the door to controversial, mandatory busing—but then invited citizens to escape busing by decamping to the suburbs. Democracy, local democracy, trumped the norm of inclusion.

Equity

So proponents of inclusion turned to the norm of equity. Even if the courts could not redraw school district lines, they could compel states to compensate for the manifestly unequal spending among school districts. Nonwhite students, who were and are concentrated in urban districts, might then receive some of the benefits promised by *Brown v. Board of Education* (1954).

Politically, the norm of inclusion had become tinged with race and "special treatment," as later disputes over affirmative action vividly confirmed. Equity had no such connotation. Although blacks strongly disagreed with whites about whether equal educational opportunity existed, both agreed that it *should*. In a 2004 Gallup Poll, 68 percent of African Americans said equal opportunity did not exist, and 63 percent of whites said it did. Nonetheless, both groups agreed on the remedy. White Americans' top solution for the "most important way" to help African American children was that blacks be held to the same standards as everyone else. African American respondents agreed.[10]

In order for public policy to move from "just a good idea" to actual legislation, policymakers have to engage in political analysis. In other words, they have to build political coalitions to shepherd the policy through representative government. Who would benefit from this policy? Educational policy seeking to bring democratic efficacy to nonwhite students through greater inclusion has a limited, though sometimes successful, political coalition. Racial desegregation had little political appeal outside nonwhite communities and schools. Advocates of financial equity, however, found a different story. Although many of the same school districts would benefit from equity as would from desegregation, so would hundreds of smaller rural and suburban school districts. The Ohio Coalition for Equity and Adequacy of School Funding (see Chapter 4) had more than 500 school districts (of 614 Ohio districts at the time) on board. Similar groups in other states have found the same widespread support.

But equity also chafed against self-rule. Americans have limited access to making actual policy decisions; most policy is made through representatives. School finance is less insulated because many states require school taxes to be approved directly by voters. The amount they approve to spend on education reflects that community's priorities. Are interests of democratic equity greater than those of self-rule? Courts were of a divided mind: the U.S. Supreme Court said no in 1973; state courts agreed only about half of the time.

Similarly, equity fell afoul of currents in the rising standards movement. Some policymakers argued that equity should apply to *inputs*. Spending should be the same, they argued, and educational quality would follow. But what if children in some districts came to school with more needs? What if their parents did not get them to school on time, read to them at night, or care if they did their homework? What if a district had a high percentage of children with learning disabilities or who were victims of crime? These districts would need *more* funding to reach the same level of *outcomes* as a suburban district. They would have to be "more equal." The Ohio Coalition took exactly this approach: "Any definition of an adequate education that does not include the identification of learning resources required for students to meet the outcome standards will result in a *fabricated* per pupil support level."[11]

Equity, then, can become unequal.

Participation

Many Americans associate the civil rights movement of the 1960s with sit-ins, demonstrations, and marches. It was participatory. Even as the movement split between nonviolent and more assertive factions in the late 1960s, it was still a broad-based social movement. Civil rights activists fully engaged the norm of participation. The marches were not permanent, and they waned as the movement's initial, concrete demands (end segregation) gave way to more abstract desires (compensation for discrimination).

Demands for democratic inclusion did not disappear, and they had not really started with the civil rights marches, either. Groups like the NAACP had long advocated inclusion. Unlike civil rights marchers, group leaders could develop expertise and relationships with policymakers and legislators. They could develop strategies to enact public policies they favored. The NAACP's Thurgood Marshall litigated dozens of cases in the years before *Brown*, including two major cases on law school admission for African Americans. He was well known in the courtroom, and he was deliberate in his strategy to challenge small inequities first.[12]

Policymakers who believed that the norms of inclusion or equity could bring faith in American democracy to nonwhites, low-performing or special-needs students, and poor school districts faced a difficult dilemma. Group politics is inherently unequal, and groups exist for the benefit of *their* members, not citizens generally. High-minded calls for equality of opportunity from an interest group seem disingenuous when members of *that* group will stand to benefit the most. Yet teachers' unions (as discussed in Chapter 5) have successfully done just that. They are most successful when Americans think of them as "teachers" but not "unions." Teachers seem above politics, but unions are in the thick of politics. A frustrated Ohio official said, "[Reforming school finance] would be easier if education leaders . . . would stop misleading us to believe that student interests always come first, as if there were no bureaucratic or professional staff interests at all."[13] When unions oppose merit pay, insist on seniority rights, and help design teacher mentor programs, they do, in fact, protect their members first. Their programs may help children learn or keep a school district financially sound, but these are not the group's main goals.

In democracies, participation through groups undercuts inclusion and thrives on inequity. But the democratic dilemma is that group politics can succeed at broadening inclusion and improving equity. E. E. Schattschneider made the point this way: "It is the losers . . . who seek redress from public authority. . . . In the school yard it is not the bully, but the defenseless smaller boys who 'tell the teacher.' When the teacher intervenes, the balance of power in the schoolyard is apt to change drastically."[14]

Understanding

The same dilemma awaits those policymakers who try to create common democratic discourse through common curriculum and national standards (see Chapter 6). Because "history, like politics, . . . is about identity," democratic understanding runs the same risks from self-rule and participation that inclusion and equity do.[15] In educational policy, democratic understanding itself poses a conflict: Should children comprehend the same history, or should they share the same interpretation of those arguments? Ironically, Nash highlighted the diversity of the American experience—but did so by recommending a common interpretation of that history. Critics contested the standards because they did not believe Nash shared *their* view of American history. The debacle surrounding the history standards serves as a warning to policymakers that democracy *cannot* have a shared understanding of the past and its politics.

The norm of participation guarantees that democracies will produce winners and losers. Indeed, the norm encourages it. The loser from Nash's proposed standards would have been the traditional, patriotic, hopeful view of American politics. "Our children need heroes," Lynne Cheney told ABC News in 1994.[16] When groups like the Family Research Council, the Eagle Forum, and other conservative organizations saw this attack on traditional history, they entered the political fray to undercut the project, and they succeeded. Even if Nash's conservative critics went too far in asserting that the history of American elites was the history of America, they, too, overlooked the power of self-rule. The genius of American democracy is not that it balances the norms of democracy well; it does not. But states, cities, and school districts can make the determination of what *their* history is. What should students in the Bronx know about American history? Those in North Dakota?

Understanding sits far more comfortably with other democratic norms when it is taken as the need for children, future voters, to parse, debate, and frame political arguments. "A democratic society cannot long sustain itself if its citizens are uninformed and indifferent about its history, its government, and the workings of its economy," wrote a critic of the original history standards.[17] When that view is taken, that democratic understanding means a common language but diverse beliefs, self-rule moves to the center of democratic discourse.

Self-Rule

"Progressive democracy needs executive leadership, because . . . it organizes and vitalizes the rule of the majority," wrote Herbert Croly, the longtime editor of *The New Republic* and a staunch Progressive, in 1914.[18] For Croly, only executive authority—presidents, governors, and mayors—could translate what the people wanted into public policy. For them, democracy was democracy only when the majority ruled; when it did not, they argued, "evil combinations" that made "corrupt bargains" did. The majority will *must* be "harmonious."[19] If it was not, it was the responsibility of leaders to make it so. Croly and other Progressives would have applauded moves by Governor Strickland in 2009 and others to concentrate the authority for American education in their offices (see Chapter 2).

Progressives tried to make American education meet the needs of every child. They thought they were enhancing democracy by giving "all American youth" an opportunity to learn appropriate skills. Progressives tried to expand educational opportunity to include the waves of immigrants flooding Ellis Island. They sought to make education modern and relevant. In all these endeavors, the Progressives forced self-rule through the "majority will." Croly illustrates the troubled relationship that Progressives had with self-rule. Experts decided what appropriate education was, not students or parents. Immigrants were taught that their own folkways were inferior to "Anglo-Teutonic" concepts of law, and reformers insistence on relevance to the modern age cut children off from the heritage of ideas and ideals of democracy. The Progressives tried to elevate self-rule by suppressing conflict, but democracy is not harmonious. The genius of the framers of the Constitution shows in the government they created, which channels those disagreements into productive policymaking.

Despite the best Progressive efforts, American educational policy has never been "one best system." It has always been fragmented and federal. Self-rule can thwart inclusion, equity, understanding, and participation— but rarely everywhere at once. Citizens are happiest not when they can rule government, but when they can choose which government will rule them.

Out of Many, One?

American federalism is slow, inefficient, and inequitable, just as democracy is slow, inefficient, and inequitable. But fifty states and 13,628 school districts have allowed diversity to bloom. It has allowed hundreds more ordinary citizens to shape educational policy than would have been possible if there were one best system. The democratic dilemmas presented in this book have played out in every state and in hundreds of school districts.

Even as school boards, superintendents of education, governors, and voters faced the democratic conflicts of the twentieth century, American educational policy passed through a less expected, deeper, and more fundamental transformation. Policymakers around the country tried to emulate the winners. Out of many conflicts, it seemed one set of solutions dominated: federal oversight with individual choice. Citizens who cared about American educational policy lost local control.

The story of growing federal influence is straightforward. When Lyndon B. Johnson signed the first Elementary and Secondary Education Act (ESEA) in 1965, he launched American educational policy on the trajectory of ever-greater federal involvement. He and many others saw local and state governments as backwaters more intent on preserving their own political power than on rectifying inequality. Johnson was right. He was also right that school districts would not really lament losing local democracy if they were compensated.

ESEA made that trade. At the time, educators were both alarmed and relieved. They were alarmed because the federal government was, for the first time, making a serious attempt to reorient school policy with financial carrots. In this case, ESEA's goal was to make schools pay attention to low-income children from families that did not participate in local democracy.

Later, the federal government added special-needs children, who were routinely ignored by schools because they were difficult to educate.

Educators were relieved to discover that the federal government really wanted almost nothing in return. So long as schools spent the money on the appropriate students, they were not accountable for how teachers taught low-income and special-needs children or for what they learned. Most school districts were pleased to take the money. Almost one-quarter of the school districts that desegregated after ESEA told federal officials that the "major" reason for desegregation was federal funding.[20]

Districts found they could bring dollars in simply by enrolling students. As the stagflation of the 1970s set in, school districts found the federal government more willing to part with money than local voters were willing to raise property taxes. So they did what the federal government wanted. William F. Buckley captured the transition in federalism well. In 1972 he wrote, "Mississippi lost the right to pass its own laws respecting schooling, transportation, hotels and restaurants. And it is, without question, a better place to live in now than before."[21]

At the same time, Americans were frightened by the nation's loss of global competitiveness. As *A Nation at Risk* percolated through the policy world, federal legislators saw a golden opportunity to turn the screws on local districts, just as Lyndon Johnson had. If ESEA could make districts pay attention to low-income students, ESEA could make districts pay attention to academic achievement, too.

Until 1994 ESEA provided virtually "free" money. According to an analyst at a prominent think tank, "Title I was primarily a funding stream that had no expectations. They counted the number of poor children in your school and sent you a check. The was no requirement from the feds that the kids actually learn anything. . . . [The] 1994 changes [signaled] impatience with the states by saying 'We want you to have accountability systems.'"[22] The 1994 reforms specified that states had to test learning, but not what, specifically, they should assess.

When President George W. Bush signed No Child Left Behind (NCLB) in 2002, districts found that they had no choice but to spend time (and money) on basic academics. NCLB specified the subject areas for standards *and* how states should assess them: through tests. If the standards could not be tested, then the federal government would not send money. Even if school voters wanted to keep the elementary strings program and shop class, many school districts simply had to defer to the federal government.[23] Self-rule in the form of local elections and school boards was overpowered by federal dollars. Indeed, the lawsuits that the NEA, school districts in three states, and the state of Connecticut brought against NCLB were not based on the grounds that democracy was threatened, but because the act allegedly did not provide enough money.[24]

Have federal policymakers become the future of educational policy, then? No, not really. The great irony of the explosion of federal education policymaking is that the federal government does not have the political power to *require* schools to change. It has to "borrow strength" from the states.[25] The U.S. Supreme Court reiterated that view when it found that education was not a "fundamental right" in the U.S. Constitution in *Rodriguez v. San Antonio* (1973). Thus, educational policy is only as effective as the states that implement it.

The federal government's prescriptions in NCLB—measuring academic outputs, highly qualified teachers, and school choice—would have been toothless if state government had not gone there first. When George H. W. Bush convened governors in 1989 in Charlottesville, Virginia, to talk about standards and choice, he did so because he needed to hear what *they* were doing. By 2001 George W. Bush argued that school districts were still ignoring the neediest students, echoing the same concern that Lyndon Johnson had and what reform-minded governors had been endlessly repeating over the previous decade.

Unlike Johnson's categorical, input-based approach, Bush wanted to monitor outputs—with a catch. The federal government could directly monitor whether ESEA funds were spent on the right students, and since the 1970s, low-income and special-needs children have benefited from this massive infusion of federal aid. Under NCLB, the federal government cannot define the outputs or even how to measure them. It seemed that the states had the last say.

Maybe. States did not have the option of tailoring standards or expectations for different students. In the name of maximum inclusion and equity, states could not respond to local concerns (*all* students must reach *proficiency* by 2014). To address these concerns, states could meet the federal goals, keep ESEA money, and keep schools open if they lowered their standards. ("Everyone can meet an easy standard.") For every Massachusetts and South Carolina that maintained high standards, there were Colorados,

Wisconsins, and Mississippis that created low academic standards that weakened the meaning of "proficient."[26] These states undermined democratic understanding simply so that all students could "succeed."

As the Obama administration geared up for the reauthorization of ESEA to replace NCLB, Secretary of Education Arne Duncan told a conference of educational policymakers: "We have sought to fundamentally shift the federal role so that the Department is playing a greater role in supporting reform and innovation in states, districts, and local communities across the nation.... [We will focus] on helping states build the capacity to implement programs successfully—instead of focusing on compliance monitoring." Duncan was offering an olive branch to educators who had chafed under NCLB, but he was reiterating what was always true: the federal government *had* to rely on the states "to implement programs successfully."

Duncan was not lamenting the loss of local democracy, though. The U.S. Department of Education might be "helping states build capacity," but Obama's Race to the Top was not a blank check. Duncan wanted state standards, charter schools, public test-based accountability, and teaching reforms like merit pay. Although states still would have to implement the actual reforms, they would not get the federal cash unless they proposed something similar to what Duncan wanted. In the first round, only Tennessee and Delaware won.[27]

While federal authority grew, policymakers built an escape hatch for individuals. They saw Americans' increasing frustration with schools that did not accommodate students' special needs and interests and schools that seemed to have lost all interest in students. As the federal government demanded standards, schools responded with narrower curricula. Enter school choice. Maybe parents disliked the emphasis on low-level reading and math that schools had to maintain to ensure every student was proficient. They could move their students to a school that offered more challenging curricula, nontraditional teaching styles, or alternative classrooms. Maybe low-income parents were tired of the difficulties their students faced in aging urban schools. In Washington, D.C., almost a third of public school students attend charter schools. The traditional system has lost over 25,000 students. So much for inclusion; parents wanted control over education.

From one perspective, this constellation of American educational policy is an attractive vision of democracy. The federal government (through the states) sets standards for students to meet, but parents of those students decide whether schools meet their needs. The federal government says it is promoting democratic understanding; parents can exercise self-rule. The stuff of education is left up to teachers and administrators—so long as their students meet the outcomes. The system seems to maximize freedom. When the model works, it brings freedom to future citizens, because they can take the reins of government confidently. It returns freedom to parents who, individually, have little say in educational policy. It gives freedom to teachers and schools to shape education in creative ways. Out of many individuals, one outcome.

But this vision of democracy also surrenders the Progressives' core success: the triumph of the norms of inclusion and equity. All students are not alike. All schools do not have equal resources. The dilemma of American democracy is that individuals need choice, but children need stability. With freedom comes the freedom to fail. Policymakers must decide whether that is worth the risk.

Appendix:
Timeline of American Educational Policy

Note: See also box 3.2.

1647   Massachusetts Commonwealth requires taxes to support schools.

1787   Northwest Ordinance authorizes the sale of public lands to support education.

1840   Horace Mann argues that schools promote economic well-being.

1857   National Teachers' Association forms in Philadelphia, forerunner to the National Education Association.

1867   Reconstruction begins. State education policy centralized in most Southern states.

1867   U.S. Office of Education created.

1870   National Education Association founded.

1893   Committee of Ten recommends standard high school curriculum for college admissions.

1906   "Carnegie units" proposed for high schools.

1916   American Federation of Teachers founded.

1916   Ellwood P. Cubberley's *Public School Administration* published.

1923   George Strayer and Roger Haig recommend that New York State adopt a minimum foundation program to fund education.

1954   Court decides *Brown v. Topeka Board of Education*, calling for an end to segregated schools.

1955   Milton Friedman suggests voucher programs.

1959   James Conant publishes *The American High School Today*.

1959   Wisconsin enacts first public employee collective bargaining law; covers teachers.

1962   One-day strike in New York City forces district to bargain with the United Federation of Teachers.

1964   Civil Rights Act enacted. Authorizes Equality of Educational Opportunity study and prohibits federal funding of segregated facilities.

1965   Elementary and Secondary Education Act enacted.

1966   Coleman releases *Equality of Educational Opportunity*, known as the "Coleman Report."

1968   Court decides *Green v. New Kent County*, requiring integrated schools.

1969   National Assessment of Educational Progress authorized.

1970   Power equalization (or guaranteed tax base) educational finance system proposed.

1971   *Swann v. Charlotte-Mecklenburg* allows busing as a remedy to integrate school districts.

1971   *Keyes v. School District No. 1* finds that school districts segregated by race without deliberate segregation may still be subject to desegregation orders.

1973   Court finds that education is not a "fundamental right" in the U.S. Constitution in *Rodriguez v. San Antonio Independent School District*.

1974   *Milliken v. Bradley* requires that mandatory desegregation remedies be confined to single school districts.

1977   Tuition Tax Credit Act is debated and fails in Congress; would have allowed taxpayers to deduct private school tuition.

1980   U.S. Department of Education becomes a cabinet-level department.

1983   National Commission on Educational Excellence issues *A Nation at Risk*.

1986   National Governors' Association issues *Time for Results*.

1989   President Bush convenes the Charlottesville Education Summit with governors. It is only the third time any U.S. president had officially met with the country's governors.

1989   Kentucky Supreme Court rules that state educational finance program must be "adequate" in *Rose v. Council for Better Education.*

1990   Milwaukee voucher program begins.

1991   First charter school law adopted.

1994   ESEA reauthorized as the Improving America's Schools Act.

1994   Goals 2000 enacted, calling for states to create academic standards.

1994   National History Standards released.

1995   National History Standards condemned by the U.S. Senate.

1995   *Missouri v. Jenkins* finds that districts cannot be compelled to correct de facto segregation, extending *Milliken v. Bradley.*

1998   National NEA–AFT merger fails at NEA national convention.

2002   ESEA reauthorized as the No Child Left Behind Act.

2002   Court agrees that parents may apply public voucher payments to religious schools in *Zelman v. Simmons-Harris.*

2004   Florida voucher program found unconstitutional in state court.

2005   Denver, Colorado, voters approve a $25 million referendum to implement ProComp, a merit-pay program.

2009   Obama administration announces the Race to the Top program.

2010   National Common Core State Standards released and adopted by most states.

2011   Public sector collective bargaining curtailed in multiple states; includes public school teachers.

Notes

Chapter 1

1. Dahl (1982).
2. National Research Council (2001).
3. Quoted in Timar (1997), 239.
4. Henig (2009).
5. See Ostrom (1990) for a detailed discussion of this concept.
6. Timar (1997).
7. *Prince v. Massachusetts* (1944), 166.
8. Kingdon (2003).
9. National Commission on Excellence in Education (1983).
10. See Gamoran and Long (2006) for an overview.
11. Kagan (2002).
12. Nathan (2007); Henry, Gordon, and Rickman (2006).
13. U.S. Department of Health and Human Services, Administration for Children and Families (2010).
14. Greene (2010).
15. Hanushek (2007).
16. Ackerman (2005).
17. Hirsch (2009).
18. For example, Orfield (2009); Spring (2000).
19. O'Brien (1999).
20. Ryan (2009), 76, 78.
21. Orfield (2009), 13.
22. Orfield (2009); Logan (2004).
23. Logan (2004), 9, 11.
24. Dahl (1982), Chapter 3.
25. National Center for Education Statistics (2009).
26. Timar (1997).

27. National Center for Education Statistics (2010b).
28. Chubb and Moe (1990); Witte (2000).
29. Clawson (1995).
30. Bracey (2000).
31. Mintrom (2000).
32. Clowes (2002).
33. Fuller and Elmore (1996); Smith and Meier (1995).
34. Petrovich and Wells (2005); Wells (2002).
35. For example, Pew Research Center (2009); Srinivasan and Ray (2009).
36. Shelley et al. (1996), 123; National Conference of State Legislatures (2010). The number cited excludes the hundreds of school finance ballot measures.
37. Berkman and Plutzer (2005), 92.
38. Schattschneider (1960); Dahl (1982).
39. Webber (2010).
40. "New Jersey Rebellion" (2010); Osborne, Rosenthal, and Turner (2000).
41. U.S. Senate, Office of Public Records (2010).
42. McCubbins and Schwartz (1984); Ringquist, Worsham, and Eisner (2003).
43. Baumgartner and Leech (2001); Schattschneider (1960); Schlozman (1984).
44. Olson (1965).
45. Baumgartner and Leech (2001); Schattschneider (1960); Schlozman (1984).
46. Leech et al. (2005).

47. Gray et al. (2004); Yackee and Yackee (2006).

48. Hess and West (2006).

49. Abernathy (2007).

50. Cronin et al. (2007); Dahill-Brown and Lavery (2010).

51. King (2010).

52. Delli Carpini and Keeter (1996).

53. Lodge and Steenbergen (1995).

54. Gilens (2001); Althaus (1998).

55. Gilens (2001), 384.

56. Lau, Andersen, and Redlawsk (2008).

57. Zaller (1992); Popkin (1994).

58. Buckley and Schneider (2003).

59. Schumpeter (1942).

60. Carpenter (2001).

61. See Downes (2002); Hanushek and Somers (2001); McGuinn (2006), Chapter 9.

62. McGuinn (2006), Chapter 9.

63. American Federation of Teachers (2006), 4.

64. Abernathy (2007), 100, and Chapter 4 generally.

65. Arrow (1963).

66. Holcombe and Kenny (2007).

67. See van der Eijk and Franklin (2009) for a thorough overview of election systems and self-governing.

68. Tiebout (1956).

69. National Center for Education Statistics (2010a); Gehring (2005); Reback (2005).

70. Greve (1999).

71. National Center for Education Statistics (2009).

72. See Buckley and Schneider (2003).

73. Weimer and Wolkoff (2001); Fischel (2001).

74. Witte, Schlomer, and Shober (2007).

75. Smith (2001).

Chapter 2

1. Huntington (1968), Chapter 2.

2. Shober (2010), 149.

3. Elliott (2008).

4. Stephens et al. (2008).

5. See Vinovskis (2008) and Henig (2009) on educational policy becoming less unique among state policy areas. Henig argues that governors now see it as simply another policy to control.

6. Shober (2010), 135.

7. Walsh (1993); Prince (1996).

8. Thompson (1995).

9. Soussan (2003).

10. National Association of State Boards of Education (2011).

11. Hernandez (2007).

12. Duncan (2009a).

13. Thompson (1995), 77.

14. See Elmore (1996) for overviews of the challenges of making policy work on the ground.

15. *DeRolph v. Ohio I* (1997), 5.

16. Madison (1788/1987), Federalist 51.

17. National Center for Education Statistics (2011), table 180.

18. Dillon and Lewin (2010).

19. Walker (1991).

20. Bandeira de Mello et al. (2009); Cronin et al. (2007).

21. Moe (1985).

22. Fischel (2001).

23. Salzer (1999); Georgia Office of Planning and Budget (2000), 183.

24. Shober (2010), 3.

25. Dunne, Reed, and Wilbanks (1997); Holcombe and Kenny (2007).

26. See Shober (2010) for a discussion of legislative dependence on bureaucracy; and Gray and Lowery (1996) for an exploration of state-level lobbying.

27. See Shober (2010), Lusi (1997), and Manna (2006) for the growth and

influence of state departments of education.

28. National Center for Education Statistics (2011), table 180.

29. Hess (2008). See also Wong and Shen (2007) and Viteritti (2009).

30. Shober (2008); Berkman and Plutzer (2005).

31. Moe (2005).

32. Raffaele (2005).

33. de Vise (2007b).

34. Aratani (2005). The case was *Citizens for a Responsible Curriculum v. Montgomery County Public Schools* (2005).

35. de Vise (2007a).

36. Finn and Keegan (2004), 15.

37. Finn and Keegan (2004); Moe (2005).

38. Hess and Meeks (2010). This document is a detailed survey of the attitudes of school board members.

39. Neal (1997); Coleman and Hoffer (1987).

40. Gill et al. (2007).

Chapter 3

1. Gordon (1994); Jencks and Phillips (1998); Odden and Picus (2008); Takei and Shouse (2008); U.S. Department of Labor (2010).

2. Ripley (1970a, 1970b).

3. Patterson (2001), 160.

4. Pierce (1972).

5. Ripley (1970b).

6. Ripley (1970a).

7. Patterson (2001), Chapter 7; Clotfelter (2004), Chapter 3.

8. Ramsey and Mitchell (2010).

9. Baumgartner and Jones (1993).

10. Stone (1989); Schneider and Ingram (1993).

11. For example, Haskins (2009).

12. For example, Wilson (1987).

13. For example, Patterson (1999).

14. Pierson (1995), especially Chapter 1; Tyack and Cuban (1995) do not discuss path dependency explicitly but imply it strongly in their discussion of educational reforms.

15. Cooper et al. (2000); Borman and Boulay (2004).

16. Kingdon (2003); Baumgartner and Jones (1993).

17. Boyer (1993); National Education Commission on Time and Learning (1994); Marcotte and Hansen (2010).

18. For example, Guthrie and Springer (2004); Smith (2001); but see Orfield (2009); Hochschild and Scovronick (2004) for a contrary view.

19. Eaton (2011).

20. Orfield (1969); Rosenberg (1993).

21. O'Brien (1999); McClatchy Washington Bureau (2010).

22. Margo (1990), 21.

23. Quoted in Patterson (2001), 65.

24. Ryan (2009), 78.

25. Patterson (2001).

26. *Education Week* (2004).

27. Jencks and Mayer (1990); Schofield and Eurich-Fulcer (2004).

28. Jencks and Phillips (1998).

29. Moynihan (1965); Wilson (1987).

30. Coleman et al. (1966), 557.

31. Coleman et al. (1966), iv.

32. Coleman et al. (1966), 22.

33. Coleman et al. (1966), Chapter 3.

34. Massey and Sampson (2009).

35. Quoted in McGuinn (2006), 29.

36. McGuinn (2006).

37. Martin and McClure (1969), 6, 8.

38. Manna (2006).

39. Graham (1984), 204.

40. Martin and McClure (1969).

41. Kirst and Jung (1980).

42. Peterson and Rabe (1983).

43. Mankiw (2010).

44. McCall et al. (2006).

45. Moynihan (1973), 240.

46. Mead (2004).

47. McGuinn (2006).

48. Shober (2010), 89.

49. Personal communication, July 2005.

50. See Manna (2011) and McGuinn (2006) for excellent overviews of the passage and consequences of No Child Left Behind.

51. Abernathy (2007).

52. National Education Association (2002), 142.

53. Associated Press (2010).

54. Center on Education Policy (2008).

55. Olson (2006).

56. For example, Price (2010); Reznick (2006).

57. Peterson (2005).

58. Bush (2002).

59. Quoted in McGuinn (2006), 171.

60. See Donovan and Cross (2002).

61. Carnoy and Loeb (2002); Hanushek and Raymond (2003).

62. Hoff and Manzo (2007).

63. Fuller et al. (2007).

64. Marsh, Pane, and Hamilton (2006).

65. Witte et al. (2007).

66. See Dee and Jacob (2009).

67. Roth (1971), 287.

68. Quoted in *Milliken v. Bradley* (1974), 733.

69. "The Nation: A Supreme Court Yes to Busing" (1971), 14.

70. *Milliken v. Bradley* (1974), 741.

71. See Clotfelter (2004); Kahlenberg (2001); Ravtich (1978); Green and Pettigrew (1976).

72. Wolters (2004).

73. Ryan (2009); Rosenberg (1993).

74. Orfield (2009).

75. Wells, Duran, and White (2008).

76. Pettigrew and Tropp (2006).

77. See Wong and Nicotera (2004).

78. Guthrie and Springer (2004), 28.

79. Rumberger and Palardy (2005).

80. Armor (2002).

81. Horsford and McKenzie (2008).

82. U.S. Commission on Civil Rights (2007).

83. Hanushek and Lindseth (2009), Chapter 6.

84. Ciotti (1998).

85. Jencks and Phillips (1998); Rothstein (2004).

86. Farkas (2003); Rumberger and Palardy (2005); Tyler and Boelter (2008).

87. Orfield (2009).

88. U.S. Department of Education (2010, 2011b).

Chapter 4

1. Ohio Historical Society (2010).

2. Shober (2010), 61; Ray (1943), 6–7.

3. Murphy (1990), 56, 161.

4. Elliott (2009); Shober (2010), Chapter 4.

5. *DeRolph v. Ohio I* (1997), 5.

6. Shober (2010), 92.

7. Ohio Department of Education (1997), emphasis original.

8. Ostrom (1990).

9. Wisconsin Department of Public Instruction (2010b).

10. Ray (1943), 51.

11. Clark (1958).

12. Orr (1950), 323; O'Brien (1999).

13. Friedman (1955).

14. Friedman recognized the dilemma between democratic inclusion and provision, as in the New Kent County plan, explained in Chapter 3. Friedman (1955), 118.

15. Witte (2000).

16. Gamoran (2001). Kozol (1991) and other books by Kozol argue this point starkly.

17. Hanushek (2007).

18. Vanneman et al. (2009); Jencks and Phillips (1998).

19. Levin (2009).

20. Bowers (2009); Grant (2007).

21. Hoxby and Leigh (2004); Allegretto, Corcoran, and Mishel (2008).

22. Gamoran (2001); Bali and Alvarez (2004).

23. See Wiley et al. (2010); Springer et al. (2010).

24. Crosnoe (2009).

25. Tyler (2004); Levin (2009).

26. Chetty et al. (2010).

27. Ludwig and Miller (2005); U.S. Department of Health and Human Services, Administration for Children and Families (2010).

28. Chetty et al. (2010).

29. *McInnis v. Shapiro* (1968), 336.

30. See, for example, National Center for Education Statistics (2003).

31. Coleman et al. (1966).

32. Hanushek (2007).

33. See National Education Association (2010a); Greene and Winters (2007); Allegretto, Corcoran, and Mishel (2008).

34. *Rodriguez v. San Antonio* (1973), 41.

35. Ohio Department of Education (2011).

36. *Rodriguez v. San Antonio* (1973), 36.

37. Quoted in Padover (1939), 89.

38. Common Core State Standards Initiative (2010).

39. *Rodriguez v. San Antonio* (1973), 35.

40. *Rodriguez v. San Antonio* (1973), 36.

41. *Rodriguez v. San Antonio* (1973), 50.

42. See Reynolds (2007).

43. Koski (2003).

44. Coons, Clune, and Sugarman (1970).

45. National Center for Education Statistics (2009).

46. Taylor (2006).

47. Ohio Department of Education (1995).

48. Price (1998).

49. Bainbridge and Sundre (1997).

50. Candisky and Leonard (2003).

51. Ohio Coalition for Equity and Adequacy of School Funding (2001).

52. Reynolds (2007).

53. Odden and Picus (2008).

54. Sielke et al. (2001).

55. Sielke et al. (2001).

56. Coons, Clune, and Sugarman (1970).

57. See National Conference of State Legislatures (2005).

58. *Connecticut v. Duncan* (2010).

59. Duncombe (2006); Reschovsky and Imazeki (1998).

60. Carey (2002).

61. Figlio and Getzler (2006).

62. Aten and D'Souza (2008); also, e.g., www.payscale.com/cost-of-living-calculator.

63. Allegretto, Corcoran, and Mishel (2008).

64. See Hanushek and Lindseth (2009); Coleman et al. (1966).

65. See Goertz and Malek (1999).

66. Ohio Office of Budget and Management (2010); personal communication (March 2011).

Chapter 5

1. National Education Association (2003).

2. Sawchuk (2011).

3. Mulvihill (2010).

4. Alex (2010)

5. Alex (2010).

6. Kahlenberg (2008), B7.

7. Podair (2002), Chapter 8.

8. Callahan (1946), 38.

9. Keaton (2010).

10. Ray (1943), 10.

11. Timar (1997).

12. Ravitch (2000); Kerchner and Mitchell (1988), Chapter 3.

13. Quoted in Murphy (1990), 59.

14. Murphy (1990), Chapter 5.

15. Kahlenberg (2006).

16. See Murphy (1990), Chapter 3.

17. Olson (1965).

18. Kerchner and Mitchell (1988).

19. Freeman and Medoff (1984).

20. Quoted in Hess and West (2006), 9.

21. Offe and Weisenthal (1980).

22. Murphy (1990), 86.

23. U.S. Congress (1916), 1529.

24. Lieberman (2000); Hannaway and Rotherham (2006).

25. McDonnell and Pascal (1979), 26; Pennsylvania School Boards Association (2008).

26. Johnson et al. (2008).

27. Shober (2010).

28. Quoted in Johnson et al. (2008), 14.

29. Blanchflower and Bryson (2004), 390.

30. Cowen (2009); Hoxby (1996); Lovenheim (2009).

31. Schneider and Ingram (1993).

32. See Sniderman and Carmines (1997).

33. Podair (2001).

34. Cameron (2005), 38.

35. See Freeman (1986).

36. Hess and West (2006), 16.

37. Murphy (1990), Chapter 11.

38. Vinovskis (2000).

39. Cameron (2005), 56.

40. Murphy (1990).

41. Snyder (1993).

42. Andrews, Duncombe, and Yinger (2002).

43. Kahlenberg (2006), 12.

44. Center for Responsive Politics (2010).

45. National Education Association (2005); American Federation of Teachers (2001).

46. Cibulka (2000).

47. Colorado Education Association (2005), 9.

48. See, for example, Coleman (2001).

49. Schnitzer (2009).

50. Schnitzer (2009); Moe (2005).

51. See Brehm and Gates (1997).

52. Shober (2010).

53. Freeman and Medoff (1984).

54. For example, Schattschneider (1960); Lowi (1979); Schlozman and Tierney (1986).

55. See Coleman (2010).

56. Hess and Leal (2005); Moe (2005).

57. Antonucci (2010); Lieberman (2000).

58. See Gray and Lowery (1996).

59. Heclo (1977).

60. Quoted in Brill (2010).

61. Obama (2008); Chennault (2010).

62. Kahlenberg (2007), 79.

63. Boyd, Plank, and Sykes (2000), 181.

64. *Fox News* (2011).

65. National Center for Education Statistics (2010b), Table 7.

66. Rasmussen Reports (2011).

67. Levenson (2011); Magyar (2011).

68. Schultze and Walker (2011).

69. Walker (2011).

70. Hetzner (2011).

71. Hetzner (2011); author's data.

72. Gilbert (2011b).

73. Stein, Stultze, and Glauber (2011); Stein (2011).

74. Schultze and Walker (2011).

75. Gilbert (2011a); Public Policy Polling (2011); Marley (2011).

76. Zaller (1992); Popkin (1994).

77. Zhou (2010), 7.

78. McGuinn (2006).

79. For example, Ravitch (2000), 417.

80. Kennedy (2008).

81. Kahlenberg (2006), 18 note 101.

82. Johnson et al. (2008).

83. Exstrom (2010).

84. For example, McCabe (2010); Cibulka (2000).

85. Casey (2006), 181.

86. Quoted in Shober (2010), 78.

87. Johnson et al. (2008).

88. For example, Aikens and Barbarin (2008); Coleman et al. (1966).

89. Cameron (2005), 174.

90. Hanushek (2007).

91. Podgursky (2006).

92. Johnson et al. (2008); Lankford, Loeb, and Wyckoff (2002).

93. Honawar (2008).

94. Lankford, Loeb, and Wyckoff (2002).

95. Farkas, Johnson, and Duffett (2003), 20.

96. Jacob and Lefgren (2005); Sanders and Horn (1994).

97. Hanushek (2007), 579.

98. Quoted in Berube (1988), 145.

99. National Education Association (2011).

100. New York City Department of Education (2010).

101. *Education Week* (2009), 8.

102. Wiley et al. (2010).

103. Springer et al. (2010).

104. National Education Association (2010a); Allegretto, Corcoran, and Mishel (2008).

105. Howell, West, and Peterson (2011), 14.

Chapter 6

1. Goodlad (1984).

2. Durden (1972).

3. Sieff (2010).

4. Jordan (1995); Durden (1972).

5. Quoted in Sieff (2010).

6. Helderman and Sieff (2010); Sieff (2010).

7. National Education Association (2010b).

8. Spady (1977, 1994).

9. Bloom (1973), 10.

10. Spady (1977), 12.

11. Bickel (1994).

12. Spady and Marshall (1991), 70.

13. Quoted in Manno (1994), 5.

14. See Manno (1994); Pliska and McQuaide (1994); Boyd, Lugg, and Zahorchak (1996).

15. Sensky (1993).

16. Quoted in Shober (2010), 114.

17. Voinovich (1993b).

18. Sensky (1993).

19. Ravitch (2000).

20. National Center for History in the Schools (1992).

21. ABC News (1994).

22. Cheney (1994).

23. Quoted in Nash, Crabtree, and Dunn (1997), 5.

24. Morrison (1995).

25. Nash, Crabtree, and Dunn (1997), 6.

26. Nash (1997).

27. U.S. Congress (1995).

28. Ravitch and Schlesinger (1996).

29. Schlesinger (1996).

30. Nash (2004).

31. Wilentz (1997).

32. Nash, Crabtree, and Dunn (1997), 6.

33. Ravitch and Schlesinger (1996); see also Wilentz (1997).

34. See Timar (1997).

35. Quoted in Timar (1997), 239.

36. Bailyn (1960).

37. See Perlmann and Shirley (1991); Cremin (1970).

38. See Gaustad (1968); Marius (1999), Chapter 25.

39. Cross (1950).

40. Orr (1950), 159.

41. O'Brien (1999).

42. Shober (2010), 61.

43. Cubberley (1909), 15.

44. Murphy (1990).

45. Cubberley (1909), 63.

46. Dewey and Dewey (1915), 32.

47. Skaife (1953), 357.

48. Conant (1959), 78.

49. Coleman et al. (1966), Chapter 2.

50. Skaife (1953), 357, 362.

51. Scott (1953), 362.

52. Burris et al. (2008).

53. See Neckerman (2007); Donelan, Neal, and Jones (1994); Oakes (1985).

54. See Ravitch (2000); Hirsch (1987).

55. O'Connor (1963), 1.

56. Sanford (1982), 26.

57. U.S. Census Bureau (2009), 33.

58. See Conant (1967); Keliher (1931).

59. Gamoran and Mare (1989).

60. Burris et al. (2008); Oakes (1985).

61. Burns and Mason (2002).

62. For example, Useem (1992); Welner (2001).

63. Gamoran and Mare (1989); see also Gamoran and Hannigan (2000).

64. Hallinan (2000).

65. For example, Hansen (1964).

66. Natriello, Pallas, and Alexander (1989).

67. Gamoran and Mare (1989).

68. See Bempechat and Wells (1989).

69. Oakes, Gamoran, and Page (1992); Oakes (1990).

70. Ravitch (2010a); Ravitch and Schlesinger (1996).

71. See Smith and O'Day (1991).

72. Hood (1998).

73. Ziebarth (2004).

74. Quoted in Shober (2010), 109.

75. Weick (1976).

76. See Borman and Dowling (2010).

77. U.S. Department of Education (2010), 5, 10.

78. Bickel (1994).

79. Abernathy (2007); Glass (1978); Cizek (2001).

80. Congressional Budget Office (1986); Harnischfeger and Wiley (1975).

81. Stedman (1996), 12; see also Stedman (2004).

82. Vinovskis (1999), 6.

83. Peaker (1975); Stedman (1996).

84. National Commission on Excellence in Education (1983).

85. Stedman and Smith (1983).

86. Stedman (2004).

87. Berliner and Biddle (1995).

88. Pew Research Center for the People and the Press (2010).

89. Clinchy and Cody (1978).

90. *Time* (1980).

91. See Grubb and Lazerson (2004).

92. See Kirp and Jensen (1986).

93. See O'Connor (2010).

94. See Osborne and Gaebler (1992); Carpenter (2010).

95. Superfine (2008), 25.

96. See Smith and O'Day (1991).

97. Shober (2010).

98. Mintrom (2000).

99. Shober, Manna, and Witte (2006); Nathan (2002).

100. Voinovich (1993a); Ohio Department of Education (1997).

101. See Lusi (1997).

102. Hall (1997).

103. McGuinn (2006), 63.

104. Quoted in Vinovskis (1999), 40.

105. McGuinn (2006), Chapter 5.

106. Ravitch and Schlesinger (1996).

107. Such as in Mintrom (2000).

108. Quoted in McGuinn (2006), 171.

109. Common Core State Standards Initiative (2010).

110. U.S. Department of Education (2010), 8.

111. Duncan (2009a), 4.

112. Duncan (2010a).

113. Banchero (2011a, 2011b).

114. See Manna (2011), Chapter 7.

115. Duncan (2009a), 7.

Chapter 7

1. Clowes (2002); Fuller (2011); Kane (2010).

2. See Weimer and Vining (2011), Chapter 1.

3. Shober (2010), 60.

4. Ravitch (2000); Tyack (1974).

5. Henig (1994); Smith and Meier (1995).

6. Manna (2011), Chapter 4.

7. "California's Parent Revolution" (2010).

8. Howell (2006).

9. Moe (1985).

10. Lubienski (2000); Gutmann (1987).

11. Cameron (2005), 180.

12. See Viteritti (2007), Chapter 9; Harry and Anderson (1994).

13. Mill (1859), 132.

14. Howell (2006), 163.

15. Lee and Burkham (2003); Grogger and Neal (2000); Neal (1997); Evans and Schwab (1995); Coleman and Hoffer (1987).

16. National Center for Education Statistics (2010a).

17. Tiebout (1956).

18. Fischel (2001).

19. Greve (1999).

20. Weimer and Wolkoff (2001).

21. Fischel (2001).

22. See Patterson (2001); Clotfelter (2004), 108–116.

23. For example, Aaronson (1999).

24. Samuels (2009).

25. Rothstein (2004).

26. General Accounting Office (2002).

27. See Witte (2000), 151; Mintrom (2000).

28. Howell and Peterson (2006), 25.

29. McGuinn (2006), 171; see also Cibulka (2000).

30. Chubb and Moe (1990).

31. Meier, Stewart, and England (1989); Smrekar (2009).

32. Henig (1994); Smith and Meier (1995).

33. See Brown et al. (2004).

34. Krueger and Ziebarth (2004).

35. National Center for Education Statistics (2010a).

36. McNeil (2009); Manna (2011), Chapter 4.

37. Wells (1993); Schneider et al. (1998).

38. Armor and Peiser (1998); Hamilton and Guin (2006).

39. Howell (2006), 157.

40. McGuinn (2006), 43–44.

41. Quoted in Witte (2000), 198.

42. Howell and Peterson (2006), Chapter 7.

43. Rubenstein, Hamar, and Adelman (1992).

44. Leithwood and Menzies (1998).

45. Witte (2000).

46. Nathan (2002); Shober, Manna, and Witte (2006).

47. Corson (1990).

48. Witte, Schlomer, and Shober (2007).

49. Maxwell (2006); Mrozowski (2009); Chambers (2011).

50. Reback (2005); Carlson, Lavery, and Witte (2011).

51. Boyd, Hare, and Nathan (2002).

52. Carlson, Lavery, and Witte (2011).

53. Mill (1859), 131; Friedman (1955).

54. Stewart et al. (2009).

55. See Figlio, Hart, and Metzger (2010); Howell and Peterson (2006).

56. Castor (2011).

57. Ellis (2011).

58. Coons and Sugarman (1978).

59. See Harrison (2010); Howell and Peterson (2006).

60. Shapiro (2011).

61. Hamilton (2008).

62. Richard (2004).

63. Allen (2011); Auge (2011).

64. Harrison (2010).

65. Hirsch (1987).

66. See Henig et al. (2005).

67. See Hess et al. (1999).

68. For example, Budde (1988); Kahlenberg (2008); Smith (2001).

69. For example, Zehr (2002); Witte, Schlomer, and Shober (2007).

70. Duncan (2009b).

71. Orfield (2010a).

72. Frankenberg, Siegel-Hawley, and Wang (2010), 99, 102–103; Zimmer et al. (2009).

73. Harambee Institute of Science and Technology Charter School (2011).

74. Chubb and Moe (1990), 217.

75. Hanushek et al. (2007); Zimmer et al. (2009); Center for Research on Education Outcomes (2009).

76. Ritter et al. (2010).

77. Frankenberg, Siegel-Hawley, and Wang (2010), 99; U.S. Census Bureau (2009).

78. See Hoxby, Muraka, and Kang (2009).

79. Wisconsin Department of Public Instruction (2010a).

80. See Hess (2010).

81. Witte et al. (2007).

82. Tuttle et al. (2010).

Chapter 8

1. Gutmann (1987); Ravitch and Viteritti (2001).

2. Arrow (1963).

3. Mann (1848).

4. Grubb and Lazerson (2004), 22.

5. For example, Mills (1956); Schattschneider (1960); Lowi (1979); Scholzman and Tierney (1986), Chapter 4.

6. Marshall (1952), 325.

7. Marshall (1952), 325.

8. Lyons (2003).

9. *Milliken v. Bradley* (1974), 741.

10. Ludwig (2004).

11. Ohio Coalition for Equity and Adequacy of School Funding (2011), emphasis added.

12. Marshall (1952).

13. Quoted in Shober (2010), 98.

14. Schattschneider (1960), 40.

15. Nash, Crabtree, and Dunn (1997), 6.

16. ABC News (1994).

17. Ravitch (2010a), 223.

18. Croly (1914), 304.

19. Croly (1914), 97.

20. Clotfelter (2004), 26.

21. Buckley (1972).

22. Quoted in McGuinn (2006), 98.

23. Ravitch (2010a), Chapter 6.

24. Peterson (2005).

25. Manna (2006).

26. Cronin et al. (2007).

27. McNeil (2010a, 2010b).

References

Aaronson, Daniel. 1999. "The Effect of School Finance Reform on School Heterogeneity." *National Tax Journal* 52 (1): 5–29.

ABC News. 1994. "Good Morning America" (October 27). http://www.h-net.org/~teach/threads/standard.html. Accessed October 15, 2010.

Abernathy, Scott Franklin. 2007. *No Child Left Behind and the Public Schools.* Ann Arbor: University of Michigan Press.

Ackerman, Debra J. 2005. "Getting Teachers from Here to There: Examining Issues Related to an Early Care and Education Teacher Policy." *Early Child Research & Practice* 7 (1, Spring). http://ecrp.uiuc.edu/v7n1/ackerman.html.

Aikens, Nikki L., and Oscar Barbarin. 2008. "Socioeconomic Differences in Reading Trajectories: The Contribution of Family, Neighborhood, and School Contexts." *Journal of Educational Psychology* 100 (2, May): 235–251.

Alex, Patricia. 2010. "Teachers Take Off the Gloves." *Bergen County* (NJ) *Record*, April 9. http://www.northjersey.com/news/education/90330609_Teachers_take_off_the_gloves.html. Accessed September 1, 2010.

Allegretto, Sylvia A., Sean P. Corcoran, and Lawrence R. Mishel. 2008. *The Teaching Penalty.* Washington, DC: Economic Policy Institute.

Allen, Jaclyn. 2011. "Douglas County Schools Approve Voucher Program." *Channel 7 News*, March 15. http://www.thedenverchannel.com. Accessed July 30, 2011.

Althaus, Scott L. 1998. "Information Effects in Collective Preferences." *American Political Science Review* 92 (3, September): 545–558.

American Federation of Teachers. 2001. *State Revenue and Taxation: Issues for Supporting Public Service in the 21st Century.* Washington, DC: Author.

———. 2006. *AFT's Recommendations for No Child Left Behind.* Washington, DC: Author.

American Federation of Teachers, President's Office. 2005. "Albert Shanker Collection Overview." http://www.reuther.wayne.edu/files/LR001553_Shanker.pdf.

Andrews, Matthew, William Duncombe, and John Yinger. 2002. "Revisiting Economies of Size in American Education: Are We Any Closer to a Consensus?" *Economics of Education Review* 21 (3, June): 245–262.

Antonucci, Mike. 2010. "The Long Reach of Teachers Unions." *Education Next* 10 (4, Fall): 24–31.

Aratani, Lori. 2005. "Contentious Sex-Ed Curriculum Halted." *Washington Post,* May 6. http://www.washingtonpost.com/wp-dyn/content/article/2005/05/05/AR2005050501189.html. Accessed May 4, 2010.

Armor, David J. 2002. "Desegregation and Academic Achievement." In *School Desegregation in the 21st Century,* by Christine H. Rossel, David J. Armor, and Herbert J. Wahlberg, 147–188. Westport, CT: Praeger Publishers.

Armor, David J., and Brett M. Peiser. 1998. "Interdistrict Choice in Massachusetts." In *Learning from School Choice*, edited by Paul E. Peterson and Bryan C. Hassel, 157–186. Washington, DC: Brookings Institution Press.

Arrow, Kenneth. 1963. *Social Choice and Individual Values*. 2d ed. New Haven, CT: Yale University Press.

Associated Press. 2010. "High Court Won't Take Up No Child Left Behind Case." *Boston Globe,* June 8. http://www.boston.com/news/education/k_12/articles/2010/06/08/high_court_wont_take_up_no_child_left_behind_case/. Accessed November 8, 2010.

Aten, Betina, and Roger D'Souza. 2008. "Regional Price Parities: Comparing Price Level Differences Across Geographic Areas." *BEA Research Spotlight* (November). Washington, DC: U.S. Bureau of Economic Analysis.

Auge, Karen. 2011. "Daniels Fund Promises up to $530,000 to Help Douglas County Schools in Voucher Case." *Denver Post*, August 31.

Bailyn, Bernard. 1960. *Education in the Forming of American Society*. New York: W. W. Norton.

Bainbridge, William L., and Steven M. Sundre. 1997. "School Aid: Where's the Logic?" Columbus *Dispatch,* July 13, sec. B.

Bali, Valentina A., and R. Michael Alvarez. 2004. "The Race Gap in Student Achievement Scores: Longitudinal Evidence from a Racially Diverse School District." *Policy Studies Journal* 32 (3, August): 393–416.

Banchero, Stephane. 2011a. "States Test Education Law." *Wall Street Journal*, July 19.

———. 2011b. "Teachers Could Defer Obama Support." *Wall Street Journal*, July 2.

Bandeira de Mello, Victor, Charles Blankenship, Don McLaughlin, and Taslima Rahman. 2009. *Mapping State Proficiency Standards onto NAEP Scales: 2005–2007*. Washington, DC: Institute of Education Sciences, National Center for Education Statistics, U.S. Department of Education.

Baumgartner, Frank R., and Bryan D. Jones. 1993. *Agendas and Instability in American Politics*. Chicago: University of Chicago Press.

Baumgartner, Frank R., and Beth L. Leech. 2001. "Interest Niches and Policy Bandwagons: Patterns of Interest Group Involvement in National Politics." *Journal of Politics* 63 (4, November): 1191–1213.

Bempechat, Janine, and Amy Stuart Wells. 1989. *Trends and Issues in Urban and Minority Education, 1989*. New York: ERIC Clearinghouse on Urban Education.

Berkman, Michael B., and Eric Plutzer. 2005. *Ten Thousand Democracies: Politics and Public Opinion in America's School Districts*. Washington, DC: Georgetown University Press.

Berliner, David, and Bruce J. Biddle. 1995. *The Manufactured Crisis: Myths, Fraud, and the Attack on America's Public Schools*. New York: Addison-Wesley.

Berube, Maurice R. 1988. *Teacher Politics: The Influence of Unions*. Westport, CT: Greenwood Press.

Bickel, Frank. 1994. "Student Assessment: The Project Method Revisited." *The Clearing House* 68 (1, September): 40–42.

Billups, Andrea. 2001. "Study Backs Jeb Bush's Voucher Program." *Washington Times*, February 16, sec. A.

Blanchflower, David, and Alex Bryson. 2004. "What Effect Do Unions Have on Wages Now and Would Freeman and Medoff Be Surprised?" *Journal of Labor Research* 25 (3, Summer): 383–414.

Bloom, Benjamin S. 1973. *Every Kid Can: Learning for Mastery*. Washington, DC: College/University Press.

Borman, Geoffrey D., and Matthew Boulay, eds. 2004. *Summer Learning: Research, Policies, and Programs*. Mahwah, NJ: Lawrence Erlbaum Associates.

Borman, Geoffrey D., and Maritza Dowling. 2010. "Schools and Inequality: A Multilevel Analysis of Coleman's Equality of Educational Opportunity Data." *Teachers College Record* 112 (5, May): 1201–1246.

Boston Public Schools. 2010. *Boston Public Schools at a Glance 2009–2010*. Report 17. Boston: Boston Public Schools.

Bowers, Alex J. 2009. "Reconsidering Grades as Data for Decision Making: More Than Just Academic Knowledge." *Journal of Educational Administration* 47 (5): 609–629.

Boyd, William Lowe, Debra Hare, and Joe Nathan. 2002. *What Really Happened? Minnesota's Experience with Statewide Public School Choice Programs*. Minneapolis: Center for School Change, Hubert H. Humphrey Institute of Public Affairs, University of Minnesota.

Boyd, William Lowe, Catherine A. Lugg, and Gerald L. Zahorchak. 1996. "Social Traditionalists, Religious Conservatives, and the Politics of Outcome-Based Education: Pennsylvania and Beyond." *Education and Urban Society* 28 (6, May): 347–365.

Boyd, William Lowe, David N. Plank, and Gary Sykes. 2000. "Teachers Unions in Hard Times." In *Conflicting Missions? Teachers Unions and Educational Reform*, edited by Tom Loveless, 174–210. Washington, DC: Brooking Institution Press.

Boyer, Ernest. 1993. "In Search of Community." Speech presented at the Annual Conference of the Association for Supervision and Curriculum Development, March 26–30, Washington, DC.

Bracey, Gerald W. 2000. "A Comparison of the Performance of the Milwaukee Public Schools and School Systems in Selected Other Cities." Report 00–03. Center for Education Research, Analysis, and Innovation, University of Wisconsin–Milwaukee.

Brehm, John, and Scott Gates. 1997. *Working, Shirking, and Sabotage: Bureaucratic Response to a Democratic Public*. Ann Arbor: University of Michigan Press.

Brill, Steven. 2010. "The Teachers' Unions' Last Stand." *New York Times Magazine* (May 17). http://www.nytimes.com/2010/05/23/magazine/23Brill.html. Accessed May 24, 2010.

Brown, Heath, Jeffrey Henig, Natalie Lacireno-Paquet, and Thomas T. Holyoke. 2004. "Scale of Operations and Locus of Control in Market-Versus Mission-Oriented Charter Schools." *Social Science Quarterly* 85 (5, December): 1035–1051.

Buckley, Jack, and Mark Schneider. 2003. "Shopping for Schools: How Do Marginal Consumers Gather Information About Schools?" *Policy Studies Journal* 31 (2, May): 121–146.

Buckley, William F. 1972. "Racial Relaxation in Mississippi." *Washington Evening Star-News*, December 19, sec. A.

Budde, Ray. 1988. *Education by Charter: Restructuring School Districts*. Andover, MA: Regional Laboratory for Educational Improvement of the Northeast & Islands.

Burns, Robert B., and DeWayne A. Mason. 2002. "Class Composition and Student Achievement in Elementary Schools." *American Educational Research Journal* 39 (1, Spring): 207–233.

Burris, Carol Corbet, Ed Wiley, Kevin G. Welner, and John Murphy. 2008. "Accountability, Rigor, and Detracking: Achievement Effects of Embracing a Challenging Curriculum as a Universal Good for All Students." *Teachers College Record* 110 (3): 571–607.

Bush, George W. 2002. "President Signs Landmark No Child Left Behind Education Bill." January 8. http://georgewbush-whitehouse.archives.gov/news/releases/2002/01/20020108–1.html. Accessed November 10, 2010.

"California's Parent Revolution." 2010. *Wall Street Journal*, December 7, sec. A.

Callahan, John P. 1946. *Education in Wisconsin*. Madison, WI: Department of Public Instruction.

Cameron, Don. 2005. *The Inside Story of the Teacher Revolution in America*. Lanham, MD: Scarecrow Education.

Candisky, Catherine, and Lee Leonard. 2003. "School-funding Suit Laid to Rest." *Columbus Dispatch*, May 17, sec. A.

Carey, Kevin. 2002. *State Poverty-Based Education Funding: A Survey of Current Programs and Options for Improvement*. Washington, DC: Center on Budget and Policy Priorities.

_____. 2010. "Is Education on the Wrong Track?" *The New Republic* (March 16). http://www.tnr.com/article/politics/education-the-wrong-track-1.

Carlson, Deven, Lesley Lavery, and John F. Witte. 2011. "The Determinants of Interdistrict Enrollment Flows: Evidence from Two States." *Educational Evaluation and Policy Analysis* 33 (1, March): 76–94.

Carnoy, Martin, and Susanna Loeb. 2002. "Does External Accountability Affect Student Outcomes? A Cross-State Analysis." *Educational Evaluation and Policy Analysis* 24 (4, Winter): 305–331.

Carpenter, Daniel P. 2001. *The Forging of Bureaucratic Autonomy*. Princeton, NJ: Princeton University Press.

_____. 2010. *Reputation and Power: Organizational Image and Pharmaceutical Regulation at the FDA*. Princeton, NJ: Princeton University Press.

Casey, Leo. 2006. "The Educational Value of Democratic Voice." In *Collective Bargaining in Education*, edited by Jane Hannaway and Andrew J. Rotherham, 181–202. Cambridge, MA: Harvard Education Press.

Castor, Betty. 2011. "Don't Endanger Our Schools." *St. Petersburg Times*, January 16. http://www.tampabay.com/news/perspective/article1145521.ace. Accessed January 16, 2011.

Center for Education Reform. 2011. *Charter School Laws Across the States 2010–11*. Washington, DC: Author.

Center for Research on Education Outcomes. 2009. *Multiple Choice: Charter School Performance in 16 States*. Stanford, CA: Author.

Center for Responsive Politics. 2010. http://www.opensecrets.org/. Accessed October 12, 2010.

Center on Education Policy. 2008. *Instructional Time in Elementary Schools: A Closer Look at Changes for Specific Subjects*. Washington, DC: Center on Education Policy.

Chambers, Jennifer. 2011. "DPS, EMU Plan for Statewide District Approved." *Detroit News* (June 22). http://detnews.com/article/20110622/SCHOOLS/106220340. Accessed July 10, 2011.

Cheney, Lynne V. 1994. "The End of History." *Wall Street Journal*, October 20, A22.

Chennault, Ronald E. 2010. "Obama-Era Education Policy." *Education Week* (May 19). http://www.edweek.org/ew/articles/2010/05/19/32chennault_ep.h29.html. Accessed October 1, 2010.

Chetty, Ray, John N. Friedman, Nathaniel Hilger, Emmanuel Saez, Diane Schanzenbach, and Danny Yagan. 2010. "How Does Your Kindergarten Classroom Affect Your Earnings? Evidence from Project STAR." Working Paper (July). http://obs.rc.fas .harvard.edu/chetty/STAR_slides.pdf. Accessed August 24, 2010.

Chubb, John, and Terry M. Moe. 1990. *Politics, Markets, and America's Schools*. Washington, DC: Brookings Institution Press.

Cibulka, James G. 2000. "The NEA and School Choice." In *Conflicting Missions? Teachers Unions and Educational Reform*, edited by Tom Loveless, 150–173. Washington, DC: Brooking Institution Press.

Ciotti, Paul. 1998. "Money and School Performance: Lessons from the Kansas City Desegregation Experiment." *Cato Policy Analysis* 296 (March 16).

Citizens for a Responsible Curriculum v. Montgomery County Public Schools. 2005. Case 05–1194. Federal Circuit, District of Maryland.

Cizek, Gregory J. 2001. *Setting Performance Standards: Concepts, Methods, and Perspectives*. Mahwah, NJ: Lawrence Erlbaum Associates.

Clark, James Ira. 1958. *Education in Wisconsin*. Madison: State Historical Society of Wisconsin.

Clawson, Linda. 1995. "Falling Dropout Rate Doesn't Satisfy Benson." *Milwaukee Journal*, January 6, B1.

Clinchy, Evans, and Elisabeth Allen Cody. 1978. "If Not Public Choice, Then Private Escape." *Phi Delta Kappan* 60 (4, December): 270–273.

Clotfelter, Charles T. 2004. *After* Brown: *The Rise and Retreat of School Desegregation*. Princeton, NJ: Princeton University Press.

Clowes, George A. 2002. Interview with Annette Polly Williams. *School Reform News* (September). http://www.heartland.org/policybot/results/10124/The_Model_for _the_Nation_an_exclusive_interview_with_Annette_Polly_Williams.html. Accessed May 12, 2010.

Coleman, James S., Ernest Q. Campbell, Carol J. Hobson, James McPartland, Alexander M. Mood, Frederic D. Weinfeld, and Robert L. York. 1966. *Equality of Educational Opportunity*. Report OE-38001. Washington, DC: U.S. Department of Health, Education, and Welfare, Office of Education.

Coleman, James S., and Thomas Hoffer. 1987. *Public and Private High Schools: The Impact of Communities*. New York: Basic Books.

Coleman, James S., Sara D. Kelly, and John A. Moore. 1975. *Trends in School Segregation, 1968–73*. Report 722–03–01. Washington, DC: Urban Institute.

Coleman, John. 2001. "The Distribution of Campaign Spending Benefits Across Groups." *Journal of Politics* 63 (3, August): 916–934.

_____. 2010. "*Citizens United* and Political Outcomes." http://users.polisci.wisc.edu/coleman/Citizens%20United%20and%20Political%20Outcomes.pdf. Accessed January 20, 2011.

Colorado Education Association. 2005. *Issue Backgrounders & Positions*. Denver, CO: Colorado Education Association.

Common Core State Standards Initiative. 2010. http://www.corestandards.org/. Accessed November 15, 2010.

Conant, James B. 1959. *The American High School Today*. New York: McGraw-Hill.

_____. 1967. *The Comprehensive High School in America*. New York: McGraw-Hill.

Congressional Budget Office. 1986. *Trends in Educational Achievement* (April). Washington, DC: Government Printing Office.

Coons, John E., William H. Clune, and Stephen D. Sugarman. 1970. *Private Wealth and Public Education*. Cambridge, MA: Harvard University Press.

Coons, John E., and Stephen D. Sugarman. 1978. *Education by Choice: The Case for Family Control*. Berkeley: University of California Press.

Cooper, Harris, K. Charlton, J. C. Valentine, and L. Muhlenbruck. 2000. "Making the Most of Summer School: A Meta-Analytic and Narrative Review." *Monographs of the Society for Research Development* 65 (1): 1–118.

Corson, Ross. 1990. "Choice Ironies: Open Enrollment in Minnesota." *The American Prospect* 1 (3, September 21). http://prospect.org/cs/articles?article=choice_ironies_open_enrollment_in_minnesota. Accessed May 20, 2011.

Cowen, Joshua M. 2009. "Teacher Union and Teacher Compensation: New Evidence for the Impact of Bargaining." *Journal of Education Finance* 35 (2, Fall): 172–193.

Cremin, Lawrence A. 1970. *American Education: The Colonial Experience*. New York: Harper & Row.

Croly, Herbert D. 1914. *Progressive Democracy*. New York: Macmillan.

Cronin, John, Michael Dahlin, Deborah Atkins, and G. Gage Kingsbury. 2007. *The Proficiency Illusion*. Washington, DC: Thomas B. Fordham Institute.

Crosnoe, Robert. 2009. "Low-Income Students and the Socioeconomic Composition of Public High Schools." *American Sociological Review* 74 (5, October): 709–730.

Cross, Whitney R. 1950. *The Burned-over District: The Social and Intellectual History of Enthusiastic Religion in Western New York, 1800–1850*. Ithaca, NY: Cornell University Press.

Cubberley, Ellwood P. 1909. *Changing Conceptions of Education*. Boston: Houghton Mifflin.

Dahill-Brown, Sara Elizabeth, and Lesley E. Lavery. 2010. "Implementing Federal Policy: Confronting State Capacity and Will." Paper presented at the Midwest Political Science Association, Chicago, IL, April 24.

Dahl, Robert A. 1982. *Dilemmas of Pluralist Democracy*. New Haven, CT: Yale University Press.

Davies, Gareth. 2007. *See Government Grow: Education Politics from Johnson to Reagan*. Lawrence: University Press of Kansas.

Dee, Thomas, and Brian Jacob. 2009. "The Impact of No Child Left Behind on Student Achievement." Working Paper 15531. Washington, DC: National Bureau of Economic Research.

Delli Carpini, Michael X., and Scott Keeter. 1991. "Stability and Change in the U.S. Public's Knowledge of Politics." *Public Opinion Quarterly* 55 (3): 538–612.

_____. 1996. *What Americans Know About Politics and Why It Matters.* New Haven, CT: Yale University Press.

de Vise, Daniel. 2007a. "Board of Education Approves New Sex-Ed Curriculum." *Washington Post,* January 10. http://www.washingtonpost.com/wp-dyn/content/article/2007/01/09/AR2007010901707.html. Accessed May 4, 2010.

de Vise, Daniel. 2007b. "The Wide Spectrum of Sex-Ed Courses." *Washington Post,* March 18. http://www.washingtonpost.com/wp-dyn/content/article/2007/03/17/AR2007031701123.html. Accessed May 4, 2010.

Dewey, John, and Evelyn Dewey. 1915. *Schools of To-morrow.* New York: E. P. Dutton.

Dillon, Sam, and Tamar Lewin. 2010. "Education Chief Vies to Expand U.S. Role as Partner on Local Schools." *New York Times,* May 3. http://www.nytimes.com/2010/05/04/education/04education.html. Accessed May 3, 2010.

DiMartino, Joseph, and John H. Clarke. 2008. *Personalizing the High School Experience for Each Student.* Alexandria, VA: Association for Supervision and Curriculum Development.

Donelan, Richarde W., Gerald A. Neal, and Deneese L. Jones. 1994. "The Promise of *Brown* and the Reality of Academic Grouping: The Tracks of My Tears." *The Journal of Negro Education* 63 (3, Summer): 376–387.

Donovan, M. Suzanne, and Christopher T. Cross. 2002. *Minority Students in Special and Gifted Education.* Washington, DC: National Academic Press.

Downes, Thomas A. 2002. "Do State Governments Matter?" In *Education in the 21st Century,* edited by Yolanda K. Kodrzycki, 143–164. Boston: Federal Reserve Bank of Boston.

Duncan, Arne. 2009a. "States Will Lead the Way Towards Reform." Speech presented to the 2009 Governors Education Symposium, June 14. http://www2.ed.gov/new/speeches/2009/06/06142009.html. Accessed December 15, 2010.

_____. 2009b. "Turning Around the Bottom Five Percent." Speech presented to the National Alliance for Public Charter Schools Conference, June 22. http://www2.ed.gov/new/speeches/2009/06/06222009.html. Accessed January 10, 2011.

_____. 2010a. "Race to the Top—Integrity and Transparency Drive the Process." Blog post, January 25. http://www.ed.gov/blog/2010/01/race-to-the-top. Accessed December 20, 2010.

_____. 2010b. "Thinking Beyond Silver Bullets." Speech presented at Building Blocks for Education: Whole System Reform Conference in Toronto, Ontario, September 13. http://www.ed.gov/news/speeches/thinking-beyond-silver-bullets-obama-administrations-vision-education-reform-remarks-s. Accessed January 2, 2011.

Duncombe, William. 2006. "Responding to the Charge of Alchemy: Strategies for Evaluating the Reliability and Validity of Costing-Out Research." *Journal of Educational Finance* 32 (2, Fall): 137–169.

Dunne, Stephanie, W. Robert Reed, and James Wilbanks. 1997. "Endogenizing the Median Voter: Public Choice Goes to School." *Public Choice* 93 (1, April): 99–118.

Durden, Robert F. 1972. *The Gray and the Black: The Confederate Debate on Emancipation.* Baton Rouge: Louisiana State University Press.

Eaton, Leslie. 2011. "Judge Jolts Little Rock: Ruling Cuts Money Meant to Desegregate Schools in City at Center of 1957 Fight." *Wall Street Journal,* June 16, A3.

Education Week. 2004. "Timeline." (February 18): 23.

_____. 2009. "Spotlight: On Pay for Performance" (May). Bethesda, MD: Editorial Projects in Education.

Elliott, Michael. 2009. "The Jennings School." *Past Pursuits* 8 (4, Winter): 2–4.

Elliott, Scott. 2008. "Strickland Rips Zelman; Wick Responds." *Dayton Daily News "Get on the Bus" Blog*, March 17. http://www.daytondailynews.com/o/content/shared -gen/blogs/dayton/education/entries/2008/03/17/strickland_rips.html. Accessed January 4, 2011.

Ellis, John G. 2011. "Vouchers Don't Mean Better Test Scores." *Indianapolis Star*, January 7. http://www.indystar.com/apps/pbcs.dll/article?AID=2011101090339. Accessed January 16, 2011.

Elmore, Richard F. 1996. "Getting to Scale with Good Educational Practice." *Harvard Educational Review* 66 (1, Spring): 1–27.

Evans, William N., and Robert M. Schwab. 1995. "Finishing High School and Starting College: Do Catholic Schools Make a Difference?" *The Quarterly Journal of Economics* 110 (4, November): 941–974.

Exstrom, Michelle. 2010. "The A+ Teacher." *State Legislatures* (September): 20–23.

Farkas, George. 2003. "Racial Disparities and Discrimination in Education: What We Know, How Do We Know It, and What Do We Need to Know?" *Teachers College Record* 105 (6, August): 1119–1146.

Farkas, Steve, Jean Johnson, and Ann Duffett. 2003. *Stand by Me: What Teachers Really Think about Unions, Merit Pay and Other Professional Matters*. New York: Public Agenda.

Figlio, David N., and Lawrence S. Getzler. 2006. "Accountability, Ability and Disability: Gaming the System." In *Improving School Accountability: Check-ups of Choice?* edited by Timothy Gronberg and Dennis W. Jansen, 35–49. San Diego, CA: JAI Press.

Figlio, David, Cassandra M. Hart, and Molly Metzger. 2010. "Who Uses a Means-Tested Scholarship, and What Do They Choose?" *Economics of Education Review* 29 (2, April): 301–317.

Finn, Chester E., and Amber M. Winkler. 2011. "The Anachronisms of School Boards." *Education Gadfly* 11 (6, February 10).

Finn, Chester E., and Lisa Graham Keegan. 2004. "Lost at Sea." *Education Next* (3, Summer): 15–17.

Fischel, William A. 2001. *The Homevoter Hypothesis: How Home Values Influence Local Government Taxation, School Finance, and Land-Use Policies*. Cambridge, MA: Harvard University Press.

The Foundation for Educational Choice. 2011. "Milton Friedman." http://www.ed choice.org/The-Friedmans/Milton-Friedman-s-Bio.aspx.

Fox News. 2011. "Christie Calls Teachers Union Thugs." (April 7). http://www.myfox philly.com/dpp/news/politics/local_politics/Christie_Calls_Teachers_Union_Thugs _040711. Accessed June 23, 2011.

Frankenberg, Erica, Genevieve Siegel-Hawley, and Jia Wang. 2010. *Choice without Equity: Charter School Segregation and the Need for Civil Rights Standards*. Los Angeles, CA: The Civil Rights Project at UCLA.

Franklin, Mark N. 2001. "Electoral Participation." In *Controversies in Voting Behavior*, 4th ed., edited by Richard G. Niemi and Herbert F. Weisberg, 83–99. Washington, DC: CQ Press.

Freeman, Richard B. 1986. "Unionism Comes to the Public Sector." *Journal of Economic Literature* 24 (1, March): 41–86.

Freeman, Richard B., and James L. Medoff. 1984. *What Do Unions Do?* New York: Basic Books.

Friedman, Milton. 1955. "The Role of Government in Education." In *Economics and the Public Interest*, by Robert A. Solow, 123–144. New Brunswick, NJ: Rutgers Press.

_____. 1985/2004. In *Lives of the Laureates*, 4th ed., edited by William Breit and Barry T. Hirsch, 65–77. Cambridge, MA: MIT Press.

Fuller, Bruce, and Richard F. Elmore. 1996. *Who Chooses? Who Loses? Culture, Institutions and the Unequal Effects of School Choice.* New York: Teachers College Press.

Fuller, Bruce, Joseph Wright, Kathryn Gesicki, and Erin Kang. 2007. "Gauging Growth: How to Judge No Child Left Behind?" *Educational Researcher* 36 (5, June): 268–278.

Fuller, Howard. 2011. "Keep Intact the Mission of Choice Program." *Milwaukee Journal Sentinel*, April 23. http://www.jsonline.com/news/opinion/120515559.html. Accessed April 24, 2011.

Gamoran, Adam. 2001. "American Schooling and Educational Inequality: A Forecast for the 21st Century." *Sociology of Education* 74 (Extra): 135–153.

Gamoran, Adam, and Eileen C. Hannigan. 2000. "Algebra for Everyone? Benefits of College-Preparatory Mathematics for Students with Diverse Abilities in Early Secondary School." *Educational Evaluation and Policy Analysis* 22 (3, September): 241–254.

Gamoran, Adam, and Daniel A. Long. 2006. "Equality of Educational Opportunity: A 40-Year Retrospective." WCER Working Paper 2006–9. Madison: Wisconsin Center for Education Research.

Gamoran, Adam, and Robert D. Mare. 1989. "Secondary School Tracking and Educational Inequality: Compensation, Reinforcement, or Neutrality?" *The American Journal of Sociology* 94 (5, March): 1146–1183.

Gaustad, Edwin Scott. 1968. *The Great Awakening in New England.* Chicago: Quadrangle Books.

Gehring, John. 2005. "Dips in Enrollment Posing Challenges for Urban Districts." *Education Week* (March 12): 1.

General Accounting Office. 2002. *Nursing Homes: Quality of Care More Related to Staffing the Spending* (June 13). Washington, DC: Author. http://www.gao.gov/new.items/d02431r.pdf. Accessed January 17, 2010.

Georgia Office of Planning and Budget. 2000. *Budget Report, Fiscal 2001.* Atlanta, GA: Author.

Gilbert, Craig. 2011a. "Loved by Republicans, Loathed by Democrats, Scott Walker Remains in a Political Class by Himself." *Milwaukee Journal Sentinel*, June 5. http://www.jsonline.com/blogs/news/123198683.html. Accessed June 6, 2011.

_____. 2011b. "Public Employees Are Wild Card on April 5 and Beyond." *Milwaukee Journal Sentinel*, March 27. http://www.jsonline.com/news/statepolitics/118750859.html. Accessed March 27, 2011.

Gilens, Martin. 2001. "Political Ignorance and Collective Policy Preferences." *American Political Science Review* 95 (2, June): 379–396.

Gill, Brian, P. Mike Timpane, Karen E. Ross, Dominic J. Brewer, and Kevin Booker. 2007. *Rhetoric versus Reality: What We Know and What We Need to Know about Vouchers and Charter Schools.* 2d ed. Santa Monica, CA: RAND Corporation.

Gillum, Jack, and Marisol Bello. 2011. "When Standardized Test Scores Soared in D.C., Were the Gains Real?" *USA Today*, March 27. www.usatoday.com.

Glass, Eugene V. 1978. "Standards and Criteria." *Journal of Educational Measurement* 15: 237–261.

Goertz, Margaret, and Edward Malek. 1999. "In Search of Excellence for All: The Courts and New Jersey School Finance Reform." *Journal of Education Finance* 25 (1, Summer): 5–32.

Goodlad, John I. 1984. *A Place Called School*. New York: McGraw-Hill.

Gordon, William M. 1994. "The Implementation of Desegregation Plans Since *Brown*." *The Journal of Negro Education* 62 (3, Summer): 310–322.

Graham, Hugh Davis. 1984. *The Uncertain Triumph: Federal Education Policy in the Kennedy and Johnson Years*. Chapel Hill: University of North Carolina Press.

Grant, Darren. 2007. "Grades as Information." *Economics of Education Review* 26 (2, April): 201–214.

Gray, Virginia, and David Lowery. 1996. *The Population Ecology of Interest Representation: Lobbying Communities in the American States*. Ann Arbor: University of Michigan Press.

Gray, Virginia, David Lowery, Matthew Fellowes, and Andrea McAtee. 2004. "Public Opinion, Public Policy, and Organized Interests in the American States." *Political Research Quarterly* 57 (3, September): 411–420.

Green, Robert L., and Thomas F. Pettigrew. 1976. "Urban Desegregation and White Flight: A Response to Coleman." *Phi Delta Kappan* 57 (6, February): 399–402.

Greene, Jay P. 2010. "So Much for the Evidence." *City Journal* (February 3). http://www.city-journal.org/2010/eon0203jg.html. Accessed May 6, 2010.

Greene, Jay P., and Marcus A. Winters. 2007. "How Much are Public School Teachers Paid?" Civic Report 50 (January). New York: Manhattan Institute.

Greve, Michael S. 1999. *Real Federalism: Why It Matters, How It Could Happen*. Washington, DC: AEI Press.

Grogger, Jeffrey, and Derek Neal. 2000. "Further Evidence on the Benefits of Catholic Secondary Schooling." In *Brookings/Wharton Papers on Urban Affairs*, 151–193. Washington, DC: Brookings Institution Press.

Grubb, W. Norton, and Marvin Lazerson. 2004. *The Education Gospel: The Economic Power of Schooling*. Cambridge, MA: Harvard University Press.

Guthrie, James W., and Matthew G. Springer. 2004. "Returning to Square One: From *Plessy* to *Brown* and Back to *Plessy*." *Peabody Journal of Education* 79 (2): 5–32.

Gutmann, Amy. 1987. *Democratic Education*. Princeton, NJ: Princeton University Press.

Halberstam, Michael J. 1952. "James Bryant Conant: The Right Man." *Harvard Crimson*, June 19.

Hall, Andy. 1997. "School Standards Get Fine-tuning; McCallum Says Out-of-State Experts Will Edit the Standards." *Wisconsin State Journal* (August 3): sec. C.

Hallinan, Maureen T. 2000. "Ability Group Effects on High School Learning Outcomes." Paper presented at the American Sociological Association, Washington, DC, August 15.

Hamilton, Laura S., and Kacey Guin. 2006. "Understanding How Families Choose Schools." In *Getting Choice Right: Ensuring Equity and Efficiency in Education Policy*, edited by Julian R. Betts and Tom Loveless, 40–60. Washington, DC: Brookings Institution Press.

Hamilton, Scott W., ed. 2008. *Who Will Save America's Urban Catholic Schools?* Washington, DC: Thomas B. Fordham Institute.

Hannaway, Jane, and Andrew J. Rotherham, eds. 2006. *Collective Bargaining in Education.* Cambridge, MA: Harvard Education Press.

Hansen, Carl F. 1964. "A Defense of the Track System." *Equity & Excellence in Education* 2 (3): 48–49.

Hanushek, Eric A. 2007. "The Single Salary Schedule and Other Issues of Teacher Pay." *Peabody Journal of Education* 82 (4, October): 574–586.

Hanushek, Erik A., John F. Kain, Steven G. Rivkin, and Gregory F. Branch. 2007. "Charter School Quality and Parental Decision Making with School Choice." *Journal of Public Economics* 91 (5–6, June): 823–848.

Hanushek, Eric. A., and Alfred A. Lindseth. 2009. *Schoolhouses, Courthouses, and Statehouses.* Princeton, NJ: Princeton University Press.

Hanushek, Eric A., and Margaret E. Raymond. 2003. "Lessons About the Design of State Accountability Systems." In *No Child Left Behind? The Politics and Practice of Accountability*, edited by Paul E. Peterson and Martin R. West, 172–151. Washington, DC: Brookings.

Hanushek, Eric A., and Julie A. Somers. 2001. "Schooling, Inequality, and the Impact of Government." In *The Causes and Consequences of Increasing Inequality*, edited by Finis Welch, 169–199. Chicago: University of Chicago Press.

Harambee Institute of Science and Technology Charter School. 2011. "Harambee Excellence!" http://www.histcs.org/. Accessed January 18, 2011.

Harnischfeger, Annegret, and David E. Wiley. 1975. *Achievement Test Score Decline: Do We Need to Worry?* Chicago: ML-Group for Policy Studies in Education.

Harrison, David. 2010. "Private-school Vouchers Return to Education Agenda." *Statesline* (December 21). http://www.statesline.org/live/printable/story?contentId =536771. Accessed January 11, 2011.

Harry, Beth, and Mary G. Anderson. 1994. "The Disproportionate Placement of African American Males in Special Education Programs: A Critique of the Process." *Journal of Negro Education* 63 (4): 602–620.

Haskins, Ron. 2009. "Moynihan Was Right: Now What?" In *The Moynihan Report Revisited: Lessons and Reflections after Four Decades*, edited by Douglas S. Massey and Robert J. Sampson, 281–314. Los Angeles: Sage.

Heclo, Hugh. 1977. "Political Executives and the Washington Bureaucracy." *Political Science Quarterly* 92 (Fall): 395–424.

Helderman, Rosalind S., and Kevin Sieff. 2010. "Va. to Reevaluate Adoption Process for Schoolbooks." *Washington Post*, October 27, sec. B.

Henig, Jeffrey. 1994. *Rethinking School Choice: Limits of the Market Metaphor.* Princeton, NJ: Princeton University Press.

———. 2009. "Mayors, Governors, and Presidents: The New Education Executive and the End of Educational Exceptionalism." *Peabody Journal of Education* 84 (3, August): 283–299.

Henig, Jeffrey, Thomas T. Holyoke, Heath Brown, and Natalie Lacireno-Paquet. 2005. "The Influence of Founder Type On Charter School Structures and Operations." *American Journal of Education* 111 (4, August): 487–522.

Henry, Gary, Craig S. Gordon, and Dana K. Rickman. 2006. "Early Education Policy Alternatives: Comparing Quality and Outcomes of Head Start and State Prekindergarten." *Educational Evaluation and Policy Analysis* 28 (1, Spring): 77–99.

Hernandez, Nelson. 2007. "Passionate as Ever, Grasmick Vows to Stay." *Washington Post*, December 16. http://www.washingtonpost.com/wp-dyn/content/article/2007/12/15/AR2007121500772.html. Accessed January 4, 2011.

Herrnstein, Richard J., and Charles Murray. 1994. *The Bell Curve: Intelligence and Class Structure in American Life*. New York: Free Press.

Hess, Frederick M. 2008. "Looking for Leadership: Assessing the Case for Mayoral Control of Urban Schools." *American Journal of Education* 114 (2): 219–245.

_____. 2010. "Does School Choice 'Work'?" *National Affairs* (Fall): 35–53.

Hess, Frederick M., and David L. Leal. 2005. "School House Politics: Expenditures, Interests, and Competition in School Board Elections." In *Besieged: School Boards and the Future of Education Politics*, edited by William G. Howell. Washington, D.C.: Brookings, 228–254.

Hess, Frederick M., and Olivia Meeks. 2010. *School Boards Circa 2010: Governance in the Accountability Era*. Alexandria, VA: National Association of School Boards.

Hess, Frederick M., and Martin R. West. 2006. *A Better Bargain: Overhauling Teacher Collective Bargaining for the 21st Century*. Cambridge, MA: Program on Education Policy & Governance, Harvard University.

Hetzner, Amy. 2011. "Protesting Teachers Force Some Schools to Cancel Class." *Milwaukee Journal Sentinel*, February 18. http://www.jsonline.com/news/education/116452478.html. Accessed February 18, 2011.

Hirsch, E. D., Jr. 1987. *Cultural Literacy*. New York: Vintage Books.

_____. 2009. *The Making of Americans: Democracy and Our Schools*. New Haven, CT: Yale University Press.

Hochschild, Jennifer L., and Nathan Scovronick. 2004. *The American Dream and the Public Schools*. New York: Oxford University Press.

Hoff, David J., and Kathleen Manzo. 2007. "Bush Claims About NCLB Questioned." *Education Week* (March 9).

Holcombe, Randall, and Lawrence W. Kenny. 2007. "Evidence on Voter Preferences from Unrestricted Referenda." *Public Choice* 127 (1, April): 197–215.

Honawar, Vaishali. 2008. "Model Plan of Merit Pay in Ferment." *Education Week* (July 30).

Hood, Christopher. 1998. *The Art of the State: Culture, Rhetoric and Public Management*. New York: Oxford University Press.

Horsford, Sonya Douglass, and Kathryn Bell McKenzie. 2008. "'Sometimes I Feel Like the Problems Started with Desegregation': Exploring Black Superintendent Perspectives on Desegregation Policy." *International Journal of Qualitative Studies in Education* 21 (5, September): 443–455.

Howell, William G. 2006. "Switching Schools? A Closer Look at Parents' Initial Interest in and Knowledge About the Choice Provisions of No Child Left Behind." *Peabody Journal of Education* 81 (1): 140–179.

Howell, William G., and Paul E. Peterson. 2006. *The Education Gap: Vouchers and Urban Schools*. Rev. ed. Washington, DC: Brookings Institution Press.

Howell, William G., Martin R. West, and Paul E. Peterson. 2011. "The Public Weighs in on School Reform." *Education Next* 11 (4, Fall): 11–22.

Hoxby, Caroline M. 1996. "How Teacher Unions Affect Educational Production." *Quarterly Journal of Economics* 111: 671–718.

Hoxby, Caroline, and Andrew Leigh. 2004. "Pulled Away or Pushed Out? Explaining the Decline of Teacher Aptitude in the United States." *American Economic Review* 94 (2, November): 236–240.

Hoxby, Caroline, Sonali Muraka, and Jenny Kang. 2009. *How New York City's Charter Schools Affect Achievement*. Cambridge, MA: New York City Charter Schools Evaluation Project.

Huntington, Samuel P. 1968. *Political Order in Changing Societies*. New Haven, CT: Yale University Press.

"The Inspector General." 1959. *Time* (September 14).

Jacob, Brian A., and Lars Lefgren. 2005. "Principals as Agents: Subjective Performance Measurement in Education." NBER Working Paper 11463. Cambridge, MA: National Bureau of Economic Research.

"James Coleman: Sociology." 1995. *University of Chicago Chronicle* 14 (March), http://chronicle.uchicago.com/950330/coleman.shtml.

Jencks, Christopher L., and Susan E. Mayer. 1990. "The Social Consequences of Growing Up in a Poor Neighborhood." In *Inner-City Poverty in the United States*, edited by Laurence Lynn and Michael McGeary, 111–186. Washington, DC: National Academy Press.

Jencks, Christopher L., and Meredith Phillips, eds. 1998. *The Black-White Test Score Gap*. Washington, DC: Brookings Institution Press.

Jensen, Arthur. 1969. "How Much Can We Boost I.Q. and Scholastic Achievement?" *Harvard Educational Review* 33 (1, February): 1–123.

Jensen, Arthur, and Frank Miele. 2002. *Intelligence, Race and Genetics: Conversations with Arthur R. Jensen*. Boulder, CO: Westview Press.

Johnson, Susan Moore, Morgen L. Donaldson, Mindy Sick Munger, John P. Papay, and Emily Kalejs Qazilbash. 2008. "The Challenge of Leading Two Generations Within the Teachers Union." Presented at the American Educational Research Association, New York City, March.

Jordan, Ervin L. 1995. *Black Confederates and Afro-Yankees in Civil War Virginia*. Charlottesville: University of Virginia Press.

Kagan, J. 2002. "Empowerment and Education: Civil Rights, Expert-Advocates, and Parent Politics in Head Start, 1964–1980." *Teachers College Record* 104 (3): 516–562.

Kahlenberg, Richard D. 2001. "Learning from James Coleman." *Public Interest* 144 (Summer): 54–72.

_____. 2006. "The History of Collective Bargaining among Teachers." In *Collective Bargaining in Education*, edited by Jane Hannaway and Andrew J. Rotherham, 7–25. Cambridge, MA: Harvard Education Press.

_____. 2007. *Tough Liberal: Albert Shanker and the Battles of Schools, Unions, Race, and Democracy*. New York: Columbia University Press.

_____. 2008. "Ocean Hill-Brownsville, 40 Years Later." *The Chronicle of Higher Education* 54 (April 25): B7.

_____. 2011. "Still Waiting for Superwoman." *Slate* (February 21). http://www.slate.com.

Kane, Eugene. 2010. "Rep. Williams Fought for MPS Kids Her Own Way." *Milwaukee Journal Sentinel*, May 24. http://www.jsonline.com/news/milwaukee/94796089.html. Accessed June 14, 2011.

Keaton, Patrick. 2010. *Numbers and Types of Public Elementary and Secondary Local Education Agencies From the Common Core of Data: School Year 2008–09* (NCES 2010–346). Washington, DC: National Center for Education Statistics, Institute of Education Sciences, U.S. Department of Education.

Keliher, Alice V. 1931. *A Critical Study of Homogeneous Grouping, with a Critique of Measurement as the Basis for Measurement.* New York: Teachers College Press.

Kennedy, Edward M. 2008. "How to Fix 'No Child'." *Washington Post*, January 7. www.washingtonpost.com/wp-dyn/content/2008/01/06/AR2008010601828_pf.html. Accessed October 1, 2010.

Kerchner, Charles T., and Douglas E. Mitchell. 1988. *The Changing Idea of a Teachers' Union.* London: The Falmer Press.

King, Neil, Jr. 2010. "Only Two States Win Race to Top." *Wall Street Journal*, March 30, A1.

Kingdon, John W. 2003. *Agendas, Alternatives, and Public Policies.* New York: Longman.

Kirp, David L., and Donald N. Jensen, eds. 1986. *School Days, Rule Days: The Legalization and Regulation of Education.* Philadelphia, PA: The Falmer Press.

Kirst, Michael, and Richard Jung. 1980. "The Utility of a Longitudinal Approach in Assessing Implementation: A Thirteen-Year View of Title I, ESEA." *Educational Evaluation and Policy Analysis* 2 (5, September): 17–34.

Koski, William S. 2003. "Of Fuzzy Standards and Institutional Constraints: A Re-Examination of the Jurisprudential History of Educational Finance Reform Litigation." *Santa Clara Law Review* 43: 1185–1298.

Kozol, Jonathan. 1991. *Savage Inequalities.* New York: Crown Publishers.

Krueger, Carl, and Todd Ziebarth. 2004. *School Choice.* Report GP-02–08W. Denver, CO: Education Commission of the States.

Lankford, Hamilton, Susanna Loeb, and James Wyckoff. 2002. "Teacher Sorting and the Plight of Urban Schools: A Descriptive Analysis." *Educational Evaluation and Policy Analysis* 24 (1, Spring): 37–62.

Lau, Richard R., David J. Andersen, and David P. Redlawsk. 2008. "An Exploration of Correct Voting in Recent U.S. Presidential Elections." *American Journal of Political Science* 52 (2, April): 395–411.

Lee, Valerie E., and David T. Burkham. 2003. "Dropping Out of High School: The Role of School Organization and Structure." *American Educational Research Journal* 40 (2, Summer): 353–393.

Leech, Beth L., Frank R. Baumgartner, Timothy M. La Pira, and Nicholas A. Semanko. 2005. "Drawing Lobbyists to Washington: Government Activity and the Demand for Advocacy." *Political Research Quarterly* 58 (1, March): 19–30.

Leithwood, Kenneth, and Teresa Menzies. 1998. "Forms and Effects of School-Based Management: A Review." *Educational Policy* 12 (3, May): 325–346.

Levenson, Michael. 2011. "House Votes to Restrict Unions." *Boston Globe*, April 27. http://articles.boston.com/2011–04–27/news/29479557_1_unions-object-labor -unions-health-care. Accessed July 25, 2011.

Levin, Henry M. 2009. "The Economic Payoff to Investing in Educational Justice." *Educational Researcher* 38 (1): 5–20.

Lieberman, Myron. 2000. *The Teacher Unions*. San Francisco, CA: Encounter Books.

Linn, Robert. 1998. *Assessments and Accountability*. Report 490. Los Angeles: Center for the Study of Evaluation at the University of California, Los Angeles.

Lodge, Milton, and Marco R. Steenbergen. 1995. "The Responsive Voter: Campaign Information and the Dynamics of Candidate Evaluation." *American Political Science Review* 89 (2, June): 309–326.

Logan, John. 2004. "Resegregation in the American Public Schools? Not in the 1990s." Report. Albany, NY: Lewis Mumford Center for Comparative Urban and Regional Research, University at Albany.

Lovenheim, Michael F. 2009. "The Effect of Teachers' Unions on Education Production: Evidence From Union Certifications in Three Midwestern States." *Journal of Labor Economics* 24 (4, October): 525–587.

Lowi, Theodore. 1979. *The End of Liberalism: The Second Republic of the United States*. 2d. ed. New York: W. W. Norton.

Lubienski, Christopher. 2000. "Wither the Common Good? A Critique of Home Schooling." *Peabody Journal of Education* 75 (1 & 2): 207–232.

Ludwig, Jack. 2004. "Race and Education: The 50th Anniversary of *Brown v. Board of Education*" (April 27). http://www.gallup.com/poll/11521/Race-Education-50th -Anniversary-Brown-Board-Education.aspx. Accessed January 21, 2011.

Ludwig, Jens, and Douglas Miller. 2005. "Does Head Start Improve Children's Life Chances? Evidence from a Regression Discontinuity Design." Working Paper 11702. New York: National Bureau of Economic Research.

Lusi, Susan. 1997. *The Role of State Departments of Education in Complex School Reform*. New York: Teachers College Press.

Lyons, Linda. 2003. "Gallup Brain: The Darkest Hours of Racial Unrest" (June 3). http://www.gallup.com/poll/8539/Gallup-Brain-Darkest-Hours-Of-Racial -Unrest.aspx. Accessed January 21, 2011.

Madison, James. 1788/1987. *The Federalist Papers*, edited by Isaac Kramnick. New York: Penguin Books.

Magyar, Mark J. 2011. "Collective Bargaining a Casualty of the Christie-Sweeney Deal." *NJ Spotlight* (June 16). http://www.njspotlight.com/stories/11/0616/0319/. Accessed July 20, 2011.

Mankiw, N. Gregory. 2010. "Crisis Economics." *National Affairs* (Summer): 21–32.

Mann, Horace. 1848. "Report No. 12 of the Massachusetts School Board." http://www2.volstate.edu/socialscience/FinalDocs/coming/hmann.htm. Accessed January 28, 2011.

Manna, Paul. 2006. *School's In: Federalism and the National Education Agenda*. Washington, DC: Georgetown University Press.

_____. 2011. *Collision Course: Federal Education Policy Meets State and Local Realities*. Washington, DC: CQ Press.

Manno, Bruno V. 1994. "The New School Wars: Battles over Outcome-Based Education." *Phi Delta Kappan* 76 (9, May): 720–726.

Marcotte, Dave E., and Benjamin Hansen. 2010. "Time for School?" *Education Next* 10 (1, Winter): 52–59.

Margo, Robert A. 1990. *Race and Schooling in the South, 1880–1950.* Chicago: University of Chicago Press.

Marius, Richard. 1999. *Martin Luther: The Christian Between God and Death.* Cambridge, MA: Harvard University Press.

Marley, Patrick. 2011. "New Poll Reflects Divide on Bargaining Limits." *Milwaukee Journal Sentinel,* September 20. http://www.jsonline.com/news/statepolitics/13017 3963.html. Accessed September 20, 2011.

Marsden, Peter V. 2005. "The Sociology of James S. Coleman." *Annual Review of Sociology* 31 (January): 1–24.

Marsh, Julie A., John F. Pane, and Laura S. Hamilton. 2006. *Making Sense of Data-Driven Decision Making in Education.* Santa Monica, CA: RAND.

Marshall, Thurgood. 1952. "An Evaluation of Recent Efforts to Achieve Racial Integration in Education Through Resort to the Courts." *Journal of Negro Education* 21 (3, Summer): 316–327.

Martin, Ruby, and Phyllis McClure. 1969. *Title I of ESEA: Is It Helping Poor Children?* Washington, DC, and New York: Washington Research Project and NAACP Legal Defense and Education Fund.

Massachusetts. 1647. *School Laws.*

Massey, Douglas S., and Robert J. Sampson. 2009. "Moynihan Redux: Legacies and Lessons." *Annals of the American Academy of Political and Social Science* 621 (1, January): 6–27.

Maxwell, L. 2006. "Detroit Schools Struggle to Stem Student Loss." *Education Week* 25 (42): 1, 20.

McCabe, Cynthia. 2010. "New Study: Merit Pay Does Not Boost Student Achievement." *NEA Today* (September 21). http://neatoday.org/2010/09/21/new-study-merit-pay -does-not-boost-student-achivement/. Accessed October 4, 2010.

McCall, Martha S., Carl Houser, John Cronin, G. Gage Kingsbury, and Ronald Houser. 2006. *Achievement Gaps: An Examination of Differences in Student Achievement and Growth.* Lake Oswego, OR: Northwest Evaluation Association.

McClatchy Washington Bureau. 2010. "Segregation Drove S. Carolina 'Golden Age' of School Spending" (February 9). http://www.mcclatchydc.com/2010/02/09/v-print/. Accessed October 19, 2010.

McCubbins, Mathew D., and Thomas Schwartz. 1984. "Policy Patrols vs. Fire Alarms." *American Journal of Political Science* 28 (1, March): 165–179.

McDonnell, Lorraine, and Anthony Pascal. 1979. *Organized Teachers in America's Schools.* Santa Monica, CA: RAND Corporation.

McGuinn, Patrick J. 2006. *No Child Left Behind and the Transformation of Federal Education Policy, 1965–2005.* Lawrence: The University Press of Kansas.

McNeil, Michelle. 2009. "Rural Areas See Policy Tilt." *Education Week* 29 (2): 1.

———. 2010a. "15 States Plus D.C. Are Named Race to the Top Finalists." *Education Week* (March 4). http://blogs.edweek.org/edweek/campaign-k-12/2010/03/ xx_states_are_named_race_to_th.html. Accessed January 20, 2011.

_____. 2010b. "Updated: Delaware and Tennessee Win Race to Top." *Education Week* (March 29). http://blogs.edweek.org/edweek/campaign-k-12/2010/03/st_st_and_st _win_race_to_the_t.html. Accessed January 20, 2011.

Mead, Lawrence. 2004. *Government Matters: Welfare Reform in Wisconsin*. Princeton, NJ: Princeton University Press.

Meier, Kenneth J., Joseph Stewart Jr., and Robert E. England. 1989. *Race, Class, and Education: The Politics of Second-Generation Discrimination*. Madison: University of Wisconsin Press.

Mill, John Stuart. 1859. *On Liberty*. 1929 ed. London: Watts & Co.

Mills, C. Wright. 1956. *The Power Elite*. New York: Oxford University Press.

Mintrom, Michael M. 2000. *Policy Entrepreneurs and School Choice*. Washington, DC: Georgetown University Press.

Moe, Terry M. 1985. "The Control and Feedback in Economic Regulation: The Case of the NLRB." *American Political Science Review* 79 (4): 1094–1116.

_____. 2005. "Teacher Unions and School Board Elections." In *Besieged: School Boards and the Future of Education Politics*, edited by William G. Howell, 254–287. Washington, DC: Brookings Institution Press.

Morrison, Bob. 1995. *Let Freedom Ring*. Washington, DC: Family Research Council.

Moynihan, Daniel Patrick. 1965. *The Negro Family: The Case for National Action*. Washington, DC: Office of Planning and Research, U.S. Department of Labor.

_____. 1973. *The Politics of Guaranteed Income*. New York: Vintage Books.

Mrozowski, Jennifer. 2009. "Detroit Public Schools' Board Drops Fight Against State Takeover." *Detroit News*, January 9. http://detnews.com/article/20090109/SCHOOLS/ 091090397. Accessed July 10, 2011.

Mulvihill, Geoff. 2010. "In NJ School Cut Debate, Insults Overshadow Issues." *Associated Press*, April 20.

Murphy, Marjorie. 1990. *Blackboard Unions: The AFT and the NEA, 1900–1980*. Ithaca, NY: Cornell University Press.

Nash, Gary B. 1997. "Reflections on the National History Standards." *National Forum* 77: 14–18.

_____. 2004. "Lynne Cheney's Attack on the History Standards, 10 Years Later." *History News Network* (November 8). http://hnn.us/articles/8418.html. Accessed December 14, 2010.

Nash, Gary B., Charlotte A. Crabtree, and Ross E. Dunn. 1997. *History on Trial: Culture Wars and the Teaching of the Past*. New York: Alfred A. Knopf.

Nathan, Joe. 2002. "Minnesota and the Charter Public School Idea." In *The Charter School Landscape*, edited by Sandra Vergari, 17–31. Pittsburgh, PA: Pittsburgh University Press.

Nathan, Richard P., ed. 2007. "How Should We Read the Evidence About Head Start? Three Views." *Journal of Policy Analysis and Management* 26 (3, Summer): 673–689.

"The Nation: A Supreme Court Yes to Busing." 1971. *Time* (May 3).

National Alliance for Public Charter Schools. 2011. "Dashboard." http://www.public charters.org/dashboard/. Accessed January 29, 2011.

National Association of State Boards of Education. 2011. *State Education Governance*. Washington, DC: Author.

National Center for Education Statistics. 2003. *Developments in School Finance: 2001–02* (NCES 2003–403). Edited by William J. Fowler. Washington, D.C.: National Center for Education Statistics, U.S. Department of Education.

_____. 2009. *Digest of Education Statistics 2009*. Washington, DC: Government Printing Office.

_____. 2010a. "Common Core of Data." http://nces.ed.gov/ccd.

_____.2010b. "National Public Education Financial Survey FY2008." http://nces .ed.gov/pubs2010/expenditures/index.asp. Accessed July 20, 2011.

_____. 2011. *Condition of Education 2011*. Washington, DC: Author.

National Center for History in the Schools. 1992. *Lessons from History*. Los Angeles, CA: Author.

National Commission on Excellence in Education. 1983. *A Nation at Risk: The Imperative for Educational Reform*. http://www.ed.gov/pubs/NatAtRisk/risk.html. Accessed April 21, 2010.

National Conference of State Legislatures. 2005. *Task Force on No Child Left Behind: Final Report*. Washington, DC: National Conference of State Legislatures.

_____. 2010. "Initiative & Referendum Legislation." http://www.ncsl.org/Legislatures Elections/ElectionsCampaigns/InitiativeampReferendumLegislationDatabase/tabid/ 16577/Default.aspx. Accessed April 27, 2010.

National Education Association. 2002. *ESEA Action Guides*. Washington, DC: National Education Association.

_____. 2003. *Status of the American Public School Teacher, 2000–2001*. Washington, DC: Author.

_____. 2005. "TABOR: A Proven Failure." www.nea.org/home/18093.htm. Accessed January 31, 2011.

_____. 2010a. "Myths and Facts about Educator Pay." http://nea.org/home/12661.htm. Accessed August 18, 2010.

_____. 2010b. "Priority Schools Campaign." *State Legislatures* (December): advertisement.

_____. 2011. "Research Spotlight on Hard-to-Staff Schools." http://www.nea.org/ tools/16917.html. Accessed January 31, 2011.

National Education Commission on Time and Learning. 1994. *Prisoners of Time*. Washington, DC: Government Printing Office.

National Research Council. 2001. *Understanding Dropouts: Statistics, Strategies, and High-Stakes Testing*. Washington, DC: Committee on Educational Excellence and Testing Equity, National Academy Press.

Natriello, Gary, Aaron M. Pallas, and Karl Alexander. 1989. "On the Right Track? Curriculum and Academic Achievement." *Sociology of Education* 62 (2, April): 109–118.

Neal, Derek. 1997. "The Effects of Catholic Secondary Schooling on Educational Achievement." *Journal of Labor Economics* 15 (1, January): 98–123.

Neckerman, Kathryn M. 2007. *Schools Betrayed: Roots of Failure in Inner-City Education*. Chicago: University of Chicago Press.

"New Jersey Rebellion." 2010. *Wall Street Journal*, April 22, editorial. http://online .wsj.com/article/SB10001424052748704133804575198141369372302.html. Accessed April 22, 2010.

New York City Department of Education. 2010. "Master Teacher and Turnaround Teacher Opportunities in Transformation and Restart Schools." http://schools.nyc .gov/Offices/DHR/masterteacher.htm. Accessed July 20, 2011.

Noble, Holcomb B. 2006. "Milton Friedman, Free Market Theorist, Dies at 94." *New York Times*, November 16, 17.

Oakes, Jeannie. 1985. *Keeping Track: How Schools Structure Inequality.* New Haven, CT: Yale University Press.

_____. 1990. *Multiplying Inequalities: The Effects of Race, Social Class, and Tracking on Opportunities to Learn Mathematics and Science.* Santa Monica, CA: RAND.

Oakes, Jeannie, Adam Gamoran, and Reba N. Page. 1992. "Curriculum Differentiation: Opportunities, Outcomes, and Meanings." In *Handbook of Research on Curriculum,* edited by P. W. Jackson, 570–608. New York: Macmillan.

Obama, Barack. 2008. "Reforming and Strengthening America's Schools for the 21st Century." http://www.barackobama.com/pdf/issues/education/Fact_Sheet_Education _Reform_Speech_FINAL.pdf. Accessed October 2, 2010.

O'Brien, Thomas V. 1999. *The Politics of Race and Schooling: Public Education in Georgia, 1900–1961.* Lanham, MD: Lexington Books.

O'Connell, Jeffrey, and Thomas E. O'Connell. 1997. "James B. Conant: A Giant on Academe's Left, Right, and Center." *Education & Law Journal* 6 (1, Spring): 109–124.

O'Connor, Flannery. 1963. "Fiction Is a Subject with a History—It Should Be Taught That Way." *The Georgia Bulletin* (March 21): 1.

O'Connor, Julie. 2010. "Flunking Out Bad Teachers." *The* (Newark) *Star-Ledger,* December 19. http://blog.nj.com/njv_impact/print.html?entry=/2010/12/flunking_out _bad_teachers.html. Accessed December 19, 2010.

Odden, Allan, and Lawrence O. Picus. 2008. *School Finance: A Policy Perspective.* New York: McGraw-Hill.

Offe, Claus, and Helmut Weisenthal. 1980. "Two Logics of Collective Action." In *Political Power and Social Theory,* edited by Maurice Zeitlin, vol. 1, 67–116. Greenwich, CT: JAI Press.

Ohio Coalition for Equity and Adequacy of School Funding. 2001. *The Time Is Now!* Columbus: Ohio Coalition for Equity and Adequacy of School Funding.

_____. 2011. "Facts and Principles." http://www.ohiocoalition.org/pdfs/Facts_and _Principles.pdf. Accessed January 22, 2011.

Ohio Department of Education. 1995. *Derivation of the Cost of an Adequate Basic Education.* Columbus: Ohio Department of Education.

_____. 1997. "State Education Leaders Respond to Supreme Court's Decision in School-Funding Case." Press release, March 24. Columbus: Ohio Department of Education.

_____. 2011. "FY2010 District Profile Report" (March 2). http://www.ode.state.oh.us/ GD/DocumentManagement/DocumentDownload.aspx?DocumentID=101457. Accessed July 21, 2011.

Ohio Historical Society. 2010. "New Straitsville Mine Fire." http://www.ohiohistory central.com/entry.php?rec=521. Accessed July 20, 2010.

Ohio Office of Budget and Management. 2010. *Executive Budget for FYs 2010 and 2011.* Columbus: Author. http://obm.ohio.gov/SectionPages/Budget/FY1011/Budget.aspx. Accessed February 1, 2011.

Olson, Lynn. 2006. "As AYP Bar Rises, More Schools Fail." *Education Week* (September 20). http://www.edweek.org/ew/articles/2006/09/20/04ayp.h26.html. Accessed November 10, 2010.

Olson, Mancur. 1965. *The Logic of Collective Action.* New York: Schocken Books.

Orfield, Gary. 1969. *The Reconstruction of Southern Education; The Schools and the 1964 Civil Rights Act.* New York: Wiley-Interscience.

_____. 2009. *Reviving the Goal of an Integrated Society.* Los Angeles: The Civil Rights Project at UCLA.

_____. 2010a. "California's Charter Schools Earn a Failing Grade on Civil Rights." *Huffington Post*, March 3. http://huffingtonpost.com/gary-orfield/californias-charter-schoo_b_484821.html. Accessed January 8, 2011.

_____. 2010b. "A Life in Civil Rights." *PS* (October): 661–670.

Orr, Dorothy. 1950. *A History of Education in Georgia.* Chapel Hill: University of North Carolina Press.

Osborne, David, and Ted Gaebler. 1992. *Reinventing Government: How the Entrepreneurial Spirit Is Transforming the Public Sector.* Reading, MA: Addison-Wesley.

Osborne, Martin J., Jeffrey S. Rosenthal, and Matthew A. Turner. 2000. "Meetings with Costly Participation." *American Economic Review* 90 (4, September): 927–943.

Ostrom, Elinor. 1990. *Governing the Commons: The Evolution of Institutions for Collective Action.* New York: Cambridge University Press.

Padover, Saul K. 1939. *Thomas Jefferson on Democracy.* New York: Appleton-Century Company, Inc.

Paine, Albert Bigelow. 1904. *Th. Nast, His Period and His Pictures.* New York: Macmillan Company.

Patterson, James T. 2001. Brown v. Board of Education: *A Civil Rights Milestone and Its Troubled Legacy.* New York: Oxford University Press.

Patterson, Orlando. 1999. *Rituals of Blood: Consequences of Slavery in Two American Centuries.* New York: Basic Books.

Peaker, G. F. 1975. *An Empirical Study of Education in Twenty-One Countries: A Technical Report.* New York: John Wiley & Sons.

Pennsylvania School Boards Association. 2008. "School Employee Strikes Lowest in Six Years." *School Leader News* (July 25). www.psba.org/issues-advocacy/issues-research/contracts-strikes/. Accessed September 14, 2010.

Perlmann, Joel, and Dennis Shirley. 1991. "When Did New England Women Acquire Literacy?" *The William and Mary Quarterly* 48 (1, January): 50–67.

Peterson, Kavan. 2005. "Rebellion Against Federal Ed Law Reignites in Utah." *Stateline* (February 16). http://www.stateline.org/live/ViewPage.action?siteNodeId=136&languageId=1&contentId=15984. Accessed November 11, 2010.

Peterson, Paul E. 2010. "A Courageous Look at the American High School," *Education Next* 10 (2, Spring): 25–33.

Peterson, Paul, and Barry Rabe. 1983. "The Role of Interest Groups in the Formation of Educational Policy." *Teachers College Record* 83 (3, Spring): 708–772.

Petrovich, Janice, and Amy Stuart Wells, eds. 2005. *Bringing Equity Back: Research for a New Era in American Educational Policy.* New York: Teachers College Press.

Pettigrew, Thomas F., and Linda R. Tropp. 2006. "Meta-Analysis Test of Intergroup Contact Theory." *Journal of Personality and Social Psychology* 90 (5, May): 751–783.

Pew Research Center. 2009. "The Global Middle Class." (February 12). Washington, DC: Pew Research Center.

Pew Research Center for the People and the Press. 2010. "Public Trust in Government." http://people-press.org/trust. Accessed December 10, 2010.

Pierce, Neal R. 1972. *The Mountain States of America: People, Politics, and Power in the Eight Rocky Mountain States.* New York: W. W. Norton.

Pierson, Paul E. 1995. *Dismantling the Welfare State?* New York: Cambridge University Press.

Pliska, Ann-Maureen, and Judith McQuaide. 1994. "Pennsylvania's Battle for Student Learning Outcomes." *Educational Leadership* 51 (6, March): 66–69.

Podair, Jerald E. 2001. "The Ocean Hill–Brownsville Crisis: New York's *Antigone.*" Presented at Conference on New York City History, City University of New York, October 6.

_____. 2002. *The Strike That Changed New York: Blacks, Whites, and the Ocean Hill–Brownsville Crisis.* New Haven, CT: Yale University Press.

Podgursky, Michael. 2006. "Teams versus Bureaucracies: Personnel Policy, Wage-Setting, and Teacher Quality in Traditional Public, Charter, and Private Schools." *Educational and Policy Analysis Archives.* epaa.asu.edu.

Popkin, Samuel L. 1994. *The Reasoning Voter: Communication and Persuasion in Presidential Campaigns.* 2d ed. Chicago: University of Chicago Press.

Price, Heather E. 2010. "Does No Child Left Behind Really Capture School Quality? Evidence from an Urban School District." *Educational Policy* 24 (5): 779–814.

Price, Rita. 1998. "The Great Debate." *Columbus Dispatch,* April 26.

Prince, Hank. 1996. "Proposal A and Pupil Equity." Lansing: Michigan House Fiscal Agency.

Public Policy Polling. 2011. "WI Voters Narrowly Against Walker Recall but Favor Feingold." Press release, August 16. http://www.publicpolicypolling.com/pdf/2011/PPP_Release_WI_0816925.pdf. Accessed August 17, 2011.

Putterman, Ethan. 2005. "Rousseau on the People as Legislative Gatekeepers, Not Framers." *American Political Science Review* 99 (1, February): 145–151.

Raffaele, Martha. 2005. "Pennsylvania Voters Oust School Board." *Washington Post,* November 9. http://www.washingtonpost.com/wp-dyn/content/article/2005/11/09/AR2005110900114_pf.html. Accessed May 4, 2010.

Ramsey, Mike, and Josh Mitchell. 2010. "U.S. Study Points to Driver Error in Many Toyota Crashes." *Wall Street Journal,* August 11. http://online.wsj.com/. Accessed October 10, 2010.

Rasmussen Reports. 2011. "Public Employee Union Members More Hostile to Republicans Than Private Sector Union Workers." Press release, March 9. http://www.rasmussenreports.com/public_content/politics/general_politics/march_2011/public_employee_union_members_more_hostile_to_republicans_than_private_sector_union_workers. Accessed March 15, 2011.

Ravitch, Diane. 1978. "Social Science and Social Policy: The 'White-Flight' Controversy." *Public Interest* 51 (April): 135–149.

_____. 2000. *Left Back: A Century of Battles Over School Reform.* New York: Simon & Schuster.

_____. 2001. "The Right Thing: Why Liberals Should Be Pro-Choice." *The New Republic* (October 8). http://www.brookings.edu/articles/2001/1008politics_ravitch.aspx.

_____. 2010a. *The Death and Life of the Great American School System.* New York: Basic Books.

_____. 2010b. "Why I Changed My Mind About School Reform." *Wall Street Journal,* March 9.

Ravitch, Diane, and Arthur M. Schlesinger Jr. 1996. "The New, Improved History Standards." *Wall Street Journal,* April 3, A14.

Ravitch, Diane, and Joseph P. Viteritti. 2001. *New Schools for a New Century.* New Haven, CT: Yale University Press.

Ray, Kenneth Clark. 1943. "The Evolution and the Reorganization of the Ohio State Department of Education." Ph.D. diss., The Ohio State University, Columbus.

Reback, Randall. 2005. "House Prices and the Provision of Local Public Services: Capitalization Under School Choice Programs." *Journal of Urban Economics* 57 (2, March): 275–301.

Reschovsky, Andrew, and Jennifer Imazeki. 1998. "The Development of School Finance Formulas to Guarantee the Provision of Adequate Education to Low-Income Students." In *Developments in School Finance 1997* (NCES 98–212), edited by William J. Fowler Jr., 121–148. Washington, DC: National Center on Education Statistics, U.S. Department of Education.

Reynolds, Laurie. 2007. "Uniformity of Taxation and the Preservation of Local Control in School Finance Reform." *University of California Davis Law Review* 40 (5): 1835–1895.

Reznick, Lauren B. 2006. "Making Accountability Really Count." *Educational Measurement* 25 (1): 33–37.

Rhee, Michelle. 2010. "What I've Learned." *Newsweek* (December 6). http://www.news week.com.

Richard, Alan. 2004. "Florida Weighs Impact Against Voucher Program." *Education Week* (October 5). http:www.edweek.org/ew/articles/2004/09/01/01voucher.h24.html. Accessed January 19, 2010.

Ringquist, Eric, Jeff Worsham, and Marc Allen Eisner. 2003. "Salience, Complexity, and the Legislative Direction of Regulatory Bureaucracies." *Journal of Public Administration Research and Theory* 13 (2): 141–164.

Ripley, Amanda. 2008. "Rhee Tackles Classroom Challenge." *Time* (November 26). http://www.time.com.

Ripley, Anthony. 1970a. "Colorado Weighs Blast Controls." *New York Times,* March 9, 10.
_____. 1970b. "Denver Blasts Destroy 24 School Buses." *New York Times,* February 7, 11.

Ritter, Gary, Nathan Jensen, Brian Kisdia, and Joshua McGee. 2010. "A Closer Look at Charter Schools and Segregation." *Education Next* (Summer): 69–73.

Roberts, Sam. 2006. "When the City's Bankruptcy Was Just a Few Words Away." *New York Times,* December 31.

Rosenberg, Gerald N. 1993. *The Hollow Hope: Can Courts Bring About Social Change?* Chicago: University of Chicago Press.

Roth, Stephen J. 1971. "Breakthrough in Detroit." *The Crisis* (November): 285–287.

Rothstein, Richard. 2004. *Class and Schools: Using Social, Economic and Educational Reform to Close the Black–White Achievement Gap.* New York: Teachers' College Press.

Rubenstein, Michael, R. Hamar, and Nancy Adelman. 1992. *Minnesota's Open Enrollment Option.* Washington, DC: U.S. Department of Education.

Rumberger, Russell W., and Gregory J. Palardy. 2005. "Does Segregation Still Matter? The Impact of Student Composition on Academic Achievement in High School." *Teachers College Record* 107 (9, September): 1999–2045.

Ryan, James E. 2009. "The Real Lessons of School Desegregation." In *From Schoolhouse to Courthouse*, edited by Joshua M. Dunn and Martin R. West, 73–95. Washington, DC: Fordham Institute–Brookings Institution.

Salzer, James. 1999. "Schrenko Defends Her Accountability." *Atlanta Journal-Constitution*, November 18, sec. E.

Samuels, Christina A. 2009. "Special Ed. Advocates Making To-Do List for Duncan." *Education Week* (February 11).

Sanders, William L., and Sandra P. Horn. 1994. "The Tennessee Value-Added Assessment System: Mixed-Model Methodology in Educational Assessment." *Journal of Personnel Evaluation in Education* 8: 299–311.

Sanford, Terry. 1982. "Remembering James B. Conant." *Change* 14 (1, January): 26, 52–53.

Sawchuk, Stephen. 2011. "Pre-Convention: NEA Executives Amend Evaluation Proposal." *Education Week* (June 30). http://blogs.edweek.org/edweek/teacher-beat/2011/06/pre-convention_nea_chiefs_amen.html. Accessed July 7, 2011.

Schattschneider, E. E. 1960. *The Semi-Sovereign People*. New York: Holt Rinehart Winston.

Schlesinger, Arthur M., Jr. 1996. "History as Therapy: A Dangerous Idea." *New York Times Book Review* (May 3): 31.

Schlozman, Kay Lehman. 1984. "What Accent the Heavenly Chorus? Political Equality and the American Pressure System." *Journal of Politics* 46 (4, November): 1006–1032.

Schlozman, Kay Lehman, and John T. Tierney. 1986. *Organized Interests and American Democracy*. New York: HarperCollins.

Schneider, Anne, and Helen Ingram. 1993. "The Social Construction of Target Populations." *American Political Science Review* 82 (2, June): 334–346.

Schneider, Mark, Paul Teske, Melissa Marschall, and Christine Roch. 1998. "Shopping for Schools: In the Land of the Blind, the One-Eyed Parent May Be Enough." *American Journal of Political Science* 42 (3, July): 769–793.

Schnitzer, Ginger Gold. 2009. "Campaign 2009: An Organizational Victory." Presentation at the National Association of Legislative and Political Specialists for Education, November.

Schofield, Janet W., and Rebecca Eurich-Fulcer. 2004. "When and How School Desegregation Improves Intergroup Relations." In *Applied Social Psychology*, by Marilynn B. Brewer and Miles Hewstone, 186–205. Malden, MA: Blackwell Publishing.

Schultze, Steve, and Don Walker. 2011. "Walker Says He Should Have Prepared Public Earlier for His Sweeping Changes." *Milwaukee Journal-Sentinel* (June 27. http://c.brightcove.com/services. Accessed June 28, 2011.

Schumpeter, Joseph. 1942. *Capitalism, Socialism, and Democracy*. New York: Harper & Row.

Scott, C. Winfield. 1953. "Why All the Fuss?" *Phi Delta Kappan* 34 (9, June): 362–366.

Sensky, Jacqui. 1993. Weekly communication, memorandum to George V. Voinovich, March 5. Series 5.1, box 1R. George V. Voinovich Papers, Ohio University, Athens.

Shanker, Albert. 1989. "Where We Stand." *New York Times*, July 23.

Shapiro, Merrill. 2011. "The Hidden Cost of Vouchers." *Forward* (January 21). http://www.forward.com/articles/134665. Accessed January 17, 2011.

Shelley, Frank M., J. Clark Archer, Fiona M. Davidson, and Stanley D. Brunn. 1996. *Political Geography of the United States*. New York: Guilford Press.

Shober, Arnold F. 2008. "Fulfilling Parents' Wishes: The Effect of School Choice on School Referenda Success." National Center for the Study of Privatization in Education, Teachers College, Columbia University, New York, New York.

_____. 2010. *Splintered Accountability: State Governance and Education Reform*. Albany: State University of New York Press.

Shober, Arnold F., Paul Manna, and John F. Witte. 2006. "Flexibility Meets Accountability: State Charter School Laws and Their Influence on the Formation of Charter Schools in the United States." *Policy Studies Journal* 34 (4, November): 263–287.

Sieff, Kevin. 2010. "Virginia 4th-Grade Textbook Criticized Over Claims on Black Confederate Soldiers." *Washington Post*, October 20, sec. A.

Sielke, Catharine, John Dayton, C. Thomas Holmes, and Ann Jefferson, eds. 2001. *Public School Finance Programs in the United States and Canada* (NCES 2001–309). Washington, DC: National Center for Education Statistics, U.S. Department of Education. http://nces.ed.gov/edfin/state_financing.asp. Accessed August 30, 2010.

Skaife, Robert A. 1953. "The Sound and the Fury." *Phi Delta Kappan* 34 (9, June): 357–362.

Smith, Daniel A. 1999. "Howard Jarvis, Populist Entrepreneur: Reevaluating the Causes of Proposition 13." *Social Science History* 23 (2, Summer): 172–210.

Smith, Kevin B., and Kenneth Meier. 1995. *The Case Against School Choice: Politics, Markets, and Fools*. Armonk, NY: M.E. Sharpe.

Smith, Marshall S., and Jennifer O'Day. 1991. "Systemic School Reform." In *The Politics of Curriculum and Testing*, edited by Susan Fuhrman and Betty Malen, 233–267. New York: The Falmer Press.

Smith, Stacey. 2001. *The Democratic Potential of Charter Schools*. New York: Peter Lang Publishing.

Smrekar, Claire. 2009. "Beyond the Tipping Point: Issues of Racial Diversity in Magnet Schools Following Unitary Status." *Peabody Journal of Education* 84 (2): 209–226.

Sniderman, Paul M., and Edward G. Carmines. 1997. *Reaching Beyond Race*. Cambridge, MA: Harvard University Press.

Snyder, Thomas D. 1993. *120 Years of American Education: A Statistical Portrait*. Washington, DC: National Center for Education Statistics, U.S. Department of Education.

Soussan, Tania. 2003. "Gov. Gets Education Chief." *Albuquerque Journal*, September 24. http://www.abqjournal.com/elex/88635nm09–24–03.htm. Accessed January 4, 2011.

Spady, William. 1977. "Competency Based Education: A Bandwagon in Search of a Definition." *Educational Researcher* 6 (January): 9–14.

_____. 1994. *Outcome-based Education: Critical Issues and Answers*. Arlington, VA: American Association of School Administrators.

Spady, William G., and Kit J. Marshall. 1991. "Beyond Traditional Outcome-Based Education." *Educational Leadership* 49 (2, October): 67–72.

Spring, Joel. 2000. *American Education*. 9th ed. Boston: McGraw-Hill.

Springer, Matthew G., Dale Ballou, Laura Hamiton, Vi-Nhuan Le, J.R. Lockwood, Daniel F. McCaffrey, Matthew Pepper, and Brian M. Stecher. 2010. *Teacher Pay for Performance: Experimental Evidence from the Project on Incentives in Teaching*. Nashville, TN: National Center on Performance Incentives, Vanderbilt University.

Srinivasan, Rajesh, and Julie Ray. 2009, August 17. "Few Voting-Age Afghans Confident Election Will Be Fair." http://www.gallup.com/poll/122360/Few-Voting-Age -Afghans-Confident-Election-Fair.aspx?version=print. Accessed April 27, 2010.

Stedman, Lawrence C. 1996. "Respecting the Evidence: The Achievement Crisis Remains Real." *Education Policy Analysis Archives* 4 (7, April). http://epaa.asu.edu/ojs/article/ download/630/752. Accessed July 20, 2011.

———. 2004. "The NAEP Long-Term Trend Assessment: A Review of Its Transformation, Use, and Findings." Paper commissioned by the National Assessment Governing Board. http://www.nagb.org/who-we-are/20-anniversary/stedman-long-term -formatted.pdf. Accessed July 20, 2011.

Stedman, Lawrence C., and Marshall S. Smith. 1983. "Recent Reform Proposals for American Education." *Contemporary Education Review* 2 (2): 85–104.

Stein, Jason. 2011. "Budget-Repair Bill Goes to Walker, After Assembly Adoption." *Milwaukee Journal Sentinel*, April 5. http://www.jsonline.com/news/statepolitics/ 119279779.html. Accessed April 5, 2011.

Stein, Jason, Steve Stultze, and Bill Glauber. 2011. "Budget-repair Bill Approved in Early-morning Vote." *Milwaukee Journal Sentinel*, February 25. http://www.jsonline.com/ news/statepolitics/116824378.html. Accessed February 25, 2011.

Stephens, Scott, Edith Starzyk, and Janet Okoben. 2008. "Strickland Wants to Appoint Education Director." *Plain Dealer*, February 7, sec. A.

Stewart, Thomas, Patrick Wolf, Stephen Q. Cornman, Kenann McKenzie-Thompson, and Jonathan Butcher. 2009. *Family Reflections on the District of Columbia Opportunity Scholarship Program*. Report of the School Choice Demonstration Project. Fayetteville: University of Arkansas.

Stone, Deborah A. 1989. "Causal Stories and the Formation of Policy Agendas." *Political Science Quarterly* 104 (2, Summer): 281–300.

Stutz, Terrence. 2005. "School Tax Repairs Ordered." *Dallas Morning News*, November 22. http://www.dallasnews.com/sharedcontent/dws/dn/latestnews/stories/112305dnt exschoolfinance.b06c3fb.html. Accessed August 28, 2010.

Superfine, Benjamin Michael. 2008. *The Courts and Standards-Based Education Reform*. New York: Oxford University Press.

Takei, Yoshimitsu, and Roger Shouse. 2008. "Ratings in Black and White: Does Racial Symmetry of Asymmetry Influence Teacher Assessment of a Pupil's Work Habits?" *Social Psychology of Education* 11 (4, November): 367–387.

Taylor, Lori L. 2006. "Comparable Wages, Inflation, and School Finance Equity. *Education Finance and Policy* 1 (3, Summer): 349–71.

Thompson, Tommy G. 1995. "Budget Address." *Journal of the Wisconsin Senate* (February 14): 77.

Tiebout, Charles M. 1956. "A Pure Theory of Local Expenditures." *Journal of Political Economy* 64 (5, April): 416–424.

Timar, Thomas B. 1997. "The Institutional Role of State Education Departments: A Historical Perspective." *American Journal of Education* 105 (May): 231–260.

Time. 1980. (June 16).

Turque, Bill. 2011. "More Than 200 DC Teachers Fired." *Washington Post*, July 15. http://www.washingtonpost.com/blogs/dc-schools-insider/post/more-than-200-dc -teachers-fired/2011/07/15/gIQADnTLGI_blog.html. Accessed July 20, 2011.

Tuttle, Christina Clark, Bing-ru Teh, Ira Nichols-Barrer, Brian P. Gill, and Philip Glea-son. 2010. *Student Characteristics and Achievement in 22 KIPP Middle Schools*. Prince-ton, NJ: Mathematica Policy Research.

Tyack, David B. 1974. *The One Best System: A History of American Urban Education*. Cambridge, MA: Harvard University Press.

Tyack, David B., and Larry Cuban. 1995. *Tinkering Toward Utopia: A Century of Public School Reform*. Cambridge, MA: Harvard University Press.

Tyler, John H. 2004. "Basic Skills and the Earnings of Dropouts." *Economics of Education Review* 23 (3, June): 221–235.

Tyler, Kenneth M., and Christina M. Boelter. 2008. "Linking Black Middle School Stu-dents' Perceptions of Teachers' Expectations to Academic Engagement and Efficacy." *Negro Educational Review* 59 (1–2, Spring–Summer): 27–44.

U.S. Census Bureau. 2009. *American Community Survey, 2005–2009 Population Esti-mates*. http://factfinder.census.gov/. Accessed January 17, 2011.

U.S. Commission on Civil Rights. 2007. *Omaha Public Schools: Issues and Implication of Nebraska Legislative Bill 1024*. Washington, DC: U.S. Commission on Civil Rights. http://www.usccr.gov/pubs/OmahaFinal.pdf. Accessed November 11, 2010.

U.S. Congress. 1916. *Final Report and Testimony Submitted to Congress by the Commis-sion on Industrial Relations*. 64th Cong., 1st sess., S. Doc. 415, 2. Washington, DC: Government Printing Office.

_____. 1995. S.R. 66, 104th Cong.

U.S. Department of Education. 2009. "The American Recovery and Reinvestment Act of 2009: Saving and Creating Jobs and Reforming Education." (March 7). http://www2.ed.gov/policy/gen/leg/recovery/implementation.html. Accessed January 25, 2011.

_____. 2010. *A Blueprint for Reform*. Washington, DC: Author.

_____. 2011a. "January 24th Education Stakeholders Forum with Secretary Duncan." http://www.ustream.tv/channel/education-department. Accessed January 24, 2011.

_____. 2011b. "Race to the Top Technical Review Form." http://www.ed.gov. Accessed April 20, 2011.

_____. 2011c. "The Nation's Report Card." http://nces.ed.gov/nationsreportcard/. Accessed January 17, 2011. U.S. Department of Health and Human Services, Admin-istration for Children and Families. 2010. "Head Start Impact Study Final Report." (January). Washington, DC: Government Printing Office.

U.S. Department of Labor. 2010. *Labor Force Characteristics by Race and Ethnicity*. Re-port 1026 (August). Washington, DC: U.S. Department of Labor, Bureau of Labor Statistics.

Useem, Elizabeth L. 1992. "Getting on the Fast Track in Mathematics: School Organi-zational Influences on Math Track Assignment." *American Journal of Education* 100 (3, May): 325–353.

U.S. Senate, Office of Public Records. 2010. "LDA Reports." http://www.senate.gov/ legislative/Public_Disclosure/LDA_reports.htm. Accessed May 10, 2010.

van der Eijk, Cees, and Mark N. Franklin. 2009. *Elections and Voters*. New York: Palgrave Macmillan.

Vanneman, Alan, Linda Hamilton, Janet Baldwin Anderson, and Taslima Rahman. 2009. *Achievement Gaps: How Black and White Students in Public Schools Perform in Mathematics and Reading on the National Assessment of Educational Progress* (NCES 2009–355). Washington, DC: National Center for Education Statistics, Institute of Education Sciences, U.S. Department of Education.

Vinovskis, Maris A. 1999. *The Road to Charlottesville*. Washington, DC: National Education Goals Panel.

———. 2000. "Teachers Unions and Educational Research and Development." In *Conflicting Missions?* edited by Tom Loveless, 211–239. Washington, DC: Brookings Institution Press.

———. 2008. "Gubernatorial Leadership and American K–12 Educational Reform." In *A Legacy of Innovation: Governors and Public Policy*, edited by Ethan G. Sribnick, 105–203. Philadelphia: University of Pennsylvania Press.

Viteritti, Joseph P. 2007. *The Last Freedom: Religion from the Public School to the Public Square*. Princeton, NJ: Princeton University Press.

———. 2009. *When Mayors Take Charge: School Governance in the City*. Washington, DC: Brookings Institution Press.

Voinovich, George B. 1993a. Letter to Ted Sanders, January 28. Series 1.2, box 50, folder 1. George V. Voinovich Papers, Ohio University, Athens.

———. 1993b. Memorandum to Ted Sanders, March 9. Series 5.1, box 1R, folder 9. George V. Voinovich Papers, Ohio University, Athens.

Walker, Jack. 1991. *Mobilizing Interest Groups in America*. Ann Arbor: University of Michigan Press.

Walker, Scott. 2011. "State of the State Address." February 1. http://host.madison.com/wsj/news/local/govt-and-politics/article_6a42ad28–2e5e-11e0–9f9e-001cc4c03286.html#ixzz1SmCcmf2L. Accessed February 2, 2011.

Walsh, Edward. 1993. "Michigan Ends Property Tax Funding of Schools." *Washington Post*, August 20, A1.

Webber, David J. 2010. "School District Democracy: School Board Voting and School Performance." *Politics & Policy* 38 (1, February): 81–95.

Weick, Karl E. 1976. "Educational Organizations as Loosely Coupled Systems." *Administrative Science Quarterly* 21 (1, March): 1–19.

Weimer, David, and Aidan Vining. 2011. *Policy Analysis*. 5th ed. Boston: Longman.

Weimer, David, and Michael J. Woloff. 2001. "School Performance and Housing Values: Using Non-Contiguous District and Incorporation Boundaries to Identify School Effects." *National Tax Journal* 54 (2, June): 231–254.

Wells, Amy Stuart. 1993. "The Sociology of School Choice." In *School Choice: Examining the Evidence*, edited by Edith Rasell and Richard Rothstein, 29–48. Washington, DC: Economic Policy Institute.

———. ed. 2002. *Where Charter School Policy Fails: The Problems of Accountability and Equity*. New York: Teachers College Press.

Wells, Amy Stuart, Jacquelyn Duran, and Terrenda White. 2008. "Refusing to Leave Desegregation Behind: From Graduates of Racially Diverse Schools to the Supreme Court." *Teachers College Record* 110 (12): 2532–2570.

Welner, Kevin G. 2001. *Legal Rights, Local Wrongs: When Community Control Collides with Educational Equity*. Albany: State University of New York Press.

Wilentz, Sean. 1997. "Don't Know Much About History." *New York Times Book Review* (November 30): 28–29.

Wiley, Edward W., Eleanor R. Spindler, and Amy N. Subert. 2010. *Denver ProComp: An Outcomes Evaluation of Denver's Alternative Teacher Compensation System.* Boulder: School of Education, University of Colorado at Boulder.

Wilson, William Julius. 1987. *The Truly Disadvantaged.* Chicago: University of Chicago Press.

Wisconsin Department of Public Instruction. 2010a. "Public School Open Enrollment Transfers and Aid Adjustments." http://www.dpi.wisconsin.gov/sms/oeaid.html. Accessed January 17, 2010.

_____. 2010b. "Sparsity Aid Program." http://dpi.wi.gov/sfs/sparsity.html. Accessed August 18, 2010.

Witte, John F., David Weimer, Arnold F. Shober, and Paul Schlomer. 2007. "The Performance of Charter Schools in Wisconsin." *Journal of Policy Analysis and Management* 26 (3): 567–588.

Witte, John F. 2000. *The Market Approach to Education: An Analysis of America's First Voucher Program.* Princeton, NJ: Princeton University Press.

Witte, John F., Paul Schlomer, and Arnold F. Shober. 2007. "Going Charter? A Study of School District Competition in Wisconsin." *Peabody Journal of Education* 82 (2, June): 410–439.

Wolters, Raymond. 2004. "From Brown to Green and Back: The Changing Meaning of Desegregation." *Journal of Southern History* 70 (2, May): 317–326.

Wong, Kenneth K., and Anna C. Nicotera. 2004. "*Brown v. Board of Education* and the Coleman Report: Social Science Research and the Debate on Educational Equity." *Peabody Journal of Education* 79 (2): 122–135.

Wong, Kenneth K., and Francis X. Shen. 2007. "Mayoral Leadership Matters: Lessons Learned from Mayoral Control of Large Urban School Systems." *Peabody Journal of Education* 82 (4): 737–768.

Yackee, Jason Webb, and Susan Webb Yackee. 2006. "A Bias Towards Business? Assessing Interest Group Influence on the U.S. Bureaucracy." *Journal of Politics* 68 (1, February): 128–139.

Zaller, John R. 1992. *The Nature and Origins of Mass Opinion.* New York: Cambridge University Press.

Zehr, Mary Ann. 2002. "Catholics Laud Voucher Decision, See Potential for Growth." *Education Week* (July 10).

Zhou, Lei. 2010. *Revenues and Expenditures for Public Elementary and Secondary Education: School Year 2007–08* (NCES 2010–326). Washington, DC: National Center for Education Statistics, U.S. Department of Education.

Ziebarth, Todd. 2004. *State Takeovers and Reconstitutions.* Denver, CO: Education Commission of the States. http://www.ecs.org/clearinghouse/51/67/5167.htm. Accessed December 18, 2010.

Zimmer, Ron W., Brian P. Gill, Kevin Booker, Stephane Lavertu, Tim Sass, and John Witte. 2009. *Charter Schools in Eight States: Effects on Achievement, Attainment, Integration, and Competition.* Santa Monica, CA: RAND Corporation.

Index